428.24 F515e c.1 EV
FINOCCHIARO
ENGLISH AS A SECOND LA[illegible] :
FROM THEORY TO PRAC[illegible]

ENGLISH AS A SECOND LANGUAGE: FROM THEORY TO PRACTICE

New Edition

by

Mary Finocchiaro, Ph.D.
Professor Emeritus
Hunter College of the City University of New York
Professor of Applied Linguistics
University of Rome

REGENTS PUBLISHING COMPANY, INC.

Copyright © 1974 by
Regents Publishing Company, Inc.

All rights reserved. No part of this book may be reproduced in any form without permission in writing from the publisher.

Published by
Regents Publishing Company, Inc.
2 Park Avenue
New York, N.Y. 10016

Printed in the United States of America

Contents

With gratitude and love to
Santo, Sal, and Rosemary,
who waited patiently.

Introduction

My experience as a teacher and teacher-trainer in the United States and my assignments in many parts of the world where I have had the good fortune to work with interested, devoted teachers and prospective teachers have reaffirmed my belief that teachers everywhere share the same concerns. With only slight variations because of factors which may prevail in a local situation, teachers voice similar doubts and hopes.

Teachers who are not native English speakers have misgivings about their linguistic competence. Native English speakers who do not know the language of their students wonder whether they can nevertheless teach effectively. Teachers everywhere are uneasy about controversies over current linguistic theories and about the realistic contributions linguistics, psycholinguistics, sociolinguistics, or other sciences can make to language learning and teaching. They are deeply concerned about keeping abreast of the "best," most "modern" methods of teaching, about the attention being given in the literature to individualized instruction and to performance objectives, about tests and grades, about homework, about uninterested pupils, and about "gifted" or "slow" pupils.

All of them are strikingly similar in that they want to become more effective teachers. Non-native and native English speakers alike express the hope that they can develop communicative competence in their pupils despite what some consider their own linguistic limitations. They want to motivate their students so that these will find language learning a pleasurable, successful activity. They are deeply aware of the fact that they can help their students or their community and country better fulfill their needs or their aspirations by providing another medium for communicating with neighbors near and far.

This Guide is dedicated to all those devoted teachers and to my students at the University whose questions and concerns have forced me to focus attention on the multiplicity of elements in the process of teaching and learning a language. It is designed for prospective teachers of English and also for experienced teachers who may find pleasure in the confirmation of some of the techniques they have undoubtedly been using. While bringing some current theories to the attention of teachers and other interested persons, the Guide will state in as many ways as possible that the *real* issue is not "modern" versus "traditional" teaching, but more efficient, more effective, or more stimulating learning. Such learning will result not only from the knowledge of various, alternative theories which the teacher may bring to bear on the solution of learning problems. It will stem also from the teacher's conviction that successful language teaching is a judicious blend of science and art—art which only the teacher can provide through his enthusiasm for his subject, his interest in his students, his creative use of the environment and of the materials at his disposal.

This Guide has been written for use both where English must be learned as a second language—that is, as the major language spoken in the community or the language of instruction in the schools—or where English is taught as a foreign language. While such factors as motivation, pace, and priorities will differ, the principles underlying learning will bear understandable similarities. After all, in both situations we are attempting to add a new mode of communication to human beings who possess similar innate physical, mental, and even psychological capabilities. Adaptations for special situations are treated more fully in Chapter VI.

I have confined myself to what I call "minimum" essentials, written in language that lay people would understand. This has been done because increased interest in the English language throughout the world and special situations within the United States and Great Britain often make it necessary for teachers or even lay people without a special background in education and in related subjects to start teaching with little or no preparation or orientation.

It is my hope that many of you will pursue even further the facts or thoughts I will outline and that you will make use of the many excellent materials which were the source of much of my knowledge and which you will find mentioned at the end of the Guide. I regret that you cannot share with me the stimulating talks on language learning that I have had with such people (and how I wish it were possible to name them all!) as Virginia French Allen, of Temple University; Douglas Beakes, Education Advisor, United States Air Force; Helen Beko, USIS; Julia Burks, Deputy Director ELT, USIS, Washington; Denis Girard, Director of BEL in France; Dr. Charles Ferguson, former Director of the Center for Applied Linguistics; Prof. Albert Marckwardt of the University of Michigan; Prof. William R. Lee, Editor of *English*

Language Teaching; Mme. Sczablowska of the Polish Ministry of Education; Prof. Ludwig Zabrocki and Prof. Alexander Sculz of the University of Poznan; Prof. Rudy Troike, Director of the Center for Applied Linguistics; Harold Urist, Ainslie Minor, and George McCready of the English Teaching Section of USIS; and Paul Weaver (Nigeria) and Donn Byrne (Italy) of the British Council. The list could fill many pages.

I am indebted to Dr. Jacek Fisiak of the University of Poznan in Poland and to Prof. Gerald Dykstra of the University of Hawaii for their careful reading of the first edition of the manuscript. Their comments, suggestions, and encouragement have been extremely valuable. Prof. Wanda D'Addio of the Ministry of Education in Rome; Donn Byrne, English Language Officer of the British Council, Rome; and Prof. Annarita Puglielli of the University of Rome have generously made suggestions for inclusions and deletions in this revised edition.

As you read, I hope you will keep constantly in mind the fact that all *any* book can do is recommend or suggest ideas or practices. *You,* and *only* you, can choose from among these suggestions those you know will work best with *you,* with *your* pupils, in *your* school, and in *your* community.

—M.F.

I. Learning A Second Language

The Nature of Language and Language Learning

If we are going to teach other people to understand and to speak a second or a third language, we should start by asking ourselves what language really is. We have all been speaking our native language since we were between the ages of one and two, but we have done so with little or no conscious thought on our part. Many of us would find it difficult or even impossible to explain what we do when we speak our language.

Fortunately, the last several decades have witnessed a tremendous upsurge of activity by scholars in this field. Definitions of language and language descriptions abound. Every few years one finds new and often contradictory theories of ways of *describing* language. There have been numerous books and articles about the advantages of describing language in traditional terms, in structural terms, in tagmemic terms, and in generative-transformational terms to name only a few. More recently a strong case has been made for describing the grammar of language in terms of cases (dative, locative, etc.) and for using semantics and functional communication as the basis for analysis.

Inevitably, new theories bring with them new terminologies and attempts to alter priorities in teaching. For example, what used to be called levels or sub-systems of language are now being called components. (One speaks today of the semantic, the syntactic, and the phonological components.) To *generate,* in generative-transformational linguistic description, does not mean to *create* in the traditional sense of the term, but to characterize a language explicitly through a series of rules which will permit the language speaker to produce and understand a theoretically infinite number of grammatically correct sentences.

Whereas with structural grammarians, phonology and structure were given priority and became the subject of intensive study while semantics (the study of meaning) was rather neglected, today the semantic component is considered central to the speech act and is given priority in description. Meaning is also paramount in teaching although syntax and phonology retain primary roles.

The Nature of Language

Some Basic Premises

Let me state them briefly:

▶Language is a uniquely human activity. It is often characterized as "species specific", i.e., it is an instrument possessed only by man.

▶All normal people in the world can speak. No group of people without a spoken language has ever been discovered.

▶Language is universal. All normal human beings in a community understand and speak well enough to carry out every activity of human life. However, many of these same people cannot read and write.

▶Every language in the world is rich enough and sufficiently complete for its speakers to carry out their daily activities. People who do not *need* iceboxes probably will have no word for *icebox.* When the need arises, new words or expressions can be borrowed from another language or can be coined with elements of the existing language.

▶Human beings can receive and transmit messages; that is, they can take the role of both hearer and speaker.

▶A speaker is free to create new utterances, but in order to be understood, his utterances must remain within the "rules" established by the linguistic system of the community.

▶Every language has its own system or code; that is, its own characteristic way of putting sounds together in order to talk about situations or events in the present, the past, or the future.

▶A speaker can hear what he says as he is saying it; in other words, he receives "feedback." (He also receives feedback by listening to the comments or watching the reactions of his hearers in face-to-face communication.)

▶Every language is composed of a limited number of distinctive sounds. With these limited sounds, the speaker can form an unlimited number of words and utterances. In other words, the same few sounds, in varying combinations permitted by the system, are used to form the infinite number of utterances needed to communicate.

▶Language reflects the socio-cultural organization and environment of its speakers. For example, the number of separate vocabulary items in a language used to express any phenomenon in the environment is an indication of the importance the speakers ascribe to it and of their needs; e.g., people living in Iceland have many different words for *snow*.

▶All languages have universal properties. All of them studied to date include signals for naming objects in the environment (nominals) and for expressing actions or states of being (verbals).

▶All languages have devices which allow speakers to talk about themselves and others, to ask questions, and to express denial and acceptance. All have *rules* which enable speakers to express and organize their ideas (the semantic and syntactic components of language) into *linear* sequences of sounds (the phonological component).

▶Writing systems originated long after spoken language existed. To the best of our knowledge, man and spoken language were created simultaneously.

▶For these reasons, the *spoken* language is considered *primary*. It is considered *primary* also because people learn to speak their native language several years before they learn to read and write it—if at all.

▶Writing is thus considered a *secondary* system, derived from speech. Would you stop to think for a moment? How much writing do *you* usually do in a day compared to the amount of speaking you do? Even as you write, don't you always think first of how you would *say* what you are putting down on paper?

Some Definitions of Language

There are several ways of characterizing language which you may wish to consider before we take a hard look at the fifth definition, the one I consider the most comprehensive. For example:

1. Language is the means by which results of human thought and action are passed on.

2. Language is a system of rules by which items are stored in the mind and manipulated so as to form infinite sets of combinations.

3. Language is learned behavior.

4. Language is a cultural product subject to laws and principles that are partially unique to it and partially reflective of general properties of the human mind.

5. Language is a *system* of *arbitrary, vocal symbols* which permits *all* people in a given culture, or other people who have learned the system of that culture, to *communicate* or to *interact*.

Let us examine the fifth definition in more detail. What is meant by such terms as *system* or *arbitrary*, etc.? Every language operates within its own *system*—that is, within its own *recurring* patterns or arrangements which are meaningful to its speakers. The sounds, which are used to form the words, which, in turn, are used in speech utterances, are always arranged in particular ways or designs which convey the same meaning to all speakers of the language. Let us examine some examples in English.

When I say the words "the man," you know I am talking of one man and of a man previously mentioned. "The men," on the other hand, conveys the meaning of more than one man. The difference was made by the /ε/ sound used in the second example. The sound /t/ at the end of "walked" gives you an immediate clue that I am referring to an occurrence that took place in the past.

When you hear "arrive," you know it would fit into the place used for verbs in a sentence. "Arrival," on the other hand, would fit into the slot used for what we generally call a noun, wouldn't it?

To continue, in English, *word order* is an important part of the *system*. Compare the two sentences: "The cat bit the lady." . . . "The lady bit the cat." The forms of the words are exactly the same, aren't they? But—what a difference in meaning! Let us take another illustration. Does the sentence "Basket with went the she" make any sense although we "know" the "meaning" of each word? No. It does not.

Any listener would know that "The boy is ill," said with the voice dropping at the end, is a statement. "Is the boy ill?" would be recognized as a question even if spoken in a monotone, because of the position of the verb *is*.

Examining another feature of the "system," we find that in English, adjectives do not "agree" with nouns. We say "The boys are tall" and "the tall boys"; "The girl is tall" and "the tall girls." In the native language of your students, changes may occur because of gender (masculine or feminine) or because of number (singular or plural).

This *system* of meaningful arrangements of sounds and forms in speech which the youngest native speaker knows by the time he reaches six or seven may differ in important respects from any other language system in the world.

Let us continue with our definition. *Vocal* means that we make sounds in our mouth using the *tongue*, the *teeth*, and the *lips*. (We use other organs, too, such as the vocal cords and the lungs to produce or make the sounds of the language.)

Every language has its own *arbitrary symbols* or *words* to express the meaning of an object or an idea. Why does "bread" mean what it does in English? Why is "horse" the name for the animal it represents? No one knows why words convey certain meanings. But *all* the speakers of the language do know and can use the general terms associated with the common objects or concepts in their environment or world. Some specialized words, related to a certain trade or profession, may be known only by those who practice that trade or profession, but the sounds within the words or the position of the words in sentences would be familiar to *all* speakers.

The words *communicate* and *interact* as used in the definition signify to *understand* and to *speak;* to be able to *hear* and to *respond* or *react* (by carrying out directions, for example) to the spoken word. They imply, too, the ability to talk about something that happened *in the past,* that is happening *at the present time,* or that may happen at some time *in the future.*

Communication through the use of the *spoken* language means understanding and reacting to what someone *says.* The response or reaction may be to make a statement; to ask a question; to agree or to disagree; to carry out a direction; to answer a question in the affirmative or in the negative with a long answer or with a short answer; e.g., "Are you going to the movies tomorrow?" "Yes" or "Yes, I am"; or to use what we call a formula in the language; e.g., the response to "Thank you" might be "You're welcome."

An extremely important function of communication is what is sometimes called its *phatic function;* that is, the ability to establish, prolong, or discontinue a conversation.

The Functions of Language: A Brief Summary

While research in the field is far from complete (tapes of actual, unrehearsed conversations are being continuously studied), the major functions of language have been subdivided by some linguists as follows: (Not all use the same basic terms but *the communicative purposes* are similar.)

personal: to express one's emotions, needs, thoughts, desires, attitudes, etc.

interpersonal: to maintain good social relations with individuals and groups—expressions of praise, sympathy, joy at another's success, inquiries about health, etc.

directive: to control the behavior of others through advice, warnings, requests, persuasion, discussion, etc.

referential: to talk about objects or events in the immediate setting or environment or in the culture.

metalinguistic: to talk about language; e.g., What does ________ mean?

imaginative: to use language creatively in rhyming, composing poetry, etc.

Where communities read and write, communication would also

include *understanding* and *conveying* messages through the printed word.

Writing, as we have said, is considered a *secondary system* derived from the spoken language. We write *symbols* (in English—the letters of the alphabet and punctuation marks) to convey the words and ideas *which are themselves* symbols of objects or ideas. For example:

referent	sound	written word	referent	sound	written word
	/hɔrs/	*horse*		/baʊ/	*bough*

Since language is the medium by which people express their experiences and their ideas of the world in which they live, it carries within it what can be called "cultural meaning." Native speakers who have been brought up in the culture or who have shared experiences in the culture are aware of differences or shades in meaning which gestures, words, or expressions may convey.

The various ways of expressing *you* in many languages are bound to the culture of the speakers of that language. To take another example, although the total expression "I'm having breakfast" has an equivalent in all languages, the sentence may evoke different thoughts or images in speakers of different native languages depending upon the time they usually eat, what they eat, where they eat, etc.

The distances maintained by speakers as they converse, the sounds or grimaces they make are also considered an integral part of culture and communication. The study of "distances" is called *proxemics;* the study of gestures, grimaces, etc. made in speaking has been termed *kinesics;* while the study of non-articulated sounds (groans) is called *paralinguistics.*

The Contributions of the Sciences

Linguistics plays a key role, as we have noted, in language learning and teaching. Equally important, some would say, are the sciences of psychology, anthropology, and those of psycholinguistics and sociolinguistics. Following are several of the principles which underlie each of these sciences. Only those which have implications for language learning and teaching are noted.

Linguistic Analyses and some Implications

While the basic premises given under the Nature of Language above are the results of linguistic research, I believe you will find it useful in teaching to be aware of the major differences (or similarities) among the principal linguistic theories discussed in current literature. Only the briefest summaries will be given, of course. You will find a bibliography for further study at the end of the text.

Traditional Analysis

1. Interprets the sentence according to meaning and according to the communicative intentions of the speaker. Thus, sentences are *declarative, interrogative, imperative,* and *exclamatory*.

2. Defines eight parts of speech (noun, verb, etc.) either according to meaning or to function; for example, a *noun* is the name of a person, place, or thing (meaning); a *preposition* is a word which relates its object to the rest of the sentence (function).

3. Describes the syntactic functions of the parts of speech in sentences; e.g., a noun may serve as subject, object of a transitive verb, complement of a linking verb, object of a preposition, etc.

4. Concerns itself primarily with the written language.

5. Ignores functional varieties of language. (See p. 5.)

6. Gave rise to the grammar (prescriptive)—translation "method."

Descriptive (Structural) Analysis

1. Distinguishes structural meaning from lexical meaning. In the nonsense sentence, *The woogles fapped adfinkly,* we know, for example, that *woogles* is a noun because it is preceded by *the* and inflected for *plurality;* that *fapped* is the *past* tense of the verb *fap* and that *adfinkly* is an *adverb.*

2. Considers grammar to be a set of formal (i.e., pertaining to the form [phonological or graphological]) patterns in which the words of a language are arranged.

3. Studies the four meaningful signals of English: word form; word order; function words; and intonation patterns from a corpus of material that *has already been said or written.*

4. Proceeds from form to meaning; from phonemes to sentences.

5. Defines the parts of speech under two general categories: form class words (nouns, verbs, adjectives, and adverbs) and function or structure words (determiners, modals, prepositions, etc.).

6. Distinguishes between the spoken and the written language, giving priority to the spoken language.

7. Recognizes and describes varieties of language. (See p. 5.)

8. Analyzes sentences and utterances into immediate and ultimate constituents through a system of binary divisions until the final two divisions (the ultimate constituents) are reached; e.g., in the sentence: *The young boys are playing,* the first binary division would split the sentence into *The young boys* and *are playing;*

The young boys // are playing.

The sentence is then divided further as follows:

The young // boys // are // playing.
The // young // boys // are // playing.
The // young // boy // s // are // play // ing.

9. Emphasizes the fact (in what is known as the tagmemic theory) that there is a definite correlation between functional positions (slots) in sentences and the constructions (or classes of words) which fill the slots.

10. Stresses the importance of contrasts within a language and between languages. This concern has given rise to numerous contrastive analyses which predict the points of conflict or interference in language acquisition; that is, in going from the source (or native) language to the target language.

11. Gave rise to the "audio-lingual" method characterized by mimicry and memorization of long dialogues; pattern practice; and the injunction against grammar- "talking about the language."

Generative-Transformational Analysis

1. Illustrates that language makes infinite use of finite means.

2. Postulates a system of finite, explicit rules potentially capable of producing all and only the grammatical sentences of the language. (The analysis does not study a fixed corpus of materials.)

3. Characterizes the "rules" as "recursive," meaning that they can be applied over and over again to similar base structures.

4. Distinguishes between *basic underlying structures** (simple, active, and declarative *"s a d"*) and *transformations* of these sentence structures through the application of rules which *add to, delete,* or *rearrange* various elements in them to produce corresponding surface forms (those that we say and hear).

5. Suggests that all human beings are born with a language acquisition mechanism which allows them to understand and apply the rules of the language. This is often called LAD (Language Acquisition Device), or Language Processing Device.

6. Helps explain ambiguities in sentences by distinguishing between deep and surface structures; e.g., the now well-known pair, *Paul*

*These have been called *Kernel Sentences.*

is easy to please and *Paul is eager to please* "look alike" on the surface but come from two different, deep structures. Note also the "deep" difference between *It's a game he never wins* and *It's a shame he never wins.*

7. Introduces the concepts of "competence" and "performance." By "competence" is meant the ability of the native speaker to judge whether utterances are grammatical or not and whether they are synonymous or not by applying the rules which he has internalized without conscious awareness. By "performance" is generally meant instances of the speaker's competence—his actual use of his native language—his overt verbal behavior.

8. States unequivocally that language is *rule-governed behavior;* that it is *stimulus-free* and *creative.* The rules are so "powerful" that any native speaker can produce sentences which he has never heard or said before.

9. Reaffirms the importance of *meaning* in grammatical analysis.

10. Gave rise to the use of short, meaningful dialogues; the teaching of alternative, creative utterances in them; the attention to descriptive rules of grammar and vocabulary; and transformations of basic sentences.

Today, linguistic research is primarily interested in the semantic aspects of language and of communication. Several theories are in a stage of development. One theory—case grammar—emphasizes the fact that the lexical meaning of the verb determines the pattern and cases (ablative, dative, genitive, etc.) of the other elements of the sentence. For example, in the sentence *Rose went to London by plane,* the verb of *motion* is followed by a *locative* and by an *ablative* of instrument. Today, "situational teaching" and "communicative competence" are gaining ground rapidly in new texts and materials.

It will be interesting to see whether similar theories based on semantic analysis will be found valuable enough to be pursued and what applications they will have to language learning. Certainly their primary focus on communication and on interpersonal relationships is entirely laudatory.

From the *psychological sciences,* we know, for example, that:

1) Learning takes place when it is related to the needs and experiences of the learner. Motivation—both integrative and instrumental*—are of primary importance in learning. By "integrative" motivation is meant the desire on the part of the learner to

---

*This concept has been the subject of numerous research studies by Lambert and his colleagues. (See p. 200.)

identify with and become accepted by the speakers of the second language. By "instrumental" is meant his desire to learn the language as a tool to acquire a better education or a better job. Both types of motivation should be fostered in the classroom.

2) Gradation and logical sequence of language within larger grammatical categories are important. The material should go from the known to the unknown and from the simple to the more difficult in small steps—often termed "incremental." All new items should be *integrated* with those the students already know.

3) Many repetitions are needed to develop correct, fluent English.

4) Repetitions should be spaced at increasingly longer intervals. (See p. 60.)

5) Knowledge that a response is correct leads to the learning of that response. Incorrect responses should be extinguished as quickly as possible.

6) Learning is favored when meaningful association is established between sounds and concepts and between concepts and cultural or social situations. The more associations made, the greater the likelihood of retention and more immediate recall.

7) Understanding of the place and function which separate elements occupy in communication promotes learning. Learners should be given insight into the place and function of various language items and skills in listening, speaking, reading, and writing activities; that is, in real communication situations.

8) Language aptitude is important if the student is to go beyond the beginning and intermediate levels of proficiency. Carroll includes the following abilities in the term "aptitude": *phonetic decoding* (the ability to discriminate among sounds or other phonetic phenomena and to remember them for some time after hearing them); *grammatical sensitivity* (the ability to be aware of the function of words in a variety of contexts); *inductive language learning* (the ability to infer rules from given language forms); and the *ability to memorize. It is important to remember,* however, that high *motivation,* the *student's active participation,* and *effective teaching* can and *do* offset poor aptitude.

9) The more and varied kinds of association built around a language item, the better learning and retention will be. The same item should be reintroduced in many *different appropriate* situations and contexts as often as feasible.

10) Since the student restructures what we teach him in his own way, he must become an active and responsible participant in the learning process; generally, the more responsibility he is given for his own learning, the more he will learn.

11) Every individual has a different learning style and a different

rate of learning. Activities in the classroom should take these different modalities into consideration.

12) Students should be helped to perceive the relationships among the elements in language. Diagrams, graphics, and visuals of all kinds will favor retention of new material.

13) Transfer of learning is not automatic. Students must be helped to recognize the shared elements of two or more language features, the recurring rules, the co-occurrence of sounds or words, or the impossibility of co-occurrence; e.g., we can say "I watched a film," but not "I watched a book."

14) Each new meaning of the same word or each form (for example, the fact that verbs of perception or knowledge are *not* used with "ing") should be taught or, at the very least, pointed out and practiced individually. We should not make statements like, "'see' and other verbs like it do not add 'ing'," without giving many examples of the other verbs in meaningful contexts.

15) Items must be contrasted constantly in order to insure retention; e.g., the simple past versus the present perfect.

The science of *anthropology*, a relatively young science, has underscored two concepts that have immediate application to English teaching: One is that culture does not refer merely to the music, literature, and arts of a people. It refers also to the sum total of its value system, its customs and mores. Although there are differences among peoples because of geography, history, or other factors, *all* people are born, speak, walk, raise children, eat, seek status, and have faith. There are *no* people without culture. In the basics of life, *all* people have the same needs and aspirations. It is important in teaching, therefore, to emphasize the basic *similarities* among human beings in various societies as well as the differences. Even within one linguistic community or within one family, *individual* differences exist. Not *every* American has ham and eggs for breakfast! Neither does every Englishman have kippers or steak!

Anthropologists' studies have emphasized that language is the central feature of culture. The words and patterns of the language often determine the way in which people can talk about their experiences.

Students should be permitted—*encouraged* would be a better term—to talk about their native culture in *English*. This will serve at least four purposes: 1) it will give them a feeling of pride in their own culture; 2) it will demonstrate that the language they are learning is a tool of communication which permits them to express emotions and facts, values and beliefs as well as does their first language; 3) it will be a meaningful experience for them since their culture is an integral part of their personality and their lives; 4) it may retard or even eliminate the feeling of "anomie"—living in a no-man's land—which affects many students as they move away from their native language community and do not as yet feel accepted by the English speaking community.

Sociolinguistics, as the term implies, is concerned with the relationship between a society—a community of speakers—and language.

1. As already noted, language reflects the socio-cultural organization of a community of speakers. It is, moreover, the only instrument adequate enough to express the needs of that society.

2. Among the characteristics which help define a community are those related to the quality of verbal behavior of its speakers. Every act of communication includes the following: the language system, the speaker, the message, the receiver, the channel (face to face and telephone), the situation (including time and place), the contexts, and the frame of reference shared by the speaker and hearer.

3. Social roles generally determine linguistic roles (teacher and student; doctor and patient) and language varieties that may be used in the speech act. Each one of us switches our way of speaking many times during the day depending on our social role at the moment (Is it one of equality, superiority, or inferiority?); the social or professional situation in which we are playing a role; the degree of formality or informality required; the topic of conversation, and other factors which govern our verbal behavior. For example, in talking about a patient, a doctor may use several varieties:

The doctor to his wife: His condition is NG (not good). I'm really worried.

The doctor to the patient: You're doing pretty well. It will take a while but you should be up and around in no time.

The doctor to the patient's family: I can't be too optimistic. He may have to be hospitalized for at least a month.

The doctor to a colleague: These are the x-rays. What do you think? I'm pessimistic. Should I try some ______________?

The doctor giving a report: X-rays showed lesions . . . He is not reacting to the prescribed medication. The prognosis is guarded.

4. Verbal behavior depends to a large extent on social conditions. Factors which condition the use of language are age, sex, social status, and social role. The environment, both home and school, and the availability of mass-media also condition verbal behavior.

5. Within the language system can be found *geographic, social,* and *stylistic* varieties. Geographic differences may be slight—with minor differences in pronunciation or in lexical items—or they may be important enough to be called dialects which differ in varying degrees with respect to pronunciation, syntax, morphology, and lexicon.

6. "Registers" are generally studied from three points of view: the *professional* or *vocational* area or field used in a colloquial, informal, consultative, or formal *situation* and the *mode* used—oral or written.

7. Sociolinguistics studies not only the evolution of language across space (geographical variation) but also across time. Languages change, as we all know. The English spoken several centuries ago would scarcely be understood today.

8. Language interference may be *interlinguistic* (between the native language and English) and *intralinguistic* (within the English that has been studied up to that point). Errors in production are often the result of 1) false analogies made by the student within the system of English; 2) partial learning of a grammatical category or class; 3) lack of knowledge of the semantic range of a word or expression; 4) unacceptable use of an expression in a given situation.

Psycholinguistics

1. The personality of each individual determines his capacity, style, and variety of speech.

2. The influence, however, is a reciprocal one, since experiences with language may help to shape the personality.

3. Language and thought condition each other; in other words, the cognitive (thinking) and expressive processes influence each other. Thoughts are organized, structured, clarified, and correlated through the help of language (which is already structured and organized).

4. The verbal behavior of an individual depends on 1) innate factors such as aptitude, personality structure, and individual rhythm of learning; 2) external factors—socially induced—such as motivation and stimuli (family, ethnic, professional, peer groups); 3) the individual's ability to restructure learning, that is, to integrate it with previous knowledge.

Crucial Factors In Learning

The Students

Our consideration of sociolinguistics and psycholinguistics cannot help but underscore the fact that the student and the community in which he lives are central to the learning process. We have stated that the individual learner restructures, in his own way, the material we may present—based on his past experiences in acquiring knowledge and in solving problems. There are other factors, too, within the students which need to be considered.

You will understand from your own reading and from your own

experience that chapters could be written under each. My intention, however, is not to discuss any characteristic at length but, through questions, to make you more deeply aware, perhaps, of the complexity of learning and teaching a language. I hope, too, that you will bear in mind the answers to some of these questions as you prepare the various parts of your lessons and as you gather together the appropriate materials of instruction.

Age—Are your students young children who can imitate you easily? Will they prefer to learn language through games, songs, etc.? Are they adults whose native language habits are more deeply established? Are they adults who can be helped to analyze the new language?

Ability—Are there wide differences among the students in your class? How can you use the abilities of the bright students? How can you help the weaker students? Can you appeal to the *ear* alone? Do you need to appeal to the *ear* and *eye*? Do you need much concrete, visual material?

Aspirations and Needs—Particularly with adults, do they need to learn English to get a job, do further study, conduct a business, take a trip? Do they need to learn English quickly in order to be able to understand other subjects which are being taught in English? Do they need to learn English because they live in an English-speaking community?

Native Language—Are there any similarities in *sounds, structure,* and *vocabulary* with English? (A caution—Some "cognates" have completely different meanings: Example—French *assister* means to be present at and *not* to assist.) What are the basic *phonemic* features of the sound system? How do these contrast with English? What devices does the language use to show meaning? (Intonation, word order, inflection, function words, etc.) What writing system is used? (Alphabet? Pictures?) How is the culture reflected in the language? (How many forms of address are used? What are these based on—sex, age, social status?)

Previous Language Experience—Have they studied any other foreign language? How much English do they know already? Did they study English in a school where you might reasonably expect the methods and materials to be the ones with which you are familiar?

I could add many more questions. It is obvious that an effective teacher needs answers to these and to other similar questions. How can a teacher find the answers? Some of them are easily recognizable. Age and ability usually need no special study. In some situations and with young learners, however, it may be important to obtain results of tests of ability (if these exist in your community) and also to find out the grades the students make in their native language studies, particularly in the language itself. These will offer some clues to discouraging lack of progress. Is it due to poor ability on their part, no motivation, poor previous teaching?

If you are teaching in an English-speaking community, it is clear that your students need to learn English as quickly as possible in order to participate in the life of the community. If your students are adults and are not living in an English-speaking community, it is very desirable (through an interpreter if you do not know their native language) to find out what their needs and aspirations are.

In order to learn about the native language of your students (I realize this may not be possible for all groups if you have more than two or three language groups in your class), you could:

1) Examine any studies that have been made comparing English and the native language of your students.

2) Ask someone (a teacher, perhaps) who speaks the native language of your students to tell you in broad terms what the language does about word order, etc.

It may be desirable for *all* teachers of English to prepare a chart of the vowels and of the consonants of the students' native language, as well as of the other phonemic features to indicate the gross patterns of its structure and vocabulary, as is done for English. (See pp. 23.)

The School and Community

In this section as in the others which have preceded it, we cannot possibly explore the topic in depth. Again, I can only ask some questions hoping that you will seek their answers by asking questions yourselves, by observing, by studying, and by examining records and other materials.

1. How long is the English program? Is it an intensive program, for example? Is it a two-year, a three-year course?
2. Is the curriculum divided into various "subjects" *within* the English program? Does *one* teacher teach Spoken English, Written English, and Reading to the same group of students, or do different teachers teach different aspects of the language?
3. What facilities exist in the school? (language laboratory, library, television)
4. What instructional materials exist?
5. Is there a testing program?
6. How are records kept?
7. Are there provisions in the school for practicing or reinforcing English? (a newspaper, assembly programs, club)
8. Does the community have large numbers of English speakers?

9. What facilities does the community have? (library, museum, etc.)

10. Is it an urban community or a rural community?

11. Are there people in the community whom you could invite to speak to your classes?

12. Are there English language newspapers, radio programs, television programs, movies in the community?

13. Are people in the community interested in social mobility?

14. Are there opportunities for the language learners to feel that they can "enter" the English-speaking group?

15. Is there a tradition of education and instruction which will motivate the learner? Is he encouraged to acquire the language by his parents or by his peers?

You, The Teacher

Most important is *your* role in the learning process. In recent literature, the teacher has been called the "facilitator" or "mediator" of learning. To me, the terms imply that machines, books, school walls, or other people come between the teacher and the students. The truth is—as all of us know—that you could be sitting in a field with a group of students and still transmit to them not only your knowledge of English, but also—more especially—your interest in them as human beings, your desire for them to learn, and your enthusiasm.

You might wish to ask yourself these and many other similar questions:

1. Are you convinced that all normal students can learn?
2. Are you enthusiastic about your subject?
3. Do you plan your lesson carefully?
   a) Is it suitable to the age and ability levels of the students?
   b) Do you make provision for individualizing instruction so that pupils can work at their own pace or respond according to their present ability?
   c) Do you provide for a variety of activities which will have meaning for the students and which will foster their desire to communicate with each other?
   d) Do you vary your patterns of student participation in the classroom?
4. Do you evaluate your students' progress periodically?
5. Do you stop to judge yourself, your attitude, your choice of materials, your interest?
6. Do you make every effort to sustain the motivation of your students by giving them many small successes, by praising them, by establishing and maintaining warm, friendly relations with them?

7. Do you make *judicious* use of audio-visual aids?

8. Do you, when absolutely necessary, when you know the language, and when the same language is spoken by everybody, use the native language of your students?

9. Do you use a system of "buddies" (student helpers from the same class) to help their peers when these have fallen behind because of such factors as absence, inattention, poor comprehension of certain basic language elements on which others will depend?

10. If there is a language laboratory, do you integrate the work done in the classroom with that done in the lab?

Theories and Principles of Language Learning

No one really knows how learning takes place. In fact, one of the major reasons for studying verbal behavior is to be able to gain insight into the mental processes of human beings. There are two major theories currently in vogue and numerous research studies in linguistics and other sciences, as we have seen, which make it possible for us to state some principles which can certainly guide us in our profession. The works of Lenneberg, Chomsky, and others (see the General Bibliography) underscore the existence in every human being of a language acquisition device. It is important to remember, however, that even in acquiring his native tongue, the child must be in an environment where *he hears* meaningful "noises" and where *other people react* to the sounds he makes. The stages of language development in all children appear to be biologically determined, but they must receive (hear) the primary data (meaningful speech) which they will then process.

Two Theories of Learning

The learner's active participation in the learning process is a fundamental premise of the two currently favored learning theories. Stated simply, one—the cognitive code theory—underscores the fact that the learner brings to the task of learning an innate mental capacity. He brings his perception of relationships and his unconscious formulation of the "rules" resulting from his discovery of the structure and organization of new material and from his perception of its relationship with known material. Closely tied in to this theory of the importance of the individual's mental organization of learned material is research which seems to indicate that the nervous system stores up images and memories which can then be evoked without a preceding stimulus.

The other theory—the association or operant conditioning theory—is based on experimentation indicating that bonds can be forged between a stimulus and a response and that responses are shaped and strengthened or extinguished by the reinforcements or rewards which should always follow the learner's response to a stimulus. Such continuous association between stimulus and response, followed immediately by confirmation of the learner's correct response by a teacher, a tape, a record, a programmed text, etc., leads to the formation of the *habits* needed for placing sounds and words in appropriate arrangements.

Both of these theories have a place in language learning. After the student has *cognitive control* of the phonological, grammatical, and lexical patterns, he will develop the *habit* of using them with facility as he practices them in numerous activities.

A Handful of Principles

1. Language items should be presented in *situations* which will clarify their meaning. Through the dramatization of a plausible, realistic situation, students should be enabled to grasp the essential features of sound, structure, words, and the arrangements of these in the utterances used in it.

▶The separate elements of the utterances—presented and understood in a situation—may then be isolated and practiced—the presentation and amount of practice at any one time depending on whether an item is *of high frequency* and *useful in many other situations* (or needed by the students in order to use their textbook profitably.)

▶The spiral approach should be used. Any new item of language should be continually *re-entered in other larger language contexts* with which it can co-occur.

▶We should distinguish between *active* and *passive* acquisition of structure and vocabulary. Active items will be learned by students for purposes of *production* (both oral and written); passive items, for *recognition* or *reception* only (listening and reading comprehension). Naturally, many passive items may be presented and practiced for active production in subsequent lessons or at more advanced levels.

2. The *sounds*—found in an utterance already understood—may be practiced one at a time in isolation and/or by contrasting them in what is called "minimal pairs." For example, "pit" and "pet" is a minimal pair because *one* sound alone makes the difference in the meaning. (See p. 56.)

▶It is important, however, that a sound which may have been practiced in isolation be inserted immediately in words, phrases, or sentences which have, in addition, the *stress, rhythm, pauses* (or *junctures*), and *intonation* which are characteristic of English.

▶The grammatical interrelationships of phonemes should be pointed out; for example, (with older learners especially), serene, serenity; divine, divinity; meter, metric.

3. In addition to the sound system, learners must be taught *the structure system* of the language. Through numerous examples, learners must be given insight into word order, inflection, derivation and into the other meaningful features of the English language (e.g., The boy is going . . . The boys *are* going; I wash every morning . . . I'm wash*ing* now . . . I wash*ed* yesterday morning . . . etc.).

▶Insight into a pattern is not enough, however. Our students have to learn the basic "rules" which govern the arrangements of sounds, structures, and words in the English language. (See p. 176.)

▶Through the application of the rules in meaningful material, they should be enabled to create similar utterances in other communication situations in which they will find themselves.

▶Learners must be taught which other words within word classes (nouns, verbs, etc.) can be used in the place (*the slot*) of each of the words in a pattern. In "Did he go to the store this morning?" for example, *she* can be used instead of *he; ride* instead of *go; office* instead of *store,* etc.

▶Such substitution of word or expression is only the beginning, however. Pupils have to be given such thorough control of the sounds and structures of the new language that they can understand, speak, and perhaps read and write without having to worry about the position of each word in the sentence or the form of each word (e.g., when do they use—sing, s*a*ng, s*u*ng?; boy, boy'*s*?; child, child*ren*?).

▶Second language learning, therefore, means acquiring new habits or ways of using the speech organs and learning the forms and the arrangements of forms required by the system. It means acquiring the habits of the language through the intensive and extensive practice of numerous examples.

▶It means, with older learners, learning the "rules"; i.e., putting to use the insight into the recurring patterns of the second language which has been gained through the study (listening, repeating, practicing) of many examples. (It is important to remember that any reference to the recurring pattern comes *after* the study of numerous examples. The reference is usually a description of what actually happens in speech and not a "rule" of grammar. We will have more to say about this later.)

▶The sounds, forms, or word sequences must be taught and practiced *systematically* in a *progression* and *order* which will permit the learners to associate each little segment of newly acquired language with every other segment they have already acquired.

▶Through listening to, repeating, and studying many examples, students should be helped to acquire a repertoire of items they may come to expect in an utterance. The ability to "anticipate" language appears to be an important factor in the development of communicative competence.

▶They should be led to notice which features are *redundant* in the English language. In an utterance such as, The *three* boy*s* *are* going to get *their* coat*s*, there are several clues to plurality. (This awareness of redundant signals will be helpful to them in *listening*, but they will still have to be given extensive practice in using each one of the signals in their speaking and writing activities.)

▶Through the study of various examples, pupils should be enabled to recognize those sentences which look alike on the surface but are not really alike; e.g., "The man was drunk by noon" and "The man was struck by lightning"; and how to resolve ambiguity by expanding the context; e.g., "Visiting relatives can be enjoyable," might be expanded to clarify its two possible meanings as: I always like to go to their homes; or We always have fun when they come to see us.

▶They should also be helped to recognize the relationships among the various possible transformations of a base sentence.

▶Students need not only knowledge about features such as those mentioned above but also practice in them in varied, stimulating, meaningful situations which will lead to really stimulus-free (creative) communication.

4. Language learning means acquiring the ability to ask and answer questions; to make statements; and to produce the normal, authentic forms used by native English speakers. For example, when someone asks, "Where did you go last night?" a possible normal response is "To the library." It is *not* "I went to the library last night."

▶The end result is "free" communication. This ideal can only be reached, however, if students are helped, through orderly presentation and extensive oral practice to communicate from the very beginning of the course. More will be said about this later.

5. It is important to reaffirm that although the new language material may be *introduced* in situations (conversations or brief narratives in which people, events, and objects in the environment are clearly delineated) you will have to do the following: 1) *select* the material for intensive "active" presentation; 2) *grade* it according to its complexity; 3) *order* it according to criteria of frequency of use; e.g., *teach* I, You, We, They first because they have the same verb form and because *I* and *You* permit immediate communication; 4) *arrange* the model utterances in a way which will permit students to perceive the recurring features and hence the underlying rule. (See p. 61.)

6. Language learning includes learning the culture, gestures, and spoken expressions which give added meaning to the words or sentences. An intonation pattern may express anger in one language but delight in another.

▶Dinner in the United States usually takes place about six or seven o'clock. In some regions of the United States, the noontime meal is called "lunch"; in others, it may be called "dinner." In Spain, one has "dinner" after 9:30 p.m.

7. The fourth and extremely important area of the English language we must help our students acquire is its vocabulary.

▶Within vocabulary (the *lexicon* of the language), we distinguish between *content* words (pen, school, go, pretty, etc.) and *function* words (with, for, may, will, etc.). The function words need to be learned as quickly as feasible (in a logical order and sequence, however). The content words can be learned in small groups around "life" situations. At the beginning stages of language learning the same words are often used repeatedly to give practice in the new structures (I need a pen; I'd like a pen; Will you buy me a pen? etc.).

▶Although vocabulary is important, its over-rapid acquisition in the early stages should be subordinated to that of the sounds and the structure (grammar) of the language. Vocabulary can be accumulated quickly as the need arises later and as wider reading is begun *after* the basic sound and structure system of the language has been learned.

On the other hand, vocabulary items—although low on a word frequency list—should be taught as soon as feasible if such teaching stimulates students to talk about the immediate environment. For example, words like *skyscraper, cow, sheep* may have to be taught immediately if the classroom window looks out on them.

The watchword is "judiciously." You should teach those items which will give the students the feeling that they are talking about the real things in their environment and which they would ordinarily talk about in their native tongue.

Each of these principles has definite implications for teaching procedure. Before examining questions, however, such as, How do pupils learn the sounds? How can we help them acquire control of the structure system? How is vocabulary taught?, it is necessary to "look at" the features of English to be taught.

Some Features of the English Language

Its Sound System

Only the briefest description, always in very simple terms, will be given. Suggestions for further study will be found at the end of this Guide.

A parenthetical statement may be in order before we proceed. Linguistics is a comparatively young science. Many experiments in the field are still in progress. Their results may not be known for years to come. It is natural, therefore, that some controversies exist among linguists about some symbols, some terms, and even some concepts. The facts given below are those *generally* accepted by a majority of linguists.

Since we will have occasion to refer to them several times in this Guide, the organs of speech, or *vocal organs*, are indicated on the following diagram.

The Vocal Organs

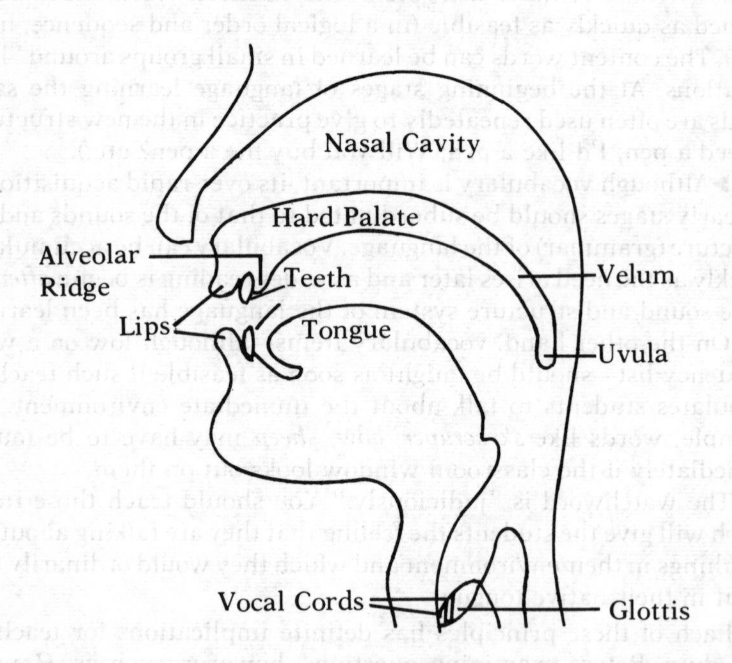

Below there are two sets of symbols representing only the significant sounds of the English language. These sounds, the *phonemes*, are those which produce a difference in meaning.

The first column (headed *IPA*) gives symbols of the International Phonetic Alphabet with slight modifications (for example, a for ɑ; y for j) since these are widely accepted. The second column (headed *T & S*) gives the symbols used by Trager and Smith in their text *An Outline of English Structure* and adopted by many American linguists with various modifications (e.g., ɑ w for aw; ɔy for oy).

Consonants

IPA	*T & S*	*English Word*	*IPA*	*T & S*	*English Word*
b	b	**boy**	s	s	**soap**
d	d	**do**	ʃ	š	**ship**
f	f	**first**	t	t	**tie**
g	g	**go**	θ	θ	**thin**
h	h	**hit**	ð	ð	**then**
k	k	**cook**	v	v	**very**
l	l	**let**	w	w	**water**
m	m	**man**	y	y	**yes**
n	n	**no**	z	z	**rose**
ŋ	ŋ	**sing**	ʒ	ž	**pleasure**
p	p	**put**	tʃ	č	**cheese**
r	r	**robe**	dʒ	j	**judge**

Vowels

IPA	*T & S*	*English Word*	*IPA*	*T & S*	*English Word*
a	ɑ	**hot**	ɔ	ɔ	**law**
æ	æ	**map**	o	ow	**hope**
e	ey	**made**	u	uw	**spoon**
ɛ	e	**let**	ʊ	u	**foot**
i	ɪy	**eat**	ə	ʌ	**but**
ɪ	ɪ	**sit**	ə	ə	**above**

Diphthongs

IPA	*T & S*	*English Word*
aɪ	ay	**tie**
aʊ	ɑw	**how**
ɔɪ	oy	**boy**

In addition to the symbols shown here, many texts contain other variations of these two major systems. It is important, therefore, that you study carefully the pronunciation symbols in any text that you use.

Since the IPA has been the basis of many of the variations and since it is widely known throughout the world, I shall use its symbols in future examples throughout this Guide. The symbols will be within slant lines / / to indicate that they are the *phonemes* of the language. Phonetic symbols, covering a much broader range of sounds, are generally enclosed within brackets [ ].

In working with phonetic and phonemic symbols, it is important to remember that *no* symbol can help a student to *make* a sound. What is significant is that we know 1) the *sound* associated with the symbol and 2) the techniques to help our students *hear* and *produce* the sound. It is also important that we and our students attach the *same* sound to a symbol or to a gesture. The symbols serve only as memory clues when the students do their assignments or as helps to them when they look up a word in a dictionary.

One of the important things we should know about the English sound system is how the sounds are made—particularly those which could cause a *difference* in meaning in the language. As noted above, we call such sounds the *phonemes* of the language. The sounds /ɪ/ and /ɛ/ between /p/ and /t/ in *pit* and *pet,* for example, are phonemes because they alone make the *meaning* different in the two words. We know that /p/ and /b/ are phonemes because in the words *pit* and *bit* only the sounds /p/ and /b/ make the meaning different. Each language has its own *phonemes.* In some cases, however, the same phoneme may exist in the native language of your learners and in English, *but* it may exist in a different position within a word. For example, we can put together (cluster) /sk/ at the *beginning* of a word (e.g., school). Spanish speakers never have that cluster at the *beginning* of a word and therefore will find it difficult to "produce."

What other features are phonemic in the sound system of English? Three: *stress, intonation,* and *pause (juncture).*

Let us examine each of the features of the English phonemic system in turn. We will start with the "vowels" and "consonants."

What makes a difference in sounds? Several things:

1) The vibration of the vocal cords. Pronounce /b/ several times putting your hands on your throat. Now pronounce /p/ several times. The vocal chords were *vibrating* for /b/. They were *not* vibrating for /p/, were they? We call sounds which are made with the vocal cords, *vibrating* or *voiced* sounds. When the vocal cords *do not* vibrate, we say the sounds are *voiceless* or *unvoiced.* All vowels are *voiced.*

The *voiced consonant phonemes* in *IPA* symbols are /b/, /d/, /g/, /l/, /m/, /n/, /ŋ/, /r/, /ð/, /v/, /w/, /y/, /z/, /ʒ/, /dʒ/.

The voiceless consonants are /f/, /h/, /k/, /p/, /s/, /ʃ/, /t/, /θ/, /tʃ/.

Notice the pairs of voiced and unvoiced consonants (the voiced consonant is first): b/p; d/t; g/k; ð/θ; v/f; z/s; ʒ/ʃ/,dʒ /tʃ.

2. Does the breath come out of the mouth or the nose? In the nasal sounds /m/, /n/, and /ŋ/, the breath comes out of the nose, doesn't it?

3. Is the air stopped in our mouths as we make a sound? Could it continue? Where is it stopped? (If it is stopped, for example, we may call the sound a *stop*.) *T* is a stop. (Try it!) *M* is a *continuant.*

4. What happens to the position of the vocal organs as we make a sound? Where do the vocal organs come together? To what other

position do they move? What is the position of the tongue, of the lips, of the teeth? In other words, what about the *articulation?*

The Vowels

Let us examine the *vowels*:

I studied French with this vowel triangle. It is just as useful in studying English. Notice how your tongue moves from front to back; notice how your lips become more rounded or less rounded as your jaw opens and closes.

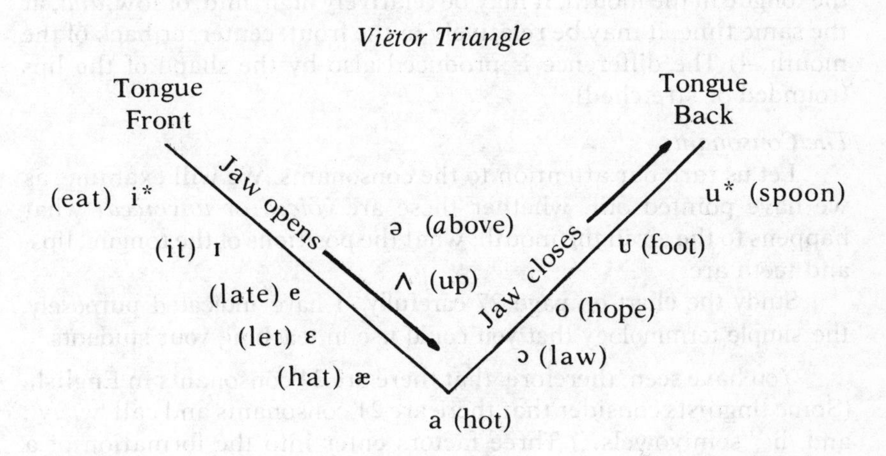

The following vowel chart, although in another form, gives you the same information about the tongue position of the phonemes shown and will help you to help your students make the sounds.

The highest part of the tongue is		*front*	*central part*	*back*	
high		i** ɪ		u** ʊ	*of the*
mid	*in the*	e ɛ	ə ʌ	o	*mouth.*
low		æ	a	ɔ	

*Some linguists do not consider these simple vowels *phonemic*.

** Simple /i/ and /u/ are not considered phonemic because some English speakers do not use them in their dialects.

As you make each vowel sound, study carefully the position of your lips. Are they rounded or stretched back? Are they tense?

All the simple vowels (above) can occur alone or with /y/, /w/, or /h/* so that the tongue glides (goes) from the vowel position to the /y/, /w/, or /h/ or from the /y/, /w/, or /h/ to the vowel position. Pronounce: *toy* /toi/, *ice* /ais/, *how* /haU/, and *hoop* /hup/.

We know, then, that in English 1) there are 9 *simple vowels,* which can be used alone or in combination with /y/, /w/, or /h/. 2) The vowels are voiced. 3) The differences in sounds are produced by the position of the tongue in the mouth. It may be relatively high, mid, or low, *and,* at the same time, it may be relatively in the front, center, or back of the mouth. 4) The difference is produced also by the shape of the lips (rounded or stretched).

The Consonants

Let us turn our attention to the consonants. We will examine, as we have pointed out, whether these are *voiced* or *unvoiced*; what happens to the air in the mouth; what the positions of the tongue, lips, and teeth are.

Study the chart on page 27 carefully. I have indicated purposely the simple terminology that you could use in teaching your students.

You have seen, therefore, that there are 24 consonants in English. (Some linguists consider that there are 21 consonants and call /w/, /y/, and /h/ "semivowels.") Three factors enter into the formation of a consonant: (1) the vibration or lack of vibration of the vocal cords; (2) the point of obstruction of air in the mouth, if at all; and (3) the points of meeting (the *articulation*) of the lips and the relation of the tongue to the teeth and the palate.

Also *phonemic,* because they produce differences in meaning, are *stress, intonation,* and *pause (juncture).* We will study each in turn.

Stress

Stress is the name given to the relative degree of loudness of a part (syllable) of a word, or of a whole word, or of a syllable within an utterance.

---

* /y/, /w/, /h/ are sometimes called semi-vowels.
These combinations with /y/, /w/, and /h/ are sometimes called "complex vowel nuclei."

Passage of air	*Vibration of Vocal Cords*	*Two Lips*	*Lower Lip-Upper Teeth*	*Tip of Tongue-Upper Teeth*	*Tip of Tongue-Back of Upper Teeth*	*Front of Tongue-Front of Palate*	*Back of Tongue-Soft Palate*	*The Vocal Cords*
Completely stopped	No—*Voiceless*	p			t		k	
	Yes—*Voiced*	b			d		g	
Two sounds: A stop followed by a continuant	No—*Voiceless*					tʃ		
	Yes—*Voiced*					dʒ		
Through a narrow opening	No—*Voiceless*		f	θ	s	ʃ		
	Yes—*Voiced*		v	ð	z	ʒ		
Through side of tongue	No—*Voiceless*							
	Yes—*Voiced*				l			
Through nose	No—*Voiceless*							
	Yes—*Voiced*	m			n	ŋ		
No stoppage	No—*Voiceless*							
	Yes—*Voiced*	w			r*	y		h

*Tongue curls toward back.

For our purpose, we may distinguish two kinds of stress. There is *word stress* and *sentence stress.* Each word or word phrase has one primary stress. We say agaín, néver, ápple tree, bús route, good býe, go ín, try ón, come báck. Word stress *can* be *phonemic.* Study, for example, "cóntract" and "contráct." Word stress is often called "accent."

There are four possible phrase* stresses in English:

1) the loudest—called primary—usually marked /

2) next to the loudest—called secondary—usually marked ^

3) the third loudest or medium soft—called tertiary—usually marked \

4) the least loud—called weak—usually marked ᴗ

(Many books, however, do not mark weak stress.)

Let us examine *sentence stress.* In a sentence like "I'm studying English," the stress is on the *E* of English, isn't it? Every sentence has at least one stress, but it may have two or more, depending on the length of the sentence or the meaning you want to convey. A sentence like "What are you doing?", for example, may have stress on *What* and stress on *do.* A short answer such as "Yes, I did" may have stress on *Yes* and on *did.* Almost any word in a sentence can be stressed depending upon the situation or on the meaning one wishes to convey; e.g., It's *my* business. It's my *business.*

Stressed syllables are usually *longer* and *louder,* giving English the *rhythm* which we say is characteristic of English.

Rhythm

Rhythm, which depends on the accented syllables in each utterance, is rather regularly spaced in English. In speaking we try to maintain the same *time* between one stressed syllable and the next stressed syllable in the utterance. In order to maintain the rhythm, we say the unstressed (unaccented) syllables *faster.* We do that by crowding the unstressed syllables together and by pronouncing all or most of the unstressed vowel as /ə/ or not pronouncing them at all. Notice how people normally say a sentence like—

What are you going to do? /wat ə yə goiŋ tə du?/

Intonation

Intonation is the name given to the levels of pitch (the relative height of the voice) in a sentence. When we talk about intonation, we include, too, the rising of the voice or the fading of the voice into silence

*No single word has four accents, but word combinations or phrases do; e.g., élĕvâtŏr òpĕrâtŏr.

at the end of an utterance as well as the sustained pitch of the voice in certain sentences we will examine later.*

There are *four* relative levels of pitch. (We use the term "relative" because the height to which the voice rises varies from speaker to speaker.) These are marked in different ways by various linguists. Some use 1 for the lowest pitch; some use 1 for the highest pitch. Some use lines. Some use arrows. I will use lines and numbers (to reinforce the lines). Most people start to speak at pitch level 2. Pitch level 2 is *normal* level. The voice then usually rises to 3 and then remains at 3 or falls to 1. Level 3 is *above normal;* level 1 is *below normal.* Level 3 is usually (but not necessarily) the level of the stressed part of the sentence. Level 4 is *way above normal.* It is usually used to express emotion, anger, surprise, delight, etc.

This is how I will mark the examples:

2 What are you 3 do ing? 1

When the word on which there is stress is the *last* word in the sentence and is a one-syllable word, we use a *diagonal* line to show that the voice glides from one position to another. Notice:

2 When did he 3 leave? 1

There are *two* important intonation patterns in English. It is desirable to concentrate *only* on these two in teaching English at the beginning and intermediate levels of the elementary and secondary schools and at the beginning college level.

1) We use *rising-falling* intonation in—

a) Simple statements

2 He came to 3 see me. 1

b) Commands

2 Go to the 3 door. 1

c) Question-word questions

2 Why did he 3 leave? 1

d) Attached questions ***sometimes (when we're *not* asking for information.)**

---

*Some linguists prefer to call these "terminal contours" since they mark the end or termination of an utterance.

**In attached questions, when we're *asking for information,* we use *rising* intonation. Notice:

2 He didn't 3 go, 2 did 3 he?

He didn't go, did he?

The fall and fade out of the voice is often designated by a /#/ (double cross).

e.g., Why did he leave? #

2) We use *rising* intonation at the end of questions which do *not* begin with a question word.

Examples: Is he there?

Can you get it for me?

Notice that in sentences with *rising* intonation, everything that follows the *rise* (the stressed syllable) is also pronounced on the high pitch or level.

The rising and fade out of the voice is often designated by a / ∥ / (double bar).

e.g., Can you get it for me? ∥

We also use *rising* intonation in direct address and in introductions. Notice:

Mr. Brown, this is Miss Jones.

How are you, Mrs. Jones?

In a *series,* we use *rising* intonation until the last item where we use *rising-falling* intonation.

I need books, pencils, and crayons.

Sustained pitch in utterances is designated by a / | / (single bar). It is used where, in *writing*, we would ordinarily place a comma or a dash. Notice:

Are you there | John?

The pitch of *there* and the pitch of *John* are the same, but if you say the sentence aloud, you will note that you have prolonged the sound of *there* more than if the sentence had been "Are you there?"

One last brief word before we leave the important subject of intonation. A contrast, such as Was he angry? and Was he angry! will show immediately that *intonation* is phonemic.

Internal Juncture or Pause

Another important feature of the English sound system which makes a difference in *meaning* is *internal juncture.* The word *pause* is often used to indicate juncture. This type of pause is unmarked in writing.

Say: The night rate /nait + ret/ is cheap.
The nitrate /naitret/ is cheap.
Say: Ice cream /ais + krim/.
I scream /ai + skrim/.

We would say that, in the first sentence, there is *plus juncture* between *night* and *rate.* In the second pair of utterances, the *plus juncture* comes between *ice* and *cream* in example 1; it comes between *I* and *scream* in example 2. There is no difference in the pronunciation of the other sounds, is there? The difference in meaning is caused *only* by the slight pause.

One other remark needs to be made about the sound system. As far as speech is concerned, what is considered a sentence? Look at this example: Question: "Where did you go yesterday?" Possible answer: "To the movies." For the purposes of *speech,* $_2$To the ^{3}mo vies$_1$ where there is a complete fading out of the voice after $_1$, may be considered a sentence.

Some linguists distinguish between *sentences* (a group of words with a subject and predicate) and *nonsentences.* In order to avoid discussion, the term "utterance" is used more and more frequently. An utterance is the name given to any meaningful act of speech which includes the features of the sound system we have been discussing (i.e., pitch, rising or fading of the voice, stress, or pause). For example, in an exchange such as "Who came in?" . . . "John.", *John* is an utterance.

We have seen that *sounds, stress, juncture,* and *intonation* are at the very core of spoken language. All are important in understanding and speaking English and all of them must be taught. Since the teacher must be concerned with helping his students learn these features, more will be said about the method of teaching them in Chapter IV.

Some Notes on Structure

In this section, I will confine myself to pointing out only some of the basic features of the English system. I will do so by presenting some examples of speech and posing some questions. Suggestions for further study will be found at the end of the Guide.

▶We noted earlier that an important aspect of the system is the use of *word order.*

Compare: Mary is home. Is Mary home?
Can you say: "Spoke to I him" and be understood?
Where is your word "not"—before or after *is*?
He is not (or he isn't) an American.
Wouldn't "I go every morning to the park" sound "foreign" to your ears?

Is *a station bus* the same as *a bus station*?

▶English uses *inflection*—that is, it may add or take away something from a word or change the form of the word to show number (singular or plural), tense (present or past)*, etc.

Notice: The *boy* is here—The *boys* are here.
The *boy* is in the classroom. The *boy's* book is in the classroom.
This is *my* book. This is *mine.*
I gave *him* a book. *He* gave *me* a book.
I *talk* to John every day. I talk*ed* to John yesterday.
I *sing* every day. I *sang* yesterday.
Sally is *pretty.* Joan is prett*ier.*

▶English uses *function words* to express relationships or meanings. There are over 150 such words in English, the number depending upon the linguist's preferences; e.g., the inclusion of pronouns. Some of those we use most frequently are:

1. *Articles* (or determiners)—a, the, an, this, some, etc.
   Give me *a* book (any). Give me *the* book (already mentioned).
2. *Auxiliaries*—do, have, be
   I want to go. I *do*n't want to go.
   I saw him. I'*ve* seen him many times.
   John wrote the letter. The letter *was* written by John.
3. *Prepositions*—at, by, for, from, of, on, in, with, to—are the most frequent.
   The book is *on* the desk. The book is *in* the desk.
4. *Conjunctions* (coordinate and subordinate)—and, but, until, although, etc.
   I want the book *and* the pencil.
   I want the book, *but* I don't want the pencil.
5. *Interrogatives*—when, where, etc. (often called "wh" words)
   When did you go? *Where* did you go?
6. *Degree words*—more, most, very, too
   May I have *more* bread?
   It's *very* hot today. It's *too* hot to go out today.

*Linguists today prefer to talk about two *tenses* only. They consider expressions like I'*ve talked* to John—or I *had talked* to John—*verb phrases.*

7. *Modals*—English uses *modals*—may, etc.—with verbs to indicate different degrees of reality or possibility.

Consider:

I *may* go to the movies.
I *might* go. (A little less probable)
I *can* go.
I *should* go. I *ought to* go.
I *must* go. I *have to* go.

Notice these additional examples of features of English structure.

1. I like *cheese.*	Give me a *cheese sandwich.*
2. Give me the *lamp oil.*	Give me the *oil lamp.*
3. It's a *long foot.*	It's a *foot long.*
4. He walked *along the street.*	He *walked along.*
5. He *took* his coat.	He *took off* his coat.
6. *Look! There's* an airplane.	*There's* an airplane in the sky.
7. *It's* cold out today.	Poor dog. *It's* cold
8. *Go* to the shop every day.	*I go* to the shop every day.
9. *Sing.*	*Let's sing.*
10. The *man's legs* are long.	The *legs of the table* are high.
11. The boy is *tall.*	The boys are *tall.*
12. He's *a tall* boy.	He's *a very tall* boy.
13. *You're* going, *aren't you?*	You're *not* going, *are you?*
14. *One* never knows.	Let me have the *one* in the window.
15. He's *un*able to speak.	His *in*ability to speak is sad.
16. You understand me.	You *mis*understand me.
17. He usually eat*s* at one.	He *can* eat at one.
18. He'*s* walk*ing* there.	He *might walk* there.

Notice these responses:

1. Are you going to be a doctor?	Yes, I *am.*
2. What did you *do* yesterday?	I *studied.*
3. Do you think it's going to rain?	I think *so.*
4. Do you have *any pencils?*	Yes. Here's *one.*
5. Who'*s* at the door?	Mary *and* John.
6. You like rice, *don't you?*	No, I *don't.* Yes, I *do.*

Basic sentence patterns in English include the following:

Two parts: Boys / eat.

The little boys at school / like to eat all the time.

Three parts: John / wrote / a letter. (This is a favorite sentence type.)

The men in the office / have had to write / long letters to their clients.

Four parts: John / wrote / me / a letter.

The women of the Colonial Association / are going to write / all the people they know / several letters.

Basic types of English sentences include:

1.	*Subject*	*Verb*	*Object*		*(Adverb)*
	He	saw	John		(yesterday).
2.	*Subject*	*Verb* (be)	*Predicate*		*(Adverb)*
	He	is	well		(now).
3.	*Subject*	*Verb* (look)	*Complement*		*(Adverb)*
	Rose	looks	fine		(again).
4.	*Subject*	*Intr. Verb*	————		*(Adverb)*
	Birds	fly	————		(gracefully).
5.	*Subject*	*Verb*	*Ind. Object*	*Dir. Object*	*(Adverb)*
	She	gave	John	a book	(last week).

Transformations include:

1. Sentences with unstressed *there*
   There's a man at the door.
   There are four books on the table.
2. Inverted questions
   Will he study later?
3. Question-word questions
   What do you want?
   Whose son is that?
4. Commands and requests
   Speak to him.
   Let's speak to him.
5. Emphatic expressions.
   He saw it *himself*.

This brief listing was obviously not intended to cover all the features of English. It will serve, however, to point up, particularly to native English speakers who have never had to think about form, order, inflection, or function, some of the more important characteristics of English which signal meaning.

Its Vocabulary

Following are several comments with respect to the *lexicon*, or the vocabulary of the language:

Words become meaningful only when studied and considered in *context*, that is, with all the other words which surround them and which help give them their meaning. Note, for example:

Show me your hand.
Hand in your papers.
Language is handed down from mother to child.

Linguistic science has pointed up the fact that our old definitions such as "A noun is the name of a person, place, or thing" are not accurate. Is *hand* a *noun* in the sentences above?

It is not even a question of the *idioms* of the language. The word *get*, for example, has over two hundred meanings. Notice:

Here's five cents. Get the paper.
Get the paper. It's on the table.
He got a good mark on the test.

One of your students' learning problems will be caused by the fact that the semantic areas in their native language do not necessarily overlap with those of English. For example, we use "thin" when talking either of a human being or of a piece of paper, while other languages have two different words to express the concept. To illustrate further, "a cake of soap" in English may be (literally) a "bread of soap" in French or a "piece of soap" in Italian.

A vocabulary item may use a different prefix to mean *not*, for example, even when the root is the same; e.g., *unable* but *inability*. Words may add formal suffixes; e.g., *man, manly, manlike, mannish* or they may change their base form completely, depending on the "register." Note, for example, *man, fellow, chap, guy, bloke*.

In *Teaching and Learning English as a Foreign Language*, Prof. Fries has divided the content* words of our language into *things, actions*, and *qualities*. He further subdivides words into *simple, compound*, and *derived*. Let us examine several examples:

Content Words

Things:

Simple — door
Compound — doorknob
Derived — arrival, goodness, ability

*In addition to *content* words, there are the *function* words studied above.

Actions:

Simple — run, walk
Compound — call up, take off, put on
Derived — enjoy, soften, harden

Qualities:

Simple — true, false
Derived — misty, childish, broken

II. The Curriculum

If you are asked to teach English in a school where no curriculum exists, if there is a need to revise the curriculum which does exist, or if you cannot obtain graded textbooks, the material in this chapter should be of particular interest to you. In most situations, however, the school will make available a syllabus or teaching guide and series of textbooks for each level of learning. You would, then, present as much of the material in each book as is recommended for each level or as much as your students can assimilate.

Even where a curriculum and textbooks exist, however, you may wish to round out the content of your English program by considering the items and suggestions in this and the following chapters. Again, comments will be brief and stated in terms which will be understood by professional teachers and by people without any training who may find themselves in a situation where they are asked to teach English in schools or to individual pupils.

Some Basic Premises In Curriculum Development

▶A curriculum guide for an English program usually includes the following for each learning level:

1) an analysis of its aims and goals (the terminal behavior the students will be expected to acquire).

2) a list of the language items to be taught (phonology, structure, and vocabulary).

3) a list of the cultural concepts to be discussed.

4) an analysis of the language skills to be developed (listening with understanding, speaking, reading, and writing).

5) a description of the activities and meaningful situations through which the language items will be introduced and practiced.

6) suggestions for evaluation (testing) of the pupils' language growth.

7) sources for teacher reference and pupils' texts.

▶The content of the curriculum at any level will depend on several factors: the *age* of the pupils, the *number of years* the English course will last, the *aims and scope* of the program. For example, will there be emphasis on listening and speaking only, emphasis on reading (for those in need of reading scientific journals), etc.?

▶With these considerations in mind, curriculum writers select and grade the material for each level, determine the number of items to be learned, and weigh the relative emphases of the skills at each level. (How much listening and speaking will be done at Level I? How much reading? How much writing? Will the same proportions in skill development be maintained after the first level?)

▶Since language learning is *cumulative,* provision is made to relate all new language skills to those which the students acquired at previous levels or in previous units.

▶No skill which has been developed (listening or speaking, for example) is (nor should it be) entirely neglected *even when* another skill is being emphasized in teaching.

▶Although each facet of a skill or feature of English may be practiced separately, these are brought together in real situations constantly so that pupils become aware of their interdependence or relationship in actual use.

▶The curriculum of the English program is so designed that it enables the pupils upon completion, to continue to study and read by themselves, to increase their skills, and to specialize in any aspect of English of their choice.

▶Unless there is some urgent reason to change the order, *priority* in the curriculum is given to: 1) all the sounds and the entire phonemic system; 2) the basic word-order structures; 3) the function words; 4) the inflections which are most frequent; 5) the vocabulary which: a) will help the students practice the structures; b) is useful in the pupils' immediate lives and environment; and c) will strengthen their conviction that English can be used to express the same ideas they express in their native tongue.

These language features are not *presented* separately. Sounds and intonation patterns are learned as they are found in a dialogue or in a reading passage; structures, function words, and arrangements of words are learned and practiced as they are found in meaningful material which duplicates the communication situations of real life. It cannot be underscored frequently enough that each item of language depends upon and is related to every other item.

▶The oral language activities which are written into the curriculum afford the students practice in understanding and in answering questions; in making statements in the affirmative and in the negative with long or with short answers; in responding by carrying out directions; in making comments (of agreement, of disagreement, of surprise, etc.); or in asking questions. The oral practice activities should enable them gradually but with perceptible progress to carry on a conversation about things they would ordinarily talk about in *their own language* with people of *their own age group*.

▶The content of the curriculum starts with the students *themselves* and with *their* environment. It is only by relating it to their own experience that a new item becomes meaningful to them. If, for example, the reading material in your text refers to transportation in a large city in the United States or in Great Britain, it is desirable to discuss transportation as *your students* see it and live it *before* proceeding to the unfamiliar concept.

▶The primary aim of language teaching is to develop "communicative competence"; that is, to help students recognize and produce language which is not only correct but also appropriate in the social situation in which it is being used.

▶Whatever the aspirations or needs of the learners, they should first be enabled to acquire the *basic common core* of English. Later, or concurrently—in situations where immediate communication is a necessity—they should be made aware of the varieties (formal, informal, etc.) and registers which would be most appropriate in a given situation. (See pp. 12–13 for further discussion.)

▶One further comment is made here and noted throughout this Guide. The selection and presentation of linguistic material should permit the learners to make functional, that is, *communicative* use of the language at *all* points of the English program from the very first day. (See p.74.) The functional and the linguistic aspects should be presented and practiced simultaneously.

Aims and Levels

Two words I have used—aims and levels—need further explanation. What should be the *aims* of the program? What do we mean by *levels?*

In the regular English program whether it starts in the elementary or secondary school or the university, we usually talk about *five* principal aims. We aim to give the student:

▶The *progressive* ability to understand the English he would use at his age when spoken by a native English speaker. (By native speaker, we mean a person who either was born and learned English in an

English-speaking country or a person who has learned English well enough to sound like a native English speaker.)

▶The *progressive* ability to carry on a conversation with a native English speaker on topics of interest to persons of his age group.

▶The *progressive* ability to read material in English with comprehension, ease, and enjoyment.

▶The *progressive* ability to write correctly and perhaps creatively in English.

▶The information, knowledge, attitude, and insight to appreciate the cultural similarities and differences (if such exist) of English-speaking people.

A brief comment should be made here. The culture need not and should not be taught systematically. When a word or a concept arises which needs special explanation, and you know the explanation, give it by all means. But, particularly at the beginning level, we should try to remember that language *is* culture, and that culture is learned automatically as the language is developed.

Since an English-learning program may start in the elementary school, the secondary school, or the university, it is desirable to talk about *levels* of English learning. The first level is the *beginning* level of English language learning; the second level is the *intermediate* level; and the third level may be considered the *advanced* level. In the regular secondary school (high school) program, the first level is the first year of high school. If the language is begun in the junior high school, * the first level may be the first two years of the junior high school. In that case, a student who has begun English in the junior high school may enter the second level or intermediate level in the high school. When language is started in the elementary school, the first level may be spread over three or four years. At the university, the first level may be of only one semester's duration. All the factors we have already discussed (age, length, and type of course, etc.) must be considered in talking about levels.

Curriculum Planning

At any rate, the name of the level is not important. Several things in curriculum planning, in addition to those we have mentioned, are important, however: 1) The material from one level should lead naturally and sequentially into the next level. 2) The material should be graded even within the situational teaching approach. For example,

*A school which pupils enter after about six years of instruction.

we would start with one modifier of a noun before giving three modifiers together; we would teach the regular "s" plural (/z/, /s/, /ɪz/) before we teach the "exceptions." 3) There should be provision for the constant reintroduction of all the material we have taught with the new material we are teaching. 4) We should not try to teach *all* the vocabulary around a topic or all the forms, meanings, or uses of an item of structure at one time. Instead, we should use what is called a "spiral approach."

Let us study an example of the "spiral approach" from a cultural topic: The first time (at the first level) we speak of "family," we may present the names of immediate family members—*father, mother, brother, sister.* At the second level, we may add to the family members list the words *grandmother, grandfather, uncle, aunt, cousins.* At the third level, perhaps, we may want to teach *mother-in-law, son-in-law, great-aunt, relatives,* etc.

Now let us look at an example in a feature of structure—the inflection of pronouns, for example. At Level I, we might teach, "*I* have a book" and "This is *my book*." At Level II, we might teach "Give *me my* book." ("Give *him his* book," etc.) At Level III, we might teach "This isn't *mine.* It's *theirs.*"

Where English must be learned quickly because it is the language of school instruction or the language of the surrounding community, attention (and priority) will have to be given to the structure and vocabulary items needed not only for participating in the other areas of the curriculum but also for making an effective personal and social adjustment to the life of the community. Again many factors will have to be taken into consideration; e.g., What is the age of the learner? Is there a bilingual program in operation in which some of the curriculum areas are taught first in the student's native tongue? What are the vocational needs of the older learner?

I will now make some *suggestions* with respect to the content at each level. Please remember that this same content may be spread over a longer period or condensed into a shorter period. If your school system uses a syllabus or books and if the year-end examinations are based on the books, *use the content of the texts,* adapting or enriching it judiciously in harmony with your students' interests.

After listing some structural items, some cultural topics (which will suggest the vocabulary content), and some features of the sound system, I will indicate generally desirable proportions for emphasis within the skills of listening, speaking, reading, and writing. For the sake of convenience, I have separated word order, inflections, etc. It is immediately obvious, however, that inflected nouns or verbs are placed in a certain "order" in an utterance and that there is overlapping.

Some Suggestions for Content

Level I

The Sound System

All the vowel and consonant sounds in English; the two basic intonation patterns (with emphasis on statements, inverted questions, and short answers); the characteristic stress and rhythm of English (reduced and contrasted forms) in the grammatical patterns you teach.

Structure*

1. The simple and continuous present of *be, have,* and "regular" verbs (eat, sing, etc.) in *statements.*
2. Questions with *be.*
3. The place of *not.* (Teach both forms. He's *not* a student; He *isn't* a student.)
4. The place of the auxiliary *do* in *questions* and *negative statements* with *have* and "regular" verbs. (Teach, Have you? etc.; i.e., the interrogative of *have* without do.)
5. The place of the noun *complement.* (I'm a student. I have a book.)
6. The place of the adjective after *be.* (He's tall. It's green.)
7. The place of the descriptive adjective before a noun, singular and plural: (I have a red pencil. She's a good student. They're good students.)
8. Question-word (Wh)** questions with *who, where, when, how, what,* etc.

Function Words

Prepositions: in, on, at, for, from, of, with, by, near.
Determiners: a, an, the, this, that, these, those.
Conjunctions (coordinating): and, but.

Inflections

Plurals of nouns: boys, girls, (some irregulars—children, men).
Regular comparisons.

---

*If other *high frequency* structures appear in the dialogues or readings, you should present and practice them too for production; i.e., active use. (See p. 60.) Students should also be helped to respond to (understand) other structures which may remain "passive" at this level. (See p. 189.)

**Some authors call these "information questions."

Pronouns

Personal: I, you, he, etc. (The major emphasis should be on the I-you alternates.)*

it, they

Possessives: my, your, his, etc.

Verbs and Verb Phrases

Simple present: I eat every day.

Present with *now*: I'm eating now.

The *going to* future: I'm going to eat.

Commands: simple and polite—Go to the door. Please go to the door.

Requests: Let's and Let's not.

Responses

Short answers—affirmative and negative with verbs taught: Yes, I am; No, I'm not; No, it's not; Yes, I do., etc.

There

There's a book on the table. There are two books on the table.

Miscellaneous Items (this is only a sampling.)

Numbers 1 to 20

Days of the week

Months of the year

Courtesy formulas; e.g.,

How are you? I'm fine.

Thank you. You're welcome.

Greetings and leavetakings

Classroom formulas; e.g.,

Show us

May I have (leave)

Time—hours and half hours

Vocabulary (Cultural) Content

1. Introductions and self-identification; names of students in room. (You may wish to assign an English name to each student.)

2. The Immediate Classroom.

Instructional materials.

Parts of the room.

Activities such as listening, reading, writing.

Subjects such as English, mathematics, social studies.

* Some linguists consider pronouns "function" words.

3. The School.
   Location of rooms.
   People in the building (names, titles [Mr., Mrs., Miss]).
   Procedures and schedules. (We come to school at eight o'clock. We come to school on Mondays.)
4. The Family.
   Names of immediate family members.
   Relationships.
   Ages (He's . . . . . years old.)
   Occupations (My father is a carpenter.)
   The house (its rooms).
   Activities (e.g., I get up at 7; I eat breakfast.)
5. Curriculum and other areas as needed.

The Skills

Suggested proportions of time. (We will discuss the "place" of reading and writing in the next chapter.)

Listening —40%
Speaking —40%
Reading —15% } Reduce or *omit* entirely in the *elementary* school
Writing — 5% } course under the second grade or year.

Level II

The Sound System

Review all the sounds and the two basic intonation patterns. Teach the change in stress when noun complements are replaced by pronouns: 2 He bought the 3 gro ceries. 1; 2 He 3 bought them. 1 Teach the intonation of attached (tag) questions (See p. 29); the stress on the second part of two-word verbs in sentences such as 2 Take it 3 off; 1 2 Turn them 3 on. 1 Teach word stress (accent) and word pause if the materials of instruction you are using contain examples of them. Work on increased fluency in increasingly longer sentences and on stress and rhythm.

Structure

Review the structures taught at Level I. In the review, strive for more accuracy, more habitual control, more immediate and fluent response.

Word Order

1. Expressions of time, such as *in the morning; at noon.*
2. Expressions of place, such as *at the office.*
3. Expressions of place and time, such as *to school in the afternoon.*
4. Frequency words, such as *usually, always.*
5. *Some, any, a lot of,* etc., before countable and non-countable nouns.
6. Comparisons with *more* and *most.*
7. Verb followed by two complements (objects): He gave *her a book;* He gave *it to them.*
8. Noun-noun combinations: Give me a *ham sandwich;* Show me a *pocket comb.*

Inflections

Pronouns:

1. Direct and indirect object (me, him, etc.): Give *him* the book. I saw *him.*
2. Possessive: *mine, yours,* etc.
3. *Whose*

Nouns:

Possessive: the *man's* hat

Countable and non-countable nouns:

Give me the *books.* Give me the *ink.* I need *water.*

Comparisons with *er* and *est.* (irregular forms.)

Adverbs: *slowly, quietly*

Verbs and Verb Phrases

Past tense: affirmative, negative, and interrogative of *be, have,* and other verbs.

Two-word verbs: (*take off; put on*)

Commands in the negative: *Don't go.* (This may have been taught at Level I.)

The verb *do* as a "substitute" word. (What did you do yesterday?)

Function Words

Modals: *can; may; must; should.*

"Will" future: negative and interrogative.

Responses and Attached Questions

Short answers—affirmative and negative: *Yes, I did; No, I didn't.*

"Tag" (attached) questions with all the verbs already studied: He's tall, *isn't he?* She isn't pretty, *is she?* I can go, *can't I?,* etc.

Miscellaneous Items

The clock: quarter hour; time *past* (after) and *to* the hour.

Intensifiers: *too, very.*

Too and *either* in: I like it *too;* I don't like it *either.*

Exclamations: *What a* pretty dress! *How* pretty!

The months of the year; the seasons. (Many of the months will have been learned "passively" as you placed the date on the blackboard each day and had the students repeat it.)

Vocabulary (Cultural) Content

(Please remember that as you review known classroom objects, places, and people in the school, you should *add* new vocabulary items within those same topics.)

The Home

1. Meals (items, hours).
2. Health and health practices (dressing, illness, bathing, etc.).
3. Clothing (include reference to seasonal changes); fabrics (wool, silk, cotton, etc.), sizes, colors; making, buying.

The Family

1. Names of more distant relatives (aunt, uncle, cousin, etc.).
2. Activities and likes or dislikes of family members.

*The Surrounding Community**

1. Transportation facilities.
2. Communication facilities.
3. Stores (kinds).
4. Shopping (money, courtesy expressions, expressions of quantity, etc.).
5. Government agencies (police station, post office).
6. Places of recreational interest (park, movie, library, theater).
7. Addresses, names, numbers to 1000, and the use of numbers in address (1822=eighteen twenty-two).

Holidays

As they occur (if possible). You should also teach the vocabulary of holidays which are *not* typically American or British but which are within *your* students' experience.

Gifts; visiting; greeting cards.

The World of Work

Occupations and some responsibilities within each.

---

*In an English-speaking community the vocabulary items in this topic would have been taught at Level I.

The Skills

Suggested proportion of time:
Listening-Speaking—40%
Reading—40%
Writing—20%

Level III

The Sound System

Review the phonemes; give extensive practice in contrasting words and phrases; teach the intonation patterns in emphatic speech, particularly those which are found in your texts; give drills in sentences of increasing length; emphasize rhythm; teach reduced forms (the use of ə) in spoken language.

Structure

Review the structures taught at Levels I and II, striving always for greater ease and fluency and for a more sustained response; that is, for more than one statement or question as a response to your question or statement—e.g.,

1: "That's a pretty dress."
Response 1: "Thank you."
2: "That's a pretty dress."
Response 2: "Thank you. It's new. I bought it last week."

Word Order

Multiple modifiers before a noun: "I bought *several very pretty white* dresses."

Prepositional phrases: The girl *with the pretty eyes;* the book *with the long title;* the legs *of the table.*

Included sentences or clauses: I'm sure *he's in the house.* The girl *who is near the table* is my friend Alice. I was eating *when he came in.* I'll study *while you eat,* etc.

Questions with *how long,* referring to both time *and* measurement; *how much;* etc.

Indirect questions and statements: Does he know where he wants to go? I know what he wants. The man asked me where I lived.

Verbs and Verb Phrases

Aspects and time in verb phrases: I've known him for a year; I've known him since Monday: I've been waiting for an hour; He shouldn't have taken the car.

Sequence of tenses after "if":
If it rains, I'll go; If it rains, I can't go.
If it rained, I wouldn't go.
If it had rained, I wouldn't have gone.

The "ing" form after verbs like enjoy, prefer; e.g., She enjoys *swimming;* he prefers *fishing;* and expressions such as "Thank you for *helping* me."

The "ing" form after adjectives; e.g., I'm interested in *learning.*

The "marked" infinitive: I'd like *to eat.* I want *to see* him. I want *you to see* him. I'm happy *to be* here. Tell her *to study.*

Short answers with the marked infinitive: Yes, I'd like to; Yes, I want to.

Special verbs taking two objects: tell, read, write, ask.

The passive with *be*: Teach only the forms commonly used in "real" speech. English speakers do *not* say, for example, "It was sewn by the tailor."

Modals: might; could; have to; ought to.

Adverbial Expressions

He went *by bus;* He did it *through hard work.*

Too, very, more, before adverbs: He drives too quickly; Speak more slowly.

Miscellaneous Items

Substitute expressions such as *I think so; I'm sure of it; I know so,* as responses to questions like: Do you think it's going to rain this afternoon? (Yes, I think so.), etc.

*Some*one; *every*one; *no*body; *one;* etc.

Linking words: however, moreover, etc.

Vocabulary (Cultural) Content*

Educational opportunities (for more advanced study).
Government, religion, social agencies.
Travel to the "wider" community (by ship, by plane).
Family—more distant relationships.
Holidays—(customs).
Vacations (mountains, beach, at home).
Music, literature, the arts.
Leisure-time activities—hobbies; community centers.
The world of work (including labor laws).
Cross-cultural concepts.

* Other topics can be added, depending upon *your students'* needs and interests.

The Skills

Suggested proportion of time:
Listening-Speaking—40%
Reading—40%
Writing—20%

The methods and devices you may wish to use to present the contents of the curriculum, the activities which will help in the development of each of the skills, and some suggestions for integrating the skills into real communication will be the subject of the next chapter.

Additional Comments on Curriculum Design

You should examine as many textbooks as possible in the field of teaching English as a second language. The sequence, organization, and content of the materials in the textbooks and a realistic appraisal of your students and community will help you in planning the curriculum for your course.

You will find that there are available many excellent textbooks in the field. It is not usually necessary to write completely new material. You can adapt existing materials to your classroom needs and add readings, dialogues, and other activities to supplement traditional or "dry" basic content. The ideal textbook for every situation will never be published, but the conscientious teacher can usually breathe life into *any* textbook. In examining any book, it is good to remember, however, that the author may not necessarily intend the book to be used at a specific level or for a specific period of time.

Using Existing Textbooks

The author's introductory remarks should always be studied carefully. An author does not usually expect a teacher to follow the items within each unit or lesson exactly as they are written. For example, a textbook may start with a conversation or reading passage containing new vocabulary; then give five grammar points; then give ten exercises; and then list the vocabulary. It is not intended that in presenting the units, the teacher will do *all* the conversation or reading first; then *all* the grammar; then *all* the exercises. For example, the new vocabulary should be clarified and practiced when it is *needed;* that is, *before* the conversations are learned or before the exercises are done.

Beginning teachers will find it desirable to study the entire text if possible but certainly each unit of work (or "lesson")* to be taught carefully. *All* the new material in the "lesson" should be listed and then divided into three or four categories: (1) pronunciation problems; (2) new structures; (3) vocabulary and culture; (4) practice activities (including reading, writing, and homework).

The teacher should then study the items of *new* material in order to decide: 1) the number of *teaching* lessons necessary to treat all of the material, 2) the review needed to relate the new work to familiar work, 3) the gradation of the material in a logical sequence. The teacher will ask himself: Which structures will be taught first? Which practice activities will be used with which new structures? When will the new vocabulary items be taught? How will the material be approached —through a conversation, through a story, through a related structure? What homework can be assigned? What materials will be needed?

Dividing a Unit of Work

Let us study a possible example. We will assume that your unit** is on the past tense (negative, interrogative, etc.), and contains a reading passage with about 30 new vocabulary words. How could you break the unit into teachable "hour" (45-60 minute) lessons? (See below for preliminary activities.)

Lesson I***

1) Motivate the need for the new material.

2) Review the simple present; the days of the week; the clock; words like *today* and *yesterday*. (Have a clock and a calendar available.)

3) Teach (in mini-situations) and practice the *function, meaning,* and *one* sound form of the past (with nouns and with I, you, etc.). You might start with the known verbs whose *past* ends in the sound /t/ (washed, walked). This starting point will permit the students to ask each other meaningful questions about their daily routines.

Lesson II

1) Review the material in Lesson I.

2) Teach and practice the /d/ past of verbs (I opened, closed, etc.). (Some of these verbs may be part of the new vocabulary.)

---

*By "lesson" here I mean the unit of work which must be divided into several teaching lessons.

**This example is based on an actual text in wide use in many school systems.

***It is expected that university students will need about three or four hours to cover the material and that younger or less able students will need more than eight hours to cover the same material.

3) Teach the interrogative of /t/ and /d/ pasts; "Did you . . . . . ?" after reviewing the "Do you . . . . . ?" form to show the similarity in word order and form.

Lesson III

1) Review Lessons I and II.

2) Teach the/ɪd/form (wanted, needed). Use questions with *why;* e.g., Why did you go to the (post office)?

3) Teach about five new vocabulary items needed to practice the structures.

4) Teach the negative after reviewing "I don't . . . . . " in order to show the similarity.

Lesson IV

1) Review Lessons I, II, and III with other time expressions (last year, a week ago).

2) Teach about five "irregular" verbs (saw, went, etc.) in the affirmative, negative, interrogative. Use these in dialogues and other situational contexts.

Lesson V

1) Review Lessons I through IV.

2) Teach the past of *be* and *have*—including the affirmative, negative, and interrogative.

3) Create brief, authentic dialogues in which the new items are inserted and dramatize them.

Lesson VI

1) Review Lessons I through V.

2) Teach some other irregular verbs (if they appear in the exercises, in the reading, or in the conversation of the textbook).

3) Teach the short answers: Yes, I did; No, I didn't; Yes, I was; No, I wasn't.

4) Begin the reading lesson. (A technique for teaching reading will be found in Chapter III.)

Lesson VII

1) Review Lessons I through VI.

2) Complete the reading lesson.

3) Dramatize the dialogues again.

Lesson VIII

1) Review the entire unit.

2) Engage in oral activities which *add* the *past tense* verbs to other structures you may have taught; e.g., I saw the man's hat; He usually went there on Wednesdays; etc.

3) Give a short test; a dictation or an aural comprehension exercise. (The procedure will be explained below.)

It goes without saying that the material within a teaching unit has to be carefully "ordered," and that we should keep constantly in mind the psychological "laws" of learning we mentioned above. We build on what our students know; we go from the simple to the more difficult; we do *not* present more than one new point at a time; we give intensive practice; we relate the new material to other known material in actual speech (and later—reading) in order to give our students the feeling that this new building block occupies an important place in our "communication" building.

A Possible Lesson Schedule

In conclusion, I should like to ask you to consider the following possible "hour" (usually 45-60 minute) schedule:

Warm-up—Recital of known material (days, dates, names, conversations, questions and answers on familiar structures) to loosen students' tongues—3-5 minutes.

Homework Correction (if homework was assigned)—short quiz—7 minutes.

Pronunciation Drill—3 minutes.

Approach to New Material (through review, related experience, or comparison or contrast with a known structure)—8 minutes.

Statement of Aim of New Lesson. (The teacher tells the students what they are going to learn or read.)

Presentation of New Material (new dialogue, new structure, new reading)—5-10 minutes.

Oral Practice Activities—15 minutes.

Summary of Lesson—2 minutes.

Overview of Homework Assignment or Review of Conversations—3-5 minutes.

Looking Ahead—"Next time, we'll talk about . . ."

And now let us turn our attention to some desirable and generally accepted practices for developing the skills of listening, speaking, reading, and writing. *Within each of these* skills we have to concern ourselves with the sound system, the structure system, and the vocabulary. We will also examine some more formal procedures for giving our students insight into the culture of English speakers.

III. Developing the Language Skills and Cultural Insights

Approaches

There are many generally accepted ways of approaching (leading into or introducing) the teaching of the sounds, structure, and vocabulary of the language and of the normal forms of conversation. Some teachers prefer to start by having students listen to and dramatize a conversation or a dialogue; some teachers prefer to start by helping students read a narrative paragraph; some start directly by presenting the new structure in authentic utterances* which are later used in a conversation; some start by telling well-known stories (fairy or folk tales); some teachers even start by dramatizing an Action Series such as "I'm getting up; I'm going to the door; I'm opening the door, etc."

The approach you use should depend on the age of your students; on their interests; and on the length and major aims of your course. Each approach has merit. Many teachers today prefer the situational (conversational) approach, in which students hear, dramatize, and perhaps memorize a short dialogue. They consider that the dialogue duplicates most closely the normal speech of native speakers. Whichever *other* approach you use to teach any feature of the language and whatever the needs of your students, provision should be made for giving them practice in the normal forms of conversation; i.e., in

---

*Let us remember that an "utterance" unit is a stretch of speech by one person before which there was silence on his part and after which there was also silence on his part. (Fries, *The Structure of English*, p. 23.)

listening to questions and answers; in making responses; and in participating in conversational exchanges of varying lengths.

You may prefer to vary your approach, depending on the structure you are going to teach. With one, you may find it most desirable to *start* with a dialogue; with another, you may wish to start with the structure and then (after you have practiced several examples) to incorporate them into a real conversation. Certainly, within every unit of work there should be provision for the study and dramatization of two or more dialogues of four to eight utterances each. These dialogues may be in addition to or they may include the questions and answers related to the structure you have been practicing. The dialogues should not be confined to questions and answers alone but should include all forms of normal speech such as statements, questions, responses, commands, formulas, complete sentences, and one-word utterances.

One dialogue could serve to *introduce* new structures (in combination, of course, with structures and vocabulary which are familiar to the students). One could serve to *reinforce* the new structures *after* these have been practiced. The cultural setting may be similar to the one in which the structures were introduced. Another dialogue may give practice in the same language items, but in different sociocultural situations.

Stages In Language Growth

Whatever the approach (conversation, story, etc.), your teaching of any language *item* should follow six sequential steps:

1. The pupils should be led to *understand* the material. This may be done through pictures, blackboard drawings, diagrams, charts; through paraphrases (sentences using familiar words which explain the new word, as for example, "A butcher is a man who cuts meat"); through dramatization of a situation in which the item is embedded; through a brief explanation in English; through an equivalent expression or a summary in the pupils' native language.

▶The use of the pupils' native tongue is a controversial issue. If all pupils speak the same native language, if you know the language, if it will save time and lift morale, no harm will come to the students if the native language is used occasionally and *judiciously*. If you *do* use the native language, do it in the following way: Say the English in a normal voice, give the native language equivalent *once* in a low voice, give the English again. In general, unless there is misunderstanding, do *not* repeat the same expression in the native language in a subsequent lesson. The use of the native language should not be allowed to become a permanent crutch. (See Appendix IV, p. 170.)

▶*Pupils should never be asked to repeat or otherwise practice material whose meaning is not clear.*

2. They should be led to *repeat* the material after you say it as often as is necessary. Do not strive for mastery at this stage.

3. They should be led to give a description of the *sounds, form, function, position,* and *meaning* of a grammatical item. This is often called a descriptive "rule" or a generalization. This step would be omitted in the lower levels of elementary school.

4. They should be led to *practice* the material in as many ways as possible.

5. They should be led to *choose* the correct word, expression, or structure (in statements, responses, or questions) from several choices.

6. They should be helped to use the new material in *every* communication situation where they can express ideas without worrying about inflections, word order, stress, or any other feature of the English language system.

As I noted earlier, an English program usually aims to develop the skills of understanding, speaking, reading, and writing while giving insight into the culture of which the language is a part. Within *each* of the skills, attention must be given to *phonology* (the *phonetic and phonemic system*), to the *grammar* (the *structure system*), and to the *vocabulary* (the *lexicon*). Each of the language skills makes use of *sounds* (even reading, as we will indicate later), *structure,* and *vocabulary.* I will therefore take these three major areas of language in turn and give some brief suggestions for teaching them. As I do so, I will make continuous reference to the six "stages" listed above. I will start with phonology since what we say and hear in any speech act is a string of sounds, the *output* of the prior mental combination of the semantic and syntactic components.

The Listening-Speaking Skills

(The Audio-Oral or Audio-Lingual Skills)

The Sound System or Component

The sound system is learned best through imitation of the teacher or of a tape or record. It goes without saying that the teacher is preferred to any electronic or mechanical device for the first *presentation* of the new material. The only situation in which we can justify the use of the tape or record *before* the teacher's live presentation is one in which he feels that his command of the language is not at all adequate. Many teachers also prefer to introduce songs through recordings.

Tapes and records are very effective, however, in making possible the *additional sustained* practice which language learning requires. Where possible, these should be used *after* the live presentation.

With older students whose ingrained native language habits may seriously conflict with the production of the new language sounds, guided imitation of the teacher is usually not enough.

After identifying the sounds which cause most difficulty to your students, you might use several techniques or a combination of techniques to teach them: 1) a *description* of the speech organs as the sound is being produced; 2) a *diagram* of the speech organs; 3) a *comparison* with the nearest sound in the students' native language (if you know the language);* 4) a *modification* of a known English sound. (This may be particularly good in teaching the voiced and voiceless pairs—b/p, f/v, s/z.)

All descriptions should be simple; e.g., for the /u/, "The lips are rounded (show yours and/or draw a sketch on the board); the tongue is back."

A diagram should be uncluttered and clear. You should learn to sketch the lips, teeth, palate, and tongue on the board. Using dotted lines, indicate the position of the tongue or the *movement* of the tongue from one sound to the other.

A very effective device is to sketch a large profile on a cardboard, indicating the lips, teeth, palate, and bottom of the mouth. Omit the tongue. Cut out the cardboard to show the mouth cavity. Make a red mitten for your right hand. As you teach a sound, use your gloved hand in the open mouth cavity to simulate the tongue. Move it against or between the teeth, bunch it up in the back, curl it up to the palate for /r/, or indicate movement from one sound to another.

After you teach one sound (the sound of *th* in "thin," for example), teach a contrasting sound (/d/ or /t/ or /ð/) in familiar words, those needed in the new lesson, and even in unfamiliar words.**Teach them in minimal pairs, if possible; that is, in words in which there is no difference except for the sound you are contrasting—for example: thin/tin; tin/din; beat/bit; Pete/pet; wine/vine; yellow/jello; zoo/sue; etc.

With older students, you may find it desirable to give the meanings of the pairs in the native language to convince them that the phonemes

---

*If a similar sound exists in the pupils' native tongue but in a position which is not similar to its position in English, you may make the students aware of the fact that they *do* know and use the sound. You will help them *isolate, extract,* and *use* it in its new English position.

**Most teachers prefer to give practice with words which students can use immediately in communication situations. When incomplete words are used, indicate the missing segment by a line, e.g., prob—(problem); —ferent (different).

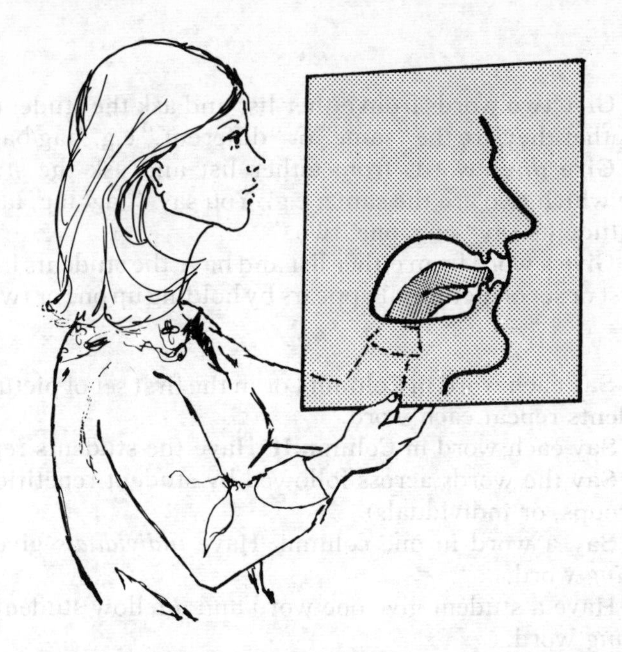

do make a meaning difference. You may find it necessary, too, to give pronunciation practice which does not exist in the textbook if your students have difficulty with certain sounds. You may even have to change the textbook order of teaching the sounds.

There are three essential steps in teaching your students to make sounds. They must be able to:

1) Hear the sound.
2) Identify the sound.
3) Produce the sound.

Following is a brief illustration of a procedure you may wish to use to insure recognition and production. Let us assume the problem is the /g/ and /k/ in final position. *Use simple pictures illustrating the words* or the words themselves (which can be placed on the board in print, or in cursive writing).

I	II
bag	back
hag	hack
rag	rack
sag	sack
tag	tack
wag	wack

1. Say all the words in Column I (or Set 1 of the pictures) two or three times.
2. Say all the words in Column II two or three times.
3. Say the words across several times.

* * *

4. Give two words from either list and ask the students to indicate whether they are the "same" or "different," e.g., bag/bag—same.

5. Give *three* words from either list and ask the students to indicate which two are the same; e.g., You say, "tag, tag, tack." Individual students say "one, one, two."

6. Give a word from either list and have the students indicate on which list or set of pictures it appears by holding up one or two fingers.

* * *

7. Say each word in Column I or in the first set of pictures. Have the students repeat each word.

8. Say each word in Column II. Have the students repeat.

9. Say the words across followed by student repetition (whole class, groups, or individuals).

10. Say a word in one column. Have *individuals* give you the *contrasting* word.

11. Have a student give one word and a fellow student give the *contrasting* word.

12. Use words from both columns in short utterances. Have the students listen to and repeat each one in ways suggested above.

A few other points about the teaching of sounds are necessary: 1) Do remember to teach minimal pairs in positions other than initial or final (e.g., miller, mirror). 2) Present minimal pairs in situations whenever feasible; e.g., Student 1: This mitt is no good. Student 2: Then don't play with it. Student 3: This meat is no good. Student 4: Then don't eat it. 3) Remember to point out the correlation between pairs like *meter* and *metric; insane* and *insanity.* 4) Teach consonant clusters in a gradual build-up of words; e.g., *were, word, world, worlds.* 5) A technique you may use to correct particularly troublesome sounds is to have some pictures available showing minimal pairs of phonemes. When a student or the class mistakes one sound for the other, point to the correct one and say, "It's this sound." (e.g., *bag, back*) or whatever picture is most appropriate in the cultural setting in which you are teaching.

The "test," of course, is Stage 6 in our language learning process: Can students *distinguish* between sentences like "The sentence is long" and "The sentence is wrong" or "I see the ship" and "I see the sheep," and can they *produce* the correct sound in "free" communication situations?

A word of caution before we proceed to the other elements in the sound system: You may have to reteach the same sound or remind the students of the pronunciation of the same sound a hundred times or more. With older students particularly, habits of using the speech organs in one's native tongue are strong. Of the three major components of language, the sound system is the most difficult to acquire.

Intonation is taught by imitation of many similar sentences. I would recommend that you teach only the two basic intonation patterns first: the *rise-fall* intonation, and the rising intonation used in inverted questions (those usually requiring a "yes" or "no" answer).

It may be desirable to indicate intonation lines on the board, or numbers 1-4; or to use an upward arm gesture to show rising intonation and a downward arm movement to show falling intonation; or to place up or down arrows (↑↓) at the end of the sentence; or to place curved arrows (↗↘) over the words having the highest or lowest pitch—or whatever helps *your* students.

Any of the techniques for indicating intonation will help. Combinations of the techniques are even more helpful.

Phonemic stress (word accent) is taught by *contrast.* Hearing; identifying the difference; producing the difference; using the words in sentences which show meaning differences; and finally using the contrasting words in "real" speech situations are the steps needed to insure a knowledge of words in which stress is phonemic.

I would reserve for the intermediate or the advanced level the placement of stress on different parts of a sentence to show varying emphases. For example:

2 "Did 3 you go to the movies yesterday?" (or your brother?)

2 "Did you go to the movies 3 yesterday? (or last week?)

2 "Did you go to the 3 movies yesterday?" (or to the library?)

The typical *rhythm* of English is learned by imitation and by practice in saying increasingly longer sentences using the words in the first sentence in the longer sentences: May I have that book? May I have that big book? May I have that big history book? May I have those two big history books?, etc.

With older students, you may also wish to teach the symbol /ə/ and to write it over words which are "weakened" or reduced in speech—e.g., "Can (/kən/) you go to the movies?" "Yes, I can." (/kaen/) (Notice the *full* value of the vowel in the *short answer.*) You may also wish to teach older students the phonemic symbols as reminders of the sounds. Whether you do or not will depend on your experience in using them, the students' writing system, their age, needs, etc.

The emphasis in language learning today is on achieving understanding. It is recognized by most authorities that the complete elimination of a "foreign accent" in the majority of adults is impossible without a tremendous expenditure of time and effort. This effort might better be given to acquiring greater fluency and control of structure.

The practice of structure patterns will automatically contribute to more accurate sound production. You should strive for *comprehensibility* at all times, however, even during those periods in the lesson when you are not giving concentrated practice on elements of the sound system.

With youngsters, the situation is different. It is always amazing to hear the accuracy with which many will mimic your speech.

The Structures

A procedure you will find useful in presenting structures for "active" use (whether or not they have been heard first in a conversation or story) is as follows:

1. *Motivate* the new structure. You may do this by dramatizing a situation; by reminding students of a familiar dialogue or narrative passage in which it was used; by asking them how they would say something in their native tongue.

2. *Review* briefly *familiar* language items which you will need in order *to present, clarify, or practice the new language item.* For example, if you are going to teach adjectives, review appropriate content words; if you are going to teach the simple present, you may wish to review expressions of time; if you are going to teach the present perfect, you may wish to review the verb *have* and also the simple past (in order to contrast the two "tenses").

3. *Use* the structure in a normal utterance.

4. Make sure the students *understand* the utterance. Do this by dramatizing an action many times; by using a picture; by giving several sentences in English with familiar words which help explain the one you are teaching; or by giving them their native language equivalent (as a last resort, however).

5. *Repeat* the utterance many times. The number of repetitions will depend on the known sounds or sound sequences in the utterance. If you have a large class, walk to various parts of the room so that all students can see your mouth.

6. *Have the utterance repeated in chorus* by *the entire class* several times. Give the model *before each* repetition you ask of the class.

7. If the sentence is long (6 or more syllables), or if the sound sequence is unfamiliar, you may wish to *break the sentence into smaller elements* for practice. Break it from the end. It is easier to keep the same intonation when you start breaking it from the end. Of course you may vary this occasionally by breaking the sentence from the beginning. Here is the procedure for breaking a sentence from the end. Let us take "He's going to read now."

a) Say the entire sentence many times.

b) Say "now." Class repeats: *now.*

c) Say "read." Class repeats: *read.*

d) Say "read now." Class repeats: *read now.*

e) Say "going to." Class repeats: *going to.*

f) Say "going to read now." Class repeats: *going to read now.*

g) Say "He's going to read now." Class repeats: *He's going to read now.*

8. *Engage in group repetition* of the same sentence (half a class; the right side; the left side; the front; each row; etc.). Indicate the group which is to repeat with a hand signal which you have devised and with which you have made your class familiar.

9. *Have individual students repeat* the same sentence. It is a good idea to start with your more able students. In that way, your less able students will have more time to listen to and repeat silently a reasonably correct sentence.

10. If there are errors in pronunciation, *you* say the sentence and engage the class in choral, group, or individual repetition again.

11. Using *familiar vocabulary only, give other sentences* which illustrate the point you are teaching and have the students repeat them. For example, if you are teaching the adjective of color after "be," say *as you show each item,* "The pencil is red. The pen is red. The book is red. The notebook is red." etc.

12. *Ask questions* which make your students "see" that the word "red" is a color; that it follows "is"; that it does not change.

a) Step 12 may be done *after* you place several sentences on the board in the form of a chart. Do *not* place the sentences on the board unless the students have heard them and can say them with reasonable accuracy and fluency. With younger students, you may prefer *not* to write sentences on the board at all.

b) The grammatical terms you use in helping your students "see" the *form* (sound; i.e., phonological or spelling; i.e., graphological), *meaning, position,* and *function* of any new item will depend to a great extent on their knowledge of grammatical terms in their native tongue. Grammatical terms are *not* necessary and neither are prescriptive "rules" of grammar. The "rule," if any, should be a description of the sounds and arrangements of sounds in the utterance. What we are striving for is 1) the automatic and habitual production of the item in speech, and 2) the internalization of its recurring, interrelated, interdependent features so that it can be used in other appropriate communication situations and in increasingly broader contexts.

c) Note a possible chart.

The	Noun	"Be"	Color (or Adjective)
The	pencil	is	red
The	pen	is	red

13. When, for example, the plurals of nouns are taught, the charts may look like this: (These should be placed next to each other.)

The	Noun	"Be"	Color
The	pencil	is	red
The	pen	is	green

The	Noun	"Be"	Color
The	pencil*s*	*are*	red
The	pen*s*	*are*	green

14. After the students are made to "see" word order, inflections, or whatever the grammar item is that we are teaching, we engage them in *varied* practice.

Basic Oral Practice Activities

While language may be rule-governed, speakers will still have to develop the habits of using their vocal organs perhaps in completely new ways, quickly and correctly; of adding inflections, prefixes, and suffixes to words; of arranging words in positions and combinations required by English; and of using the registers or varieties appropriate in the particular communication situation. Listeners, of course, will have to learn to recognize and react to the oral signals they hear in a message. Only intensive practice can bring about the competence and performance needed to encode (transmit) and to decode (understand) a message.

Oral drills—about five for each new item—should follow the presentation of the item in a communication situation, its rote repetition, and its description or rule. Most oral drills fall into the following categories: *substitution, expansion* (including embedding), *deletion,* and *transformation.* There are numerous variations of these as we shall see.

Other distinctions are often made among these drills. They may be subdivided into *mechanical* or *manipulative; meaningful* and *communicative.* (At any level, the three types, including the mechanical substitution drill, can be used with profit.) Here is an example of the distinction made among them:

Mechanical substitution: Teacher: He arrived at *seven.* (Cue: nine) Student: He arrived at nine. (Cue: eleven, etc.)

Meaningful response: Teacher: What time did you arrive? Student: I arrived at nine.

Communicative response: Teacher: What have you done this morning? Student: (time of getting up, leaving for school, etc.) We will have more to say about communicative practice later. (See p. 74.)

A few other general remarks should be made about oral practice. (Incidentally, drills particularly appropriate in developing reading and writing will be given in subsequent sections although *any drill* will contribute to the growth and reinforcement of the abilities to read and write.)

1. The utterances used in the drills should be authentic (e.g., those that a native speaker would use; those that make sense; those that are relevant to the students' interests and lives).

2. You should relate the utterances (after the mechanical substitution drills) either with respect to structure or to the vocabulary area. This will make a real conversation —hence communication —possible more quickly.

3. Substitution drills should *precede* all other types of drills so that students will get into the habit of arranging words in certain positions.

4. You should practice other drills—where feasible—in mini-situations; e.g., Be careful. I will be. ; or Take care . . . Don't worry, I will.

5. In the drills immediately following the initial presentation, the change to be made should be *minimal* (only *one* change) and it should be *consistent;* e.g., the instruction might be: Use the word *never* in each of these sentences. (Each of the sentences would contain the verb BE *or* a "regular" verb.)

6. You should give at least five examples—*after* the two you will do with your students.

7. You should present only the most appropriate drills for the item being practiced. For example, in teaching adjectives, *substitution, expansion, transformation,* and *embedding* (integration) drills would be effective—as well as questions and answers, of course.

8. You should present the drills briskly. This is possible 1) if you have prepared a small card to fit into your *left* hand (leaving your right hand free for gesturing, calling on students, etc.) which will contain the cue words you plan to use; 2) if you have given clear instructions; and 3) if you have modeled two examples.

9. Some drills should *not* be attempted *orally* unless the timing and pauses are perfect; *I went --- the store* (requiring the response *to* or *into*) would give students a distorted aural impression of the sentence. Moreover, it would call for an isolated word in the response that could not be considered a true utterance. *If* tried at all, students should be asked to repeat the entire sentence.

10. The use of oral reconstruction drills depends on extensive previous practice and good timing. Students should *see* the cues for the sentence you want them to reconstruct: *John/ not/ eat/ yet.* This eliminates the danger that they may develop a form of pidgin English.

11. You can do all drills—especially in the early stages—with five kinds of cues: 1) the spoken word and the object shown simultaneously; 2) the spoken word; 3) the object; 4) a picture or sketch of the object; 5) the written word. For obvious reasons, it is desirable to start with spoken words and to reinforce the association of the spoken word and its referent.

12. You should avoid giving students jumbled words to be placed in the correct order, especially if they are printed in linear sequence; e.g. Went a park the to basket I with, etc. If you do want to have students place words in proper position, it is more desirable to list them vertically. This type of drill, however, is time-consuming and not the best drill to practice word arrangements.

13. Before asking students to "choose" between such contrasting items as verb forms, pronouns, or placement of adverbs of time, I would give them *the entire series* of utterances I plan to use which they would then listen to and repeat.

14. There should be an appropriate pause between the base sentence and the oral cue so that students do not hear (in a drill, for example, in which they are to transform the present continuous to the simple past) a string of words such as, I'm going there. (yesterday)

15. Some authors may also subdivide drills under *recognition* and *production*. Examples of both were given under the Sound System (p. 21), and will be found under Writing (p. 85). With syntactical and lexical items, most recognition drills (e.g., the multiple choice or True and False) are best *seen* by the students.

16. In order to avoid possible different responses which may cause confusion, the entire group should not be asked to respond to a cue. (The responses of individuals might, however, be confirmed by a choral response.)

Following are the commonly agreed upon names and some examples of oral pattern practice activities which help students grow in their control of the *patterns* of language. In doing any drill, *you* should give the model sentence two or three times and show the students, *by doing it yourself*, exactly what you expect them to do.

Substitution: In this drill, students use another word of the same class in the place of a word in the sentence. A noun is replaced by another noun; a verb by another verb; an adjective by another adjective; a determiner (the, a, some, each, any) by another determiner; etc.

Let us assume you are teaching the present of *have.* Give a sentence: "I have a pencil." Say in English (at the beginning, you may use their native tongue to make sure they understand the directive), "Now, I'll give you another word. Put it (or use it) in the place of *pencil.*" (Remember to do at least two examples *with* them.)

1. Say "I have a pencil." Show the pencil. Pause for a moment. Say "ruler." The student called upon will say "I have a ruler." Say "notebook." The student will say "I have a notebook." Continue in this way, practicing about ten sentences. Then proceed to "You have," "We have," etc., using the same or similar vocabulary items.
2. Use the same spoken words without showing the object.
3. Instead of the word, now show an object. As above, *say a sentence;* then show an *object;* then call on a student.
4. Instead of the word or object, show a picture or a chart of pictures. Give the base sentence; then point to one of the pictures —sometimes in sequence, sometimes at random. At times, have students come up and point to the pictures. They will call on their classmates to give the sentences.
5. Instead of the spoken word, object, or picture, use flashcards on which individual words are written. (Use this fifth cue only *after* reading has been taught.) You may also write a list of words on the board.

Replacement or *Restatement:* The students will be expected to replace one element by another, e.g., *nouns or names* by a pronoun (he, she, etc.); or to restate the sentence using a synonymous expression.

1. Give a sentence: "John has a pencil." The students will be expected to say, "*He* has a pencil." Do *not* change the object (pencil) in any of the sentences in the drill. In the drills we will describe (except the Progressive Replacement Drill), only *one* element in the sentence is to be changed at one time.
2. Give sentences with *often,* for example. The students will give the same sentences with *many times a week;* e.g., I *often* speak to him. I speak to him *many times a week.*
3. Give sentences such as "I see *the man.*" Students will say "I see *him.*" (Remember that intonation changes here.)
4. Give sentences such as "I *have to* go now." Students will say "I *must* go now."

Paired Sentences: In this drill, you will give a sentence and then ask a question. For example, you will say, "Mary likes to study. What about you?" or "What about the boys?" A student would say, "I like to study too" or "They like to study too." This is a good drill for practicing verb forms or adjectives. For example, "Joan is pretty. What about Helen?"—"Helen is pretty, too."

Transformation (sometimes called *conversion*): The students will be given practice in changing from affirmative to negative or to interrogative and later from present to past or to future, etc. Give the model sentence and say, for example, "Now we're going to make questions from these sentences." Say, "He has a pencil." The student will say, "Does he have a pencil?" (or, "Has he a pencil?" depending on the book you are using or the form *you* use in your speech.)

It is *not* necessary to use words like *negative, past,* etc. You can say instead, "Let's start each sentence with *No,*" or "Let's use *not* in these sentences" (even though you may ask them to use the *contracted* form of *not*), or "Let's use *yesterday,*" or "Let's use *going to,*" etc.

Expansion: The students will be given a word or expression *to be added to* a sentence you give them. For example, "Let's add the word *always* to these sentences." Say, "I have a pencil." The student says, "I always have a pencil." In later stages, they may be asked to place expressions such as "I'm sure," "I think," "I know" before other sentences.

They may also be asked to make *multiple expansions* (one at a time, however), to noun phrases or verb phrases. For example, say: "I see a boy." (cue) *good-looking;* (cue) *with red hair.* Students called upon would give the entire sentence with each new cue added.

With advanced classes, you may ask them to *expand* a sentence with a word or expression which will necessitate a change in verb form; e.g., "Use *yesterday* in these sentences. Make the necessary changes." "I'm eating . . . (I ate yesterday)" or, "Place 'The man asked me' in front of these sentences . . . 'How old are you?' (The man asked me how old I was.)"

Reduction: This drill is a form of replacement drill because you "reduce" a sentence by changing an expression to a word. For example, "I have *the pencil*" to "I have *it;*"* "I'm going to the *library*" to "*I'm going there*"; "Come *to my house*" to "Come *here*." Later you can practice substitute expressions. "I'd like one of the books in the window" to "I'd like one of those"; "I see all the people" to "I see everyone"; "I think it's raining" to "I think so." When appropriate, you can give practice in "reducing" clauses to phrases; e.g., "All the people who were in the store" to "All the people in the store."

Directed Practice: A student is directed (asked) to ask another student a question. The second student is directed to answer. This drill needs a lot of help from you at the beginning. It should be done in three stages:

*Notice the change in intonation.

Stage I—Teacher: "X, ask Y, 'Do you have a pencil?' "
Teacher: "Y, tell X, 'I have a pencil,' or 'Yes, I do.' "

Stage II—Teacher says, "X, ask Y if he has a pencil."
Teacher whispers to X, "Do you have a pencil?"
X says aloud, "Do you have a pencil?"

The teacher says to the second student, "Y, tell X you have a pencil." He whispers: "Yes, I have a pencil," and the student says, "Yes, I have a pencil" aloud.

Stage III—You do *not* whisper the direct question (that is, you do not prompt the students). If the students do not know what to say, help them, of course. If these drills are built up gradually over a long series of lessons, however, you will find that you have little or no prompting to do in Stage III.

A student is asked to "tell" or "ask" something, requiring transformation; e.g., "Ask him how he came to school." "Tell us what you did last evening."

Integration: Students are asked to put two short sentences together to make *one* sentence. For example, "I have a pencil. It's red" becomes "I have a red pencil"; "The woman is in the store. She's my sister" becomes "The woman who is in the store is my sister." or "The woman in the store is my sister."

Progressive Replacement: This drill needs much teacher help at the beginning, but students enjoy doing it after they have learned the trick of it. This is a *multiple substitution* drill. Whereas in the substitution drill, only *one* element was changed each time (the noun or the adjective or the verb), in this drill a new element is changed in each sentence. The students have to *remember* what is said in each sentence in order to form the new sentence. Notice:

Teacher	*Student*
I have a red pencil.	I have a red pencil.
green	I have a green pencil.
He	He has a green pencil.
pen.	He has a green pen.
Mr. Jones	Mr. Jones has a green pen.
four	Mr. Jones has four green pens.
They	They have four green pens.
need	They need four green pens.
	etc.

Translation: I have deliberately left this practice activity to the end of this series of drills for several reasons. First, there is controversy as to the advisability of doing translation. Only the teacher who knows the native language of his students can engage in this drill because the students should generally not use the native language. If translation is to be done at all, it should always be on a *limited* structure point, and on *one* point only. The *equivalent* is always given; never, of course, a literal translation. Notice:

Teacher	*Student*
(Native Language)	I have a few pencils.
(Native Language)	I have a few books.
(Native Language)	I have a few notebooks.

or:

Teacher	*Student*
(Native Language)	I've been studying for an hour.
(Native Language)	I've been waiting for an hour.
(Native Language)	I've been resting for an hour.

With "slow" students and especially with structures which contrast markedly with those in the native language, you may wish to precede the type of exercise just described with one in which *you* will give the English and individual students will give the native language. This type of exercise must again be done *judiciously;* that is, if you know the native language and if all the students speak the same language. *Most importantly,* it should be done for two or three minutes *only* and *after* all/other appropriate drill activities have been carried out.

Since many school systems throughout the world include a translation from English to the native language and vice-versa on achievement or proficiency examinations, the "equivalents" proposed above will serve several purposes: they will 1) heighten the morale of students; 2) give you firm assurance that the contrasting features have been internalized; and 3) prepare students for the often dreaded examination. As usual, the key word is "judiciously."

Question-Answer Practice: There are several basic types of question-answer drills. Moreover, *each* drill can be done in several ways: 1) The teacher asks all the students a question; *one* student answers.* 2) A student asks the teacher a question; the teacher answers. 3) A student asks another student a question. (See also p. 152 for paired practice activities.) 4) Pairs of students question each other in chain fashion. This too has several variations:

a) Student 1 asks Student 2 a question. Student 2 answers. Student 3 asks the same question of Student 4.

b) Student 1 asks Student 2 a question. Student 2 answers and asks the same question of Student 3.

*A choral answer may lead to confusion unless the teacher models both the question *and* the answer.

c) Student 1 asks Student 2 a question; e.g., "Do you have a pencil?" Student 2 answers, "Yes, I do" or "Yes, I have a pencil." Student 3 asks Student 4, "Does he (or she) have a pencil?" referring to Student 2.

Let us examine some basic question and answer drills which can be used effectively in teaching *structure.* (Questions which can be used in developing the skill of reading will be discussed later in this chapter.)

1. Answer *Yes* or *No.* "Do you have your book?"

2. Answer *Yes. Give a long answer* (or a complete sentence). "Do you have a pencil?" "Yes, I have a pencil."—A substitution drill can be combined effectively with this question-answer practice.

3. Answer *Yes. Give a short answer.* "Do you have a pencil?" "Yes, I do."

4. Answer *No. Give a long answer.* "Do you have a pencil?" "No, I don't have a pencil."

5. Answer *No. Give a short answer.* "Do you have a pencil?" "No, I don't."

6. Answer *No. Give a short answer and a long answer.* "No, I don't; I don't have a pencil."

7. Answer *No. Tell what you have (or tell what it is).* "Do you have a pencil?" "No, I don't have a pencil. I have a pen." "Is this a table?" "No, it's not (or it isn't) a table. It's a chair."

At the beginning, you or an able student may give the cue which tells the students what to answer. For example, "Do you have a pencil?" You or a student will say "pen" (or show the picture, object, or word *pen*), and the student will answer, "No, I don't have a pencil. I have a pen."

8. *Choose one or the other.* "Do you have a pencil or a pen?" . . . "I have a (pen)."

9. *Patterned Response.* You will ask a question such as "Do you have a pencil?" or "May I borrow your pencil?" The student *always* answers with the sentence being practiced; for example, "Yes, here it is." "Do you like salad (ice cream, swimming, etc.)?" "Yes, very much."

At more advanced levels, the patterned response drill can be used to practice changes in word order or substitute expressions. Notice:

I'm hungry . . . So am I; or I am too.
I'm thirsty . . . So am I; or He is too.

or

Do you think she's pretty? . . . Yes, I think so.
Do you think it's going to rain? . . . Yes, I think so.

or

Would you like one of these lovely pictures? . . . Yes, I'd like one very much.

10. *"Wh" or Information Questions.* You or individual students will ask questions with *who, whose, where, how long,* etc. Other students may be asked to reply with an utterance or with a complete sentence, depending on what you wish to practice.

11. *Free Response.* You may ask "What do I have on my desk?" (or in my hand). A student would answer, "You have a pencil, a pen," etc. You would ask, "What do you have on your desk?" or "What do you always bring to school?" or "What do we have in this room?" or anything you are practicing. In this activity, you (or a student) can again use *spoken words, pictures, objects,* or *written words* to elicit the response desired.

Other Comments on Oral Drills

Some drills lend themselves better than others, of course, to the items we are practicing. It is important to vary the drill activities and to conduct them briskly in order to prevent monotony. As soon as interest in one type of drill lags, you should either proceed to another type of drill, change the cue, or vary the type of student participation involved; that is, proceed from choral repetition; to chain repetition; to your questioning students; to students' questioning you or each other. (See p. 152.)

When you start a chain, break it after four to six learners have spoken. Begin the chain again in another part of the room, using the same sentences or, if you wish, changing some part of the sentence but maintaining the same pattern.

Drills should lead gradually to the normal use of language items in real situations. "Formulas" of the language, as well as rejoinders of all kinds (agreement, surprise, disagreement), should be practiced. For example:

"Does my speaking bother you?" "No, not at all."

"Do you mind if I leave now?" "No, of course not."

"Hello! We thought we'd come to visit you." "What a nice surprise. Do come in!"

The principle of the "spiral" approach should be kept in mind in planning drill activities. As we have said, after repetition and intensive pattern practice, new material should always be practiced with familiar material. For example, when *ask* followed by a person is taught, we can go back to "having a pencil"—with sentences such as "He asked me if I had a pencil" or "I asked him if he had a pencil" or "Please ask him for his pencil," etc.

In addition to the dialogues or exchanges in which each speaker in turn makes one statement or where one asks and the other answers a question, multiple responses should be practiced as soon as the students are able to make them. Whereas at the beginning, the stimulus statement can be "That's a nice tie," and the response "Thank you," the second time the response may be "Thank you. I'm glad you like it," or "Thank you. It's new," or "Thank you. It's a gift from my wife," or anything else you have practiced previously in *pattern practice* drills.

With advanced classes you may devise a code or a format for dialogues which students will follow with little or no prompting on your part. The following (or even a longer list) may be placed on a chart or on the board:*

S (Stimulus)	*R (Response)*
Q (Question)	St (Statement)
Q and St	Q
Q, St and St	St and St (Two utterances)
St, St and Q	St, St and Q

Your advanced students can use any of the above combinations to prepare increasingly longer conversational exchanges within the list of cultural situations given in Chapter II. You may wish to prepare another easily accessible chart with a list of twenty or more topics of interest. (See p. 162.) Thus students can select a topic and be guided to speak about it utilizing the cues in the chart above to practice the normal forms of conversation of native speakers. Following is a simple illustration of this technique.

Topic: A Suit

1. Is that a new suit?
2. Yes, it is.

* * *

1. Is that a new suit? It looks very good on you.
2. Do you really like it?

* * *

1. Is your suit new? I've never seen it before. It looks very good on you.
2. Yes, it is new. It's the first time I'm wearing it.

* * *

1. I've never seen that suit. Brown is a good color for you. When did you buy it?
2. I bought it last week. Brown is my favorite color. Do you really like the suit?

*The words in parentheses need not be on the chart. They are noted here for your use only.

It is essential that students, particularly those in advanced classes, be given practice in recognizing and using the polite forms and appropriate responses of the language. For example:

Would you like (a cup of tea)?—Yes. Thank you.
Won't you have another (sandwich)?
  Yes, thank you very much.
  No, thank you. I can't now.
May I get you (a cup of coffee)?
  Yes, thank you. I'd like one.
I'd be very grateful if you got me (a cup of tea).
  Of course. I'll be glad to., etc.

Other items which give the language its authentic "ring" are words like *so, well, then, of course, as a matter of fact,* which many native speakers use to begin their utterances. Systematic practice should be given in these as they arise in the texts you are using. You should make provision to teach them, however, whether or not they appear in the formal instructional materials.

We have talked about *understanding, repetition,* and *practice,* the first three steps in our language learning process. We have also indicated how *conscious* selection operates. When the student has to choose between "he" and "she," or "here" and "there," or any other contrasting feature in English in a practice activity, such as a chain drill, he is *consciously* choosing between one form and the other.

We have touched upon *unconscious,* or free, selection of structures in the preceding paragraphs. Another technique you may wish to use is the following: Give the students some sentences about a situation and then ask, "What would you say?" or sometimes, "What would you do?" For example, say, "You meet someone in the street who invites you to a party at his home. You've never been to his home. What would you say? What would you ask?" ("Thank you, I'd like to come. Where do you live?" etc.) Additional communication activities will be suggested on p. 76.

Before leaving the topic of oral drills permit me to express a few words of caution:

1. Try to minimize student errors. This is possible if you: a) give many models; b) prompt the answers; c) engage in choral repetition first; d) call on your more able students first; e) give the correct response, statement, or answer yourself by saying simply "Listen" or "Ask me the question."; f) do not expect your students to "create" sentences or to "improvise" in the early stages.

2. Correct errors immediately by giving the *correct* form (except during the *motivation* stage of your lesson when you may overlook minor mistakes *temporarily*. You will make a mental note of them, of

course, and give practice which will eliminate them, later in that lesson or in the next lesson). Merely say, "Listen" and give the correct form.

3. Start the drills, but then give your students every opportunity to ask questions, give answers, etc. Remember that *they* are the language learners, *not* you.

The Vocabulary

As we noted above, the importance of meaning has gained increasing currency in the last few years. Everything that has been said to this point presupposes a primary vocabulary or semantic base. Messages between speakers and listeners; in other words, *communication,* must include meaningful words, a content of shared referents, shared experiences, and shared culture.

At the beginning level we should concentrate on the function words and the more frequently used vocabulary items which are needed to give practice in the basic structures and sounds of the language. Precedence, however, should be given to the vocabulary which is intimately related to the environment and experiences of the pupils. While our major concern may seem to be with sounds and syntax, a store of content words from everyday life situations can make practice of the structures much more interesting to the students.

A question frequently asked is "How many new words can be taught in one lesson?" As is true of other questions related to teaching, there is no *one* answer. Children of eight or nine may learn four or five new words; children of ten or eleven may learn seven or eight; secondary school students may learn fifteen to twenty; while highly motivated university students may "absorb" thirty or more words.

Several premises and comments related to the teaching of vocabulary follow:

▶Not all of the words a student hears during any lesson need become a part of his "active" vocabulary during that lesson or even in later lessons. Some words in the new language (and in our native language) will remain "passive"; that is, we understand them when we hear them or read them, but we don't use them ourselves in speaking or in writing. The vocabulary for active use should be systematically presented and practiced.

▶Vocabulary should always be taught in *normal speech utterances.*

▶New vocabulary items should *always* be introduced in *known* structures.

▶Whenever possible, the vocabulary items should be centered about one topic. Words about food should be given in one lesson;

words about clothing in another; words about weather in still another; etc. All the words around a "center of interest" (food, clothing, recreation, etc.) should *not* be taught at one time or at one level. Other words within the same "center" can always be added when they fit logically with the other socio-cultural topics being studied or when they are met in reading.

In the beginning stages, the same context (situation or topic) should be used with a new word so that students will learn to associate the word with the situation in which it is usually used. For example, "What *mark* did you get on that test?" "The teacher gave me my *mark*."

▶Whenever a familiar word is met in a *new* context, it should be taught again and practiced. A review or mention of the known meaning of the word should be made so that students will understand the contrast. If possible, only one context should be taught at one time.

▶Vocabulary items should be taught in the same way we teach everything else. We give our students an understanding of the meaning in many ways. We dramatize; we illustrate using ourselves and our students; we show pictures; we paraphrase; we give the equivalent if necessary; we use any appropriate technique.

▶Vocabulary should be *practiced* as structures are practiced—in substitution drills, transformation drills, questions and aswers, etc.

▶Vocabulary items should be reintroduced many times with all the structures and in all the situations in which they can logically be used.

▶Students should be encouraged to learn and use *nouns, verbs, adjectives,* and *adverbs* which contain the same roots. We can help the learner prepare four-column word charts: e.g.,

Noun	*Verb*	*Adjective*	*Adverb*
difference	(to) differ	different	differently

We give extended practice in their use in order to reinforce position (slot), function, and meaning.

A Few Additional Words About Communication Activities

Since many teachers feel that oral practice activities leading to communicative competence are at the very heart of the language learning process, it may be useful to summarize some of what has already been said and to pinpoint activities which may be considered more properly "communicative." First of all, what are some of the responsibilities of the language teacher in this regard? Let me note several:

1) *To know* intimately the students and the community in which

they live in order to relate new language and cultural material to the probable experiences and interests of the students.

2) *To broaden* the students' experiences through discussion of music, art, hobbies, and other areas of interest in the school curriculum or in the community.

3) *To enrich* the students' vocabulary not only through studies of antonyms, synonyms, cognates and words of the same family, but also by giving them—from the outset—the words and expressions they will need to talk about their communities and their backgrounds; e.g., stores, farming, dating.

4) *To teach* as quickly as feasible the formulas of English—words like: *By all means, How do you do,* and to create situations in the classroom in which the use of such formulas will be appropriate.

5) *To present* all new vocabulary and structures in easily demonstrable situations or in a meaningful, self-explanatory context and to make sure that students understand these thoroughly.

6) *To exploit* every language learning activity so that it will reinforce and facilitate communication.

7) *To proceed* from tightly controlled drill to freer, more authentic, creative expression from the very *first* day of the language program. For example, if names have been taught, you could ask: What's his name? . . . Student: I don't know . . . or I don't remember . . . You: Ask him. . . . Student: What's your name? . . . Student 2: It's ________. You: What's his name? . . . Student: It's ________.

8) *To reintroduce* structures and vocabulary of high frequency as often as possible after their initial presentation in as many appropriate situations as feasible so that students will be able to recall them with ease when needed for communication.

9) *To add* to textbooks authentic, meaningful language activities and short, two or three line dialogues for frequent dramatization.

10) *To suggest*—or encourage students to suggest—alternate sentences in the dialogue utterances so that they will not always expect the responses they will have learned in the original dialogue, e.g., depending on the class, your rapport with the students and their rapport with each other—Dialogue: Student 1: What did you do last night? Student 2: I went to the movies . . . or I studied.—A possible alternate sentence might be: It's none of your business. The students can be as creative as possible, but they should be helped to avoid giving offense.

11) *To modify*, if necessary, the sequence and order of materials in textbooks so that *questions* of all kinds and the pronouns *I* and *you* are introduced and practiced very early.

12) Last, but very important is *to remember* that understanding the meaning of any utterance depends upon knowing its single ele-

ments of *pronunciation,* of *grammar,* of *vocabulary,* and of *culture.* While, very often, the first understanding of a dialogue or reading passage may be global, teachers must eventually make provision for teaching and practicing most of the single elements within the material. The learning of dialogues and of reading passages, for that matter, should generally proceed in *two parallel streams.* In order to engender *motivation,* a global understanding of partially unfamiliar but authentic material may be given. I consider that Stream I, the one of greater importance. In Stream II, I would provide for the *systematic, ordered* presentation of the individual elements within the longer, live material. How boring for us and for our students if we waited to introduce authentic, real-life material until students had mastered all the individual items within it!

Now let us turn for a few minutes to some language learning activities which will hopefully lead to verbal communication. I shall omit questions and answers. Students may be asked to:

1) Develop a new, brief dialogue using utterances from two or more previously learned dialogues, e.g., the new dialogue "Where did you go yesterday?" "I went shopping for a hat," may be adapted from the following two dialogues: "I went shopping for a hat yesterday." "Did you buy one?" and "Where did you go yesterday? I didn't see you." "I had to go to the library."

2) Dramatize a dialogue with varying emotions; e.g., "Look at my new coat!" (excitedly, angrily). "What a funny joke!" (humorously, sarcastically).

3) Dramatize a telephone conversation—when the person called is there; when the person is not there.

4) Take part in role-playing activities (older students especially); e.g., A student applies for a job giving his name, address, date of birth, experience, etc. The same student may be called back for a further interview. The "employer" may make numerous errors of fact; e.g., "Ah, you're Mr.______________." The applicant would then have to say, "No, I'm not______________. I'm______________," or "My name's______________."

5) Describe hobbies and activities, how they do or make something—stamp collecting, fishing, cooking.

6) Talk about a film or TV program. Several students may contribute one sentence each to the description.

7) Describe a picture, a set of pictures, or a wall chart. (A series of pictures will be found on p. 101.)

8) Summarize what a previous speaker has said.

9) Develop increasingly sustained conversation for each of the situations you will create, situations such as going to the post office,

the market, a tourist agency, etc. by means of pictures or a magnet or flannel board.

10) Tell you and their classmates what they had done on a holiday, before they came to school, or after they got home yesterday.

11) Perform some actions in the classroom. You or another student may ask, "What is he (she) doing?" or "What has he just done?" "What do you think he'll do now?" or whatever you are practicing.

12) Prepare (in groups) a short talk on some aspect of culture. They will give the prepared talk and then answer questions (put by you or their classmates) about what they have said.

The activities I have mentioned are primarily listening-speaking activities. It goes without saying, however, that reading and writing activities—also communication skills—lend themselves very well to the further stimulation of listening and speaking.

Often you may wish to read a passage several times and have students reproduce orally what they remember of it, or you may ask them to predict the outcome, particularly if it is a brief, humorous incident.

Letter writing or composition writing should, of course, be preceded by a discussion of ideas to be included in the letter or composition and by class discussion of a possible logical information sequence for the ideas suggested.

Let me say that, *ideally,* communication implies the absence of external controls or stimuli. I feel that this is an unrealistic expectation in our secondary schools or even at the university for students who are not working for a degree in English. Teachers must be prepared with audio-visual aids, everyday situational topics, themes of interest, and suggested formats for eliciting longer sentences or multiple responses.

Communication is at the very core of success in language acquisition but more important in interpersonal relationships—in communion with our fellow men. It is our responsibility to make sure in every way possible that pupils will not only have *something to talk about* but also that they will develop the increasing desire to do so whenever the opportunity arises.

Reading

The third skill we help our students develop is that of reading—of getting meaning from printed or written material. In addition to helping students comprehend the written material in the texts we are using, we should give them the knowledge and the ability to be able to read other material with ease and enjoyment. With guidance, they should be able to turn to books freely with a feeling of pleasure —and eventually perhaps to read the literature of America and of England in the original.

Before proceeding to the stages or techniques in reading, I should like to state several facts which result from observation and experimentation:

1. Listening and speaking should *always* precede reading. It is only *after* students can say material with reasonable fluency that they should be permitted to see it.

The length of time the teaching of reading should be deferred has been a matter of some controversy among language specialists. Again, it has been my experience that there is no one answer which will suit every situation. Before being asked to teach a language television program for children of ten and eleven, I had considered it desirable to defer the teaching of reading to children for one or two years. The letters the television viewers sent me indicated that they tried to write what I said using their own "native" language spellings. The spelling was completely distorted, of course.

Certainly language learners should hear *many* times and be able to repeat with reasonable accuracy any material before they see it, but the number of class hours which should elapse between hearing, saying, and reading must perforce be flexible and should depend on several factors. The chart below is *not* designed to provide the definitive answer to this knotty question but to help you arrive at your own conclusions.

Age	Duration of Course	Principal Aims	Length of Time of *Possible* Deferment of Reading
7-10	6 years	The four skills	1 year
11-14	5 years	The four skills	1 month
14-18	2 years	The four skills	2 weeks
	3 years		4 weeks
18 and over	1 year or less	Reading or translation	1 day
	2 years	The four skills	1 week
	More than 2	The four skills	2-4 weeks

2. In reading, and this happens in reading our native tongue, too, we make sounds in our throat. We read faster, therefore, if we know how to say the sounds and if we don't stumble over them.

3. You should *always* read aloud for the students any reading you are going to assign to them. (This is true at any level but especially at the beginning one.) Since English is *not* written the way it sounds in many cases, it is important that you read aloud so that your students: a) don't reinforce incorrect sounds in their silent speech; b) will comprehend words they meet in their reading which they have heard spoken and vice versa. If you are not convinced, pause for just a moment and say the following words ending in *ough*: enough, through, though, bough, dough, hiccough. Now say these words: I, machine, pie, piece, it, ice, island. We could multiply the examples, but anyone who teaches English as a second language will appreciate the difficulties of students and, therefore, the necessity for *oral* reading by the teacher (or for listening to the material on a tape or other recording).

"Free" reading is a complex skill. In order to "get" meaning and to read with ease and enjoyment, students must know the sounds of the language, its structures, and its vocabulary. In addition, they must be familiar with any allusion to an aspect of culture. This is as true in reading one's native language as it is in reading a second language.

What is the responsibility of you, the teacher, in developing reading skills? You may have to extend the experiences of the pupils so that they will understand the cultural allusions; you will have to teach the sounds and meanings of new words; you will have to help them understand the more difficult structures ("included sentences" are usually not easy for language learners); you will have to teach them the comprehension skills; you will have to help them increase their speed in reading.

With beginners; with those who cannot read their native language; or whose native language uses different symbols, you, the teacher, will have additional responsibilities. I should point out that many specialists advocate that initial reading should always be done in the native tongue. I cannot go into the advantages and disadvantages of that principle in this small Guide (e.g., the native tongue may *not* have a writing system; the illiterate learner of fifteen or sixteen in an English speaking community may need to read signs [Exit, Entrance, etc.] *immediately).* I should like to underscore again that the decision should be arrived at by *a committee* of experts (linguists, psychologists, education specialists, classroom teachers, community leaders) after studying such factors as age, needs, morale, motivation, and educational resources in the community.

Again, using the parallel stream concept *(systematic* teaching of individual elements *at the same time* that interesting, *meaningful material* is heard and read with your guidance), you will have to do the following:

Help the students:

1. *Coordinate* their eye movements.

2. *Link symbols* they are accustomed to hearing (i.e., acoustic symbols) to those they see in print (i.e., visual symbols).

3. *React* only *to the significant characteristics* of the visual symbols.

4. *Recognize grammatical units.* (This process will be facilitated if you read aloud to them and if you point out, where feasible, the reason for the pauses; e.g., Read *I will go in spite of the weather* pausing first after *go;* then after *in;* then after *spite.* You get three different meanings, don't you?)

5. *Read in thought groups.*

6. *Learn the spelling patterns* which are basic to reading; e.g., syllable words containing a consonant, a vowel and a consonant; the same words with a final *e* added; digraphs (e.g., ch, sh, th); consonant clusters (initial and final); silent letters (know, gnaw, write).

7. *Grasp the full meaning* of an utterance through the signals and symbols (phonological, grammatical, and lexical) used in it.

Developing the Skills

How can you, the teacher, help students develop the skills they need in reading? In several ways:

1. You can help them *enrich their vocabularies* by giving them cognates (if their native language is one with similar word roots), paraphrases, antonyms, synonyms, words of the same family (e.g., bed, bedspread, bedclothes, or jewels, jewelry, jeweler, jewelry store); you can help them "see" little words in bigger words (able, unable, inability); you can help them recognize prefixes (unkind, unable, unaccustomed, or retell, redo) and suffixes (childish, mannish or quietly, slowly, kingly); you can help them guess meanings of words from the surrounding words, or in other words, you can help them use "contextual clues." You can sometimes give the meaning of abstract words in the native language of the students if you know the language. You can find out from a speaker of the language the native term for important abstract words which cannot be pictured and either say them yourself or place them on the board or have a student say them.

2. You can help students *arrive at the meaning of structures* in any of the ways mentioned above and give limited practice in their use.

3. As simply as possible in English and with the help of pictures, clocks, calendars, or any other appropriate item, you can give the pupils some *insight into the cultural allusions.* If you can, and if you consider it necessary, you may give a *brief* explanation in the students' native tongue.

4. You can *insure comprehension* in various ways. I will mention only a few at this point:

▶Ask many *different kinds* of questions on the *same* sentence. For example, with "John is an engineer," you can ask:

a) Inverted question: "Is John an engineer?"

b) Question-word questions with "who" and "what," etc. "Who is an engineer? What is John?"

c) In later stages, you will ask "why" questions and inferential questions on the reading material; e.g., "What do you think . . . .? or How do you think . . . .?"

▶Ask questions, the answers to which the students can find verbatim (word for word) in the material being read.

▶Ask for a summary of a paragraph. The summary should include the important ideas in the *sequence* in which they appeared in the paragraph.

▶Ask for the *main idea* of the paragraph.

▶Ask the students to find words which describe a person or a process—which show that the person talked about was in a hurry or angry or whatever the passage is about.

▶Give sentences in the passage out of order and ask the students to place them in the proper order.

5. How can you *increase the students' speed?* a) When you have them read silently, time the reading. b) Keep decreasing the time judiciously throughout the year. c) Discourage lip movements. d) Give them a *definite purpose* for reading. They must find the answer to some questions, or some words, or an idea, or a title, or the central thought, etc.

Some Detailed Techniques*

1. For *judging recognition* and *comprehension* of *vocabulary:*

a. Choosing from among three or four words the one that has the *same* meaning as the one given.

b. Choosing from among three or four words the one that has the *opposite* meaning of the one given.

c. Indicating whether pairs of words are synonyms or antonyms.

d. Giving the negative prefix of a list of words.

e. Completing a sentence with the correct negative word.

f. Completing tables of words; e.g.,

Noun	*Verb*	*Adjective*	*Adverb*
ability	to be able to	able	ably

*Some of these were suggested in an article by William Norris in "English Teaching Forum," September 1971, pp. 6-13.

g. Finding a sentence from among three which illustrates the same use of the underlined word; e.g., He *spared* the prisoner.

1) I cannot spare the money now.
2) Use the food sparingly.
3) We must spare the women.

h. Using contextual clues, indicate the *synonym* (from among three given) of the underlined word in a sentence.

i. Using words in original sentences.

2. For *judging* and *giving practice in sentence structure:*

a. Using the appropriate preposition in this sentence; e.g., He lives ____ Main Street.

b. Completing the paragraph using appropriate words. (Every fifth or sixth word can be deleted. These may be nominals, prepositions, conjunctions, etc.)

3. For *judging sentence comprehension:*

a. Completing the sentence using one of the four words given; e.g., He's used to a spacious house. This place is too _____ (large, cramped, old, modern).

4. For *insuring comprehension of the entire selection:*

a. Giving an outline of the text when sentences are given out of order.

b. Using comprehension questions (as noted above on p. 81).

1) Indicating whether a statement is true or false.
2) Choosing the correct word to complete a sentence.
3) Asking Wh questions.
4) Formulating Wh questions, either when *specific parts of the sentence are underlined* or when they are not.
5) Asking questions with *or.*
6) Asking questions which will force students to make inferences; e.g., How do you think _____ felt about that? Why?
7) Asking questions to elicit the students' viewpoint; e.g., What do you think should have been done?

The Stages in Reading Growth

We have talked about the process of reading. Let us talk now about the stages in the teaching and learning of reading. There are several stages. These should be followed wherever possible.

Stage I—Students read the material they have learned to say very well* or material they have memorized. This may be a dialogue, a series of action sentences, a simple story of an experience the

*This might not be true for students whose only immediate interest is the translation of scientific material, for example.

class members have had and which they have discussed, or model sentences containing some of the structures taught.

You will have the students say the known material without looking at it. Then you will read the material aloud as the students look at it. They can read in *chorus* after you.* Next, you may ask groups and individuals to read it.

Stage II—You and/or a group of English teachers in the school combine the *known* words and structures to make a *different* dialogue or paragraph. The students are helped to read this newly organized material in which *all* the elements are familiar to them.

Stage III—The students start to read material in which some of the words and structures are unfamiliar to them. A committee of teachers can write this type of material, or existing texts with a low vocabulary and structure level, but at an interest level in harmony with the age of the students, may be used. Experimentation has shown that students experience little or no difficulty when one "new" word is interspersed among about thirty familiar words. Often "grammar" texts contain paragraphs and selections which are suitable for reading at this level. A detailed technique for teaching reading at Stage III will be explained below.

Stage IV—Some people recommend the use of simplified classics or magazines. There are others who object to the use of simplified texts on the grounds that they do not convey the style or the spirit of the author. I have found excellent simplified books on the market, however, which can be used to great advantage with students who are still not advanced enough to read the originals. The technique used for teaching this simplified or adapted material will be the same as the one for Stage III outlined below.

Stage V—Unlimited material. The whole world of books should be open to your students.

When do learners reach Stage V? Some may never reach it as they would not reach it in their native language. Some may reach it after a six-year program in the junior and senior high school. Some may reach it after one or two years of university training. All the factors in learning which we have stated several times must be considered in discussing the "mastery" of this skill as of any other.

A Procedure

You may wish to use the following procedures in teaching reading at Stages III and IV:

1. Divide the reading for that day into two or three sections so that you can vary your techniques.

*The number of times this is done depends on the students' age, ability, etc.

2. Motivate the reading. *Relate it to the pupils' own experiences,* or if the reading is part of a longer story, *relate it to the longer story.*

3. State the purpose of the reading. "What do you think will happen? . . . Let's find out," or "Let's read more about . . . ."

4. Deal with any difficulties in the first portion. Place (or have placed beforehand) the new words on the board. Say them; have the students say them after you. Explain them in the ways we have mentioned. You may even wish to give a short summary of the reading portion weaving in the words on the board. (This is the most interesting way.)

5. After the difficulties have been clarified, you may do several things: You may use Technique A (below) for the three portions of the day's reading; or you may use Technique B for the three portions; or use ABA or BAB. When you first start Stage III reading with your students, it is desirable to use A for most of the reading.

Technique A

Read *each line* aloud, and as outlined above (see p. 81) ask simple questions on each line. Make sure the answer is on the printed page.* At the end of the paragraph, ask for a summary (with various students contributing an idea). The use of the exact words of the text will minimize the possibility of errors. If the summary is difficult, ask questions to help your students summarize.

Technique B

Read the portion aloud; then ask the students to read it silently. (Time the reading.) After they have read, ask them questions; or have them complete sentences which you have placed on the board, (use multiple choice or cued responses); or ask them if statements you make are True or False, (if they are false, they are to give the true answer); or ask for a summary.

6. Ask for a complete summary of the day's reading.

7. Now you may want to do one of several things:

a) Distribute 4 or 5 sequential questions you have prepared. Have one student read a question; another answer it; another place it on the board. When all the answers are on the board, correct any mistakes with class cooperation** and *then* read them. The students can read them in chorus after you.

---

*The question of "books opened" or "closed" is also controversial. If time permits, have students close their books while you read the first time. Have books open during your second *oral* reading. (*Vary* your techniques!) But remember that "reading" means *looking at* printed material. Reading should be distinguished from practice in listening comprehension.

**See the procedure for correction in the section on "Writing."

b) Read the selection, one sentence at a time, and have the class read in chorus after you.

c) Have the new words (see Step 4) used in other sentences.

d) Do word study drills with the students—e.g., "Find the synonym of . . . . in Line 1. Make a noun from the word . . . ."

e) Have the students formulate questions on the story which they will ask their classmates to answer. (Place question words—*who, what, when, where, how, how much,* etc.—on the board to help them, if necessary.)

One other word should be said about reading. You may wish at the intermediate or advanced level to assign supplementary reading to your more able students. Suggest books in their area of interest; give them sufficient time to read a book. (You may wish to assign different parts of the same book, or books with different points of view, to several students.) Give them the opportunity to tell you and their classmates what they have read. Make the supplementary reading the stimulus for discussion and "free" communication.

Writing

The fourth and last of the communications skills we help develop in our students is that of writing. When we say "writing," we mean primarily the carefully *guided* marks on paper that we assist our students in making unless we are teaching a course in creative writing or advanced composition.

We lead them through several stages over a long period of time —the length depending, as usual, on their age, interests, capacities, needs—to a freer stage where they are able to write a "composition" or "essay" on a topic of interest.

Specialists in the field of second language teaching and learning usually recommend that in the secondary schools, this "freer" type composition be deferred until the middle of the third year. At the university level it may well come in the middle of the second year.

Naturally, the type of writing system (alphabet, picture) which exists in the native language is an important factor in determining the ease or speed with which students learn to write. The students may have to learn an entirely new writing system.

Some of Your Responsibilities

▶Progressively, and in small steps, you should teach students:

1) The sound-spelling correspondences

2) The mechanics of writing (punctuation, capitalization, spelling)

3) Letter writing, formal and informal (greetings, endings, other mechanics)

4) Practical, functional writing needed for note-taking, outlining, summarizing

5) The organization and expression of an idea which will convey its desired meaning and permit the reader to understand the message

6) The differences (where such exist) between speaking and writing, between informal and more formal styles of writing, and between "modes of discourse"

In English, for example, we generally contract and elide sounds in speech but we do not necessarily do so in writing. The vocabulary we use may differ depending on the message we are attempting to convey and the person(s) to whom we are addressing the message. (These variations have been termed "registers," as you know.)

There are two major types of writing, both overlapping: practical and creative. Practical writing is found in letters as well as in outlines, summaries, or a series of notes; creative writing, in literature. Many of your students will never write "creatively" as they would not in their native tongue, but creativity, where observed or suspected, should be encouraged and carefully nurtured. *All* students can be taught to express their ideas clearly and correctly.

Students should be helped to recognize and to use different "modes" of discourse. The mode may be narrative, expository, critical, or a combination of these. Any of these "modes" may be found in letters, dialogues, poems, essays, or plays.

▶Writing has been characterized as written thinking. Students should be encouraged to express their ideas, experiences, thoughts, and feelings. Any free or creative writing they are required to do should have a content in harmony with their evolving interests.

The ideas may be suggested by you directly but, better still, they should result from many experiences and oral discussions which you will provide. When this is feasible, students should listen to recordings of music, plays, or speeches. They should look at and discuss works of art; they should examine pictures for details of color, shape, and form; they should view films, slides, and filmstrips; they should read material in many fields of interest; they should listen to talks and lectures by guest speakers.

A Few General Considerations

Before discussing several types of writing activities which give practice in correctness and which help lead to creativity, let me mention a few general considerations.

▶Little or no writing should be *practiced* in class.* Class time should be devoted to listening and speaking; that is, to activities which the students *cannot* do by themselves outside of class. (It goes without saying that with students who are not accustomed to alphabet writing, some class time may be devoted to the holding of paper, pen, and pencil and to the writing of the alphabet. This need be done only when writing is introduced, however.)

▶Occasionally dictations and simple aural comprehension exercises should be done in class. Procedures for giving these will be explained below.

▶Writing should *reinforce* the structural and lexical items which have been taught as well as the listening, speaking, and reading skills.

▶All writing done by students, whether at home or in class, should be corrected as quickly as feasible.

▶The correction of written work need not constitute a heavy chore for the teacher. Here are some suggestions for "checking" written work:

Correcting Written Work

Homework

1. Permit students who have not done their homework to tell you so *before* you start your regular lesson.

2. If you wish, with young students, assign the first person in each row to check the performance of homework.

3. If blackboard space permits, send two or three (or more) of your *more able* students to place a designated segment of their completed homework on the board.

4. When all the work has been placed on the board, ask *another* able student to go to the board and to ask his classmates questions such as "Is there an error in line 1?" "Who sees a mistake?" He will *cross out* the incorrect word and write the correct word *above* it. While this is being done, you may walk around the room, making sure the students are correcting the work in their notebooks.

5. When the work has been completely corrected, ask still another student to read it *from the board*.

6. If time permits, have several students read their corrected work *from their notebooks*.

*Any writing of "rules"—paradigms, charts, dialogues, etc., form a chart or blackboard—should be done during a *specific* period of time (preferably toward the end of the lesson). Anything else slows down the lesson considerably and may lead to behavior problems.

Dictations and Aural Comprehension Exercises

1. Use steps 3, 4, and 5 above.

   or

2. Have students exchange papers with their neighbors. Follow the procedure for correction outlined above.

"Free" Compositions

1. Ask your students to leave a one- or two-inch margin on the left-hand side of their papers.
2. Have them divide this margin into four columns. The first will be Sp (Spelling); the second may be P (Punctuation); the third Str (Structure); the fourth V (Vocabulary).
3. When you collect the compositions, perhaps once every two weeks, merely *underline* the error and *place a check* on the appropriate line in the appropriate column.
4. You may wish, on a 10-point scale, to deduct ¼ point for each error, or you may deduct ½ point for structure and ¼ for vocabulary, etc. You may prefer, if ideas are important, to give two points for ideas. (If you think four ideas are necessary, give ½ point for each.) In later stages, and if you have given practice in word study, you may also wish to give one or two points for richness and variety of vocabulary.
5. Have the students rewrite the composition and return the original and corrected copies to you.

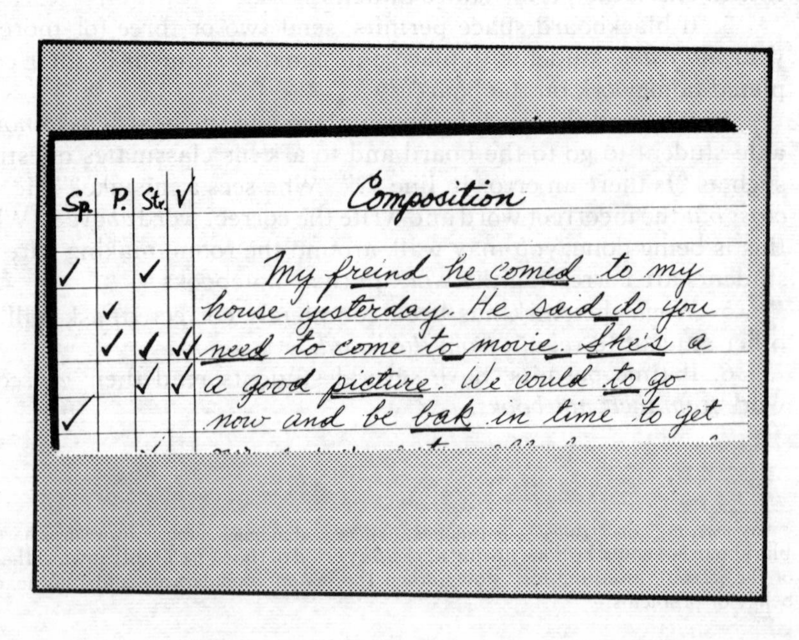

Guided Writing Activities*

What are some of the *guided writing* activities which lead to correctness and ease in writing? Students may:

1. *Write out in full* the pattern practice sentences they have practiced orally. Say, for example, "Use the words in the list to write sentences like sentence 1."

I went to the store
to the library, etc.

2. *Write out in full* a number of pattern practice sentences using elements from each group. Say, "Write ten sentences using any word from each column." (It is important to choose words carefully so that the combinations will be logical.)

I	bought	a	pen.
John	wanted	a	pencil.
Mr. Jones	found	a	notebook.
The boy	paid for	a	ruler.

When your students reach the stage of conscious selection, prepare columns which will "force" them to choose appropriate items from each of the columns; e.g., "Make five sentences using these words:"

The boy	drank	the bread.
The old woman	ate	his dinner.
The man	threw away	the milk.

3. *Change* the sentences in a known dialogue, short paragraph, or series of action sentences in the following way:

a) Change the subject. (The name of the person or pronoun.)
b) Change the subject and verb to the plural.
c) If the subject and verb are in the plural, change them to the singular.
d) Change by adding *yesterday* or *later* or *tomorrow.*
e) Change the point of view of the paragraph; e.g., "I went to the movies. I liked the film. The hero was excellent" to: "I went to the movies. I didn't like the film. The hero was terrible," etc.

4. *Add to* a known related dialogue using newly learned structures and vocabulary.

5. *Answer* a series of specific questions on any activity or on a reading passage. (Wherever possible, the questions should be in logical sequence.)

---

*For other suggestions, see Testing, p. 125.

6. *Complete* a series of related sentences. The completed sentences will constitute a short composition. Example:

I went . . . .
. . . . went with me.
The music was . . . .
We heard . . . .
After the concert, we went to . . . .

7. *Write a summary* of material which has been read.

8. *Write an outline* of material which has been read.

9. *Write a letter* (after the appropriate form has been taught and practiced) in which they expand the ideas you have given them. For example, "Write a letter to your friend. Tell him the subjects you are studying; the ones you enjoy; your plans for the future. Ask him about his plans."

10. *Write an original ending* to a story which they have read.

11. *Write an ending* to a story they have *not* yet completed reading or hearing.

12. Write simple dialogues using (recombining) known structures.

13. *Complete a dialogue* when the first few lines have been given.

14. *Prepare a narrative paragraph* from a dialogue. This activity, as will the next, will require much teacher guidance and patience. (Many similar sentences should be changed to indirect discourse and should be linked together with appropriate connectors over a long period of time in preparation for this activity. (See p. 119.)

15. *Prepare a dialogue from a narrative paragraph.*

16. *Reconstruct a dialogue* from one or two words given in each utterance.

17. *Reconstruct a passage* in which every fifth (or sixth) word has been omitted.*

Other writing activities—many of them combined with listening, speaking, and reading activities—will also be found effective in preparing students for the "freer" expressional writing which we hope many of our language learners will be able to engage in. You may find one or more of the suggestions below helpful to your students.

Ask the entire class, small groups, or individuals as the need arises to:

1. *Combine clauses or sentences* using connectors such as *and, but, although, unless.* (Two sentences only should be combined at first, then three, then four, etc.) Needless to say, extensive practice should have been given with each connector before students are asked to choose among them.

---

*This is generally termed a "cloze" procedure.

2. *Use connectors between sentences or paragraphs* such as *on the other hand, nevertheless, however, furthermore, similarly,* etc.

3. *Transform base sentences* to note the different stylistic effects possible through various transformation rules.

4. *Proofread paragraphs* you will compose or that students have written containing some mechanical errors, inappropriate vocabulary items, or incorrect structure, etc. (These may be flashed on a wall or screen or they may be duplicated for distribution.)

5. *Take a dictation.* (A procedure will be suggested below.)

6. *Take notes* on a reading passage. Learners will need extensive help in determining what the key words are.

7. *Do a listening comprehension* exercise in which the answers are to be written. (A procedure will be suggested below.)

8. *Add an explanation* or appropriate details to a statement that has been given.

9. *Place a series of sentences* in a logical sequence. This may follow reading and oral discussion.

10. *Study a model paragraph* several times in order to note the central thought, the connecting words, the transitional sentences, the details explaining the topic sentences, or the sequence of steps.

11. *Supply* the missing words in a model paragraph which has been studied.

12. *Paraphrase a model paragraph* substituting not only individual words but structures and phrases. (These words may be supplied by you, or the students may be expected to recall them from previous learning activities.)

13. *Write a paragraph* based on a model but on a different topic suggested by you (but using the same organization and structures).

14. *Memorize carefully* chosen sentences or brief paragraphs.

15. *Reconstruct* a paragraph using key words which you will supply.

16. *Rewrite* a paragraph using a different register or style (more formal or colloquial, etc.).

Freer Writing

As I noted above, this is a much more difficult activity. Students normally need a lot of help before they can be asked to "go home and write a composition." As we all know, such an assignment often causes panic even in writing one's native tongue.

The following *pre*-writing steps are essential:

1. Select a topic. (The students may help suggest a topic based on something of interest which has occurred or is about to occur.) Place the title on the board—(Top center)—Divide the board in thirds.

2. Engage in oral discussion of the topic. Have students give several ideas that should be included. (Have an able student under

your direction list these on the left third of the board as they are suggested.)

3. Discuss with the students the *logical* sequence of ideas. Have the ideas listed in Column 2 (with adequate space between them) in the sequence in which they will be written.

4. Next to each idea, write in Column 3, the structures, idioms, and vocabulary items needed to write about each. Some items will be suggested by the students; some may have to be supplied by you.

a) Pronounce the new words.

b) Give numerous examples of each structure.

c) Give *brief* pattern practice when time permits (I enjoy boating; I enjoy fishing; I enjoy swimming; etc.) using pictures, words, etc. (The important thing is to get to the writing.)

5. Have individual students compose a few sentences under each idea. When this has been done, you may wish to ask the students to write the first paragraph. As the students write, you may quietly look at several papers and ask one or two students to read to the entire class a paragraph which you consider a good model.

Give the students several days to write the composition at home. Tell them not to expect the corrected material before seven to ten days. After compositions are corrected in the manner indicated previously or any other you prefer, ask the students to make the corrections and to return the compositions to you.

Before leaving the subject of writing, there are three additional matters which should be mentioned:

1. In order to assist your students in developing a rich vocabulary and more ideas, you may wish to reinforce through writing some of the techniques we mentioned under reading—broaden their experiences by having them listen to music, look at paintings, or discuss ideas found in books. Give them practice in paraphrasing sentences. Give them synonyms for simple, overworked words like "said" (exclaimed; stated; observed; cried; shouted; etc.).

2. Give, at least once a week, *short dictations,* first on familiar material and then on combined new and familiar material. After you have motivated your students and explained all of the difficulties, dictate the material at *normal* speed. Then dictate the material again but in logical breath groups. Have students write during this second dictation. (One or two students may write on the back or side board or even on the front board.) Say the material again at normal speed. Give the students one or two minutes to look over their papers before correcting the material in one of the ways suggested previously.

Some teachers prefer to indicate punctuation marks during the second and third readings. Others feel that students ought to learn to write the punctuation marks by listening to the rise and fall of the voice.

The skill of transferring spoken intonation to written punctuation marks has to be *specifically* taught and practiced. *Transfer* of learning does *not* normally occur automatically.

If you have time and appropriate facilities, you may wish to prepare copies of paragraphs for dictation* leaving blank spaces in various places. In that case, students (at the *second* reading) will write on their separate answer paper only the words that are missing.

3. *Aural comprehension* exercises also provide excellent practice in understanding and writing. The paragraph chosen for this activity should be short and, if possible, should constitute a complete idea about which you can ask four or five questions, the answers to which can be taken word for word (or nearly so) from the paragraph.

The procedure for conducting an aural comprehension activity is as follows:

a) Motivate by giving a brief summary.

b) Clear up any difficulties.

c) State your aim *and* the procedure you will follow.

d) Read the paragraph through *twice* at normal speed.

e) Read a question *twice.* Give the students the opportunity to write the answer. (One or two students may write on the board.)

f) Continue until you have given all the questions.

g) Read the paragraph again at normal speed.

h) Read the questions again at normal speed.

i) Give the students one or two minutes to check their own work.

j) Correct the material in one of the ways suggested before.

4. *Dicto-comps,* as the name implies, are a combination of dictation and composition. Here is a possible procedure:

a) Select two or three sequential paragraphs around a topic of interest.

b) Motivate the topic by relating it to a familiar experience.

c) Clarify any difficulties in it. (You may leave the words on the board, particularly the first few times you use the technique.)

d) Read the paragraphs sequentially four or five times.

e) Ask your students to reconstruct the paragraphs sequentially *using the words they remember* in them. (Permit them to look at the words on the board.)

f) For checking, either distribute a sheet on which the paragraphs appear or use a device to flash them on the screen. If the paragraphs will be used later, you may wish to write them on a chart which can be used for such activities as choral recitation, structure and word study, and especially, as a model for the composition of paragraphs on a related theme. For example, a dicto-comp on a trip to the mountains

*This is generally termed "spot dictation."

can be rewritten (with new words given, of course) as a trip to the seaside.

It is important to underscore again, as we conclude this brief review of writing activities, that any of the procedures noted above can and should be modified according to your students' needs and interests. For example, in saying the dictation the second time (in logical breath and writing groups), you may have the students say the words aloud *before* writing them. Listening to you, followed by their oral repetition and feedback, will undoubtedly be of help to them as they write the words.

No procedure given in this book or in any other book should be considered immutable. As we said above, needs, modalities of learning, and interests of *your* students should always be taken into consideration in selecting and conducting any activity.

Developing Cultural Insights

And now, what are some of the ways in which cultural insights can be provided? Any one of the techniques noted below and, preferably, a combination of them should be used. These are listed in no particular order. Some are possible at every learning level. Some such as the reading of literary masterpieces will only be possible at the fourth or fifth level, if at all.

1. The classroom should reflect the culture of the English-speaking world. (This is possible, we realize, only when one or more rooms in the school are set aside for language instruction.)

a) At the beginning levels, parts of the room may be labeled in English.

b) Maps and posters of English-speaking countries should be attractively displayed.

c) A bulletin board should include newspaper or magazine clippings of current events, taken either from English or native language sources, advertisements, comic strips, proverbs, pictures, songs, and music.

d) A windowed closet or a table may contain objects related to English culture such as a collection of dolls, money, stamps, menus, costumes, and other artifacts.

e) A library corner should contain books and magazines *in English* at the reading and interest levels of the students. Books in the curriculum areas used in English-speaking schools are of particular interest to students. There should also be books about English-speaking countries written in the students' native language. Wherever possible, a piece of literature in English and its equivalent in the students' native language should be provided.

It is also informative to have books written by English speakers. What is their view of us? Why? If it is unfavorable, could it be changed? How?

Newspapers, where possible, can be a source of study for format, style, point of view, attitude towards others, etc.

The magazines should be on sports, adventure, science, love, and anything else that is of interest to the students and which will motivate them to learn the language while developing cultural awareness.

f) A record player and records of contemporary music or folk songs should be available for frequent use.

2. Individuals and groups of students should carry out projects related to English-speaking culture which will then serve for class reporting and discussion. The projects may include the preparation of:

a) Maps—physical, economic, geographic—showing the relation of English-speaking countries to the one in which you are teaching; the location of important cities, monuments, and places of interest; regions where natural resources are found or certain foods produced; and areas which are the setting for well-known literary masterpieces.

b) Itineraries for actual trips to pertinent places of interest in the community or for trips to English-speaking lands.

c) Floor plans of houses and other buildings—with appropriate labels.

d) Menus of food eaten on special occasions.

e) Calendars indicating special holidays.

f) "Information Please" or quiz programs.

g) Word study materials (English words and expressions in the native tongue, native words and expressions in English, common word origins [where feasible, of course]).

h) An English language newspaper.

i) A scrapbook (current events, art, science, etc.).

j) Filmstrips or picture series.

k) A play reading.

l) The preparation of an original skit or playlet.

m) A book fair.

n) Forms, documents, and other pertinent materials related to commerce and industry between English-speaking countries and the country in which you are teaching.

3. The culture of English speakers may be studied and/or experienced in:

a) An assembly program (songs, dances, backdrops, talks).

b) A festival to which community members are invited.

c) Songs and dances which are heard and learned.

4. The showing of visual materials and the language laboratory should be used as vehicles for:

a) Listening to recitals or readings by contemporary authors.

b) Viewing filmstrips and films on any aspect of English-speaking culture.

c) Listening to spoken descriptions of museum materials as students view works of art or artifacts.

d) Seeing short films of interviews with people in the news.

5. Masterpieces of literature should be read and studied (adapted when necessary), since a real work of literature reflects, as perhaps no other art form or material, the character of the people, the situations in which people interact, the historical or geographical rationale for their behavior, the values to which people are attached; in short, the entire gamut of the values, customs, and beliefs included in the term "culture."

Moreover, the study of a literary masterpiece permits discussion of linguistic style and aesthetics and perhaps of language registers, dialects, and idiolects which no other art form can exemplify as well.

Although this is a controversial issue, I am convinced that a good translation of a masterpiece is better than not exposing the students to English literature at all.

6. The possibility of correlation with other areas in the curriculum should be explored continuously. For example, the relationship between the study of the native tongue and English can be emphasized through the study of plays, stories, and films which are translated and shown in your country or in the English-speaking community.

The music department in your school, if one exists, will be delighted to cooperate with you and your students as they learn about any outstanding composers and their works or as they learn the songs and dances of the English-speaking world. The social studies department will welcome your support in discussions of the interrelationships of governments in world economy, production, imports, exports, etc. The impact of geography and history on the culture of any society would be a fruitful field of correlation between the social studies and English departments.

7. Resource people should be invited to speak to the class on cultural topics. If the talk is in English, it would be desirable to ask the speaker to explain important words or to show visual materials to clarify his topic. His delivery (gestures, distance maintained, facial expressions, use of certain expressions, intonation) will still be helpful to the students whether or not they understand everything.

If the visit is preceded by a letter of invitation and followed by a letter of thanks, the authentic formulas used in letter writing (including the writing of dates, numbers, salutations, closing remarks, etc.) will be another example of cultural knowledge the students will acquire.

8. A pen pal project should be initiated very soon after the students learn to write. The first letter need not be elaborate but may simply indicate: "My name is so and so. I'm sending you a picture. I go to X school. Please write to me."—with appropriate headings and closing, of course. (Sources of "Pen Pals" will be found on p. 214.)

9. Teachers of art, science, and social studies may give brief lectures in the native language.* You can then engage the class in oral activities in English related to the topic.

10. Last, but most essential, you can give a twenty minute illustrated lecture in English on any cultural topic, followed by questions and a summary.

Summary

In summary, I would like to emphasize again several premises on which the development of communication is based:

1. The sequence in which the four skills are taught is listening, speaking, reading, writing. The first approach to language should be through the ear. Students should be asked to read only the material they can say with *reasonable* fluency.

2. The principal aim of any lesson may be the development of *one* skill only, but there will be necessary overlapping with other skills. For example, we usually speak after listening or reading. We may write as a result of listening or reading.

3. Since it is impossible to teach all the sounds or structures at one time, we should hold our students to a higher degree of correctness *only* for those features of language which we have practiced intensively. Let us assume we have practiced intensively only the sound /ɪ/. In teaching "What's this," we should expect only reasonably good imitations of "What's" and of /ð/ and /s/, but a more correct production of /ɪ/.

4. Within each of the skills, attention must be given to the sound system, the structure system, and the vocabulary.

5. In the beginning stages of language learning, the teacher's role is to have the students reproduce correct responses which he has modeled and to help them make carefully cued substitutions or transformations. Creativity or improvisation, before the students are ready, will cause unnecessary errors which necessitate an expenditure of time for correction and eradication and will result in frustration.

*The usual cautions must be exercised, of course.

6. As soon as possible and with every technique or tool at our command, our students must be made to feel and see the relationship between each of the separate language features and each of the separate skills within the total act of communication. They should be enabled to understand and to use in English the normal forms of speech they would use in their native tongue. They should, in addition, be enabled and motivated to develop further the basic skills of reading and writing which we have initiated.

7. No skill is developed without continuous and intensive practice. No skill can be maintained unless it is used frequently. The planning for continuous and intensive practice in which the material which has been taught is constantly *reintroduced* and *consolidated* with known material is one of the major responsibilities of the teacher of English as a second language.

8. Communicative competence—the primary objective of the majority of English as a Second Language programs—will result from our efforts to give learners opportunities for practice which will insure accuracy, fluency, and appropriateness in a variety of social situations.

9. Since language reflects the culture of English speakers, students should be given insight into the habits, customs, and values which are similar to or different from their own. It is imperative, however, that they appreciate that *all* people have culture and that there are no "good" or "bad" cultures. More important for the student than the acquisition of any item of language is that he retain pride in his own culture as he moves toward the acceptance of the language and culture of native English speakers.

10. Cultural insights are acquired incidentally as students dramatize conversations, using not only different varieties of language, but also the appropriate gestures, expressions, and distances which duplicate those of a native speaker. They are acquired also as a result of the learners' group activities and your direct teaching of the values, beliefs, art forms, and literature of English speakers.

IV. Materials and Techniques of Instruction

Let us begin this chapter on teaching aids by reaffirming our belief that the teacher is the most important single factor in the teaching-learning process. There can be no question that given students with some interest in language learning, it is what we as teachers do—to promote a friendly environment in the classroom; to create and organize materials; to overcome shortcomings in our textbooks; to stimulate and maintain interest through varied practice activities; to emphasize certain enjoyable aspects of language learning while minimizing other features—which will determine their growth toward communication.

In many instances, the desire to learn a new mode of communication can be fostered even in students who do not have a strong initial interest in language study. By the same token, alas, many students who approach the study of English with enthusiasm are often deflected by teachers who follow the textbook slavishly or who follow, in a mechanical manner, some of the learning steps we have outlined above.

There are so many devices and approaches which can supplement the textbook and often even the teacher's voice that it seems a pity for the alert teacher not to make use of them. In this section, therefore, will be indicated some of the materials and techniques which will help bring motivation into the language learning classroom. Let us start with *materials*.

Some Materials of Instruction

1. The Picture File

Every classroom should contain a file of pictures which can be used not only to illustrate the aspects of the socio-cultural topics listed in Chapter II, but also to give interesting, meaningful practice in the sounds, structures, and vocabulary of English.

The file should contain three kinds of pictures: 1) pictures of individual persons and of individual objects; 2) pictures of situations in which persons are "doing something" with objects and in which the relationship of objects and/or people can be seen; 3) a series of pictures (6 to 10) on one chart. You may wish to create several of these charts; for example, one for count nouns (the objects in the classroom for example); one for mass nouns (food, for example); one for count and mass nouns placed at random; one for words illustrating difficult consonant clusters without regard to "count" and "mass"; one for work activities; one for verbs which cannot add "ing"; one for verbs like "seem"; many with four scenes depicting four situations which will enable pupils to create a sequential dialogue or oral (and then written) narrative paragraph. An example will be found in Appendix II on p. 158.

The file should contain *more than one picture* of individuals and of objects. This is necessary if students are not to assume that your finger touching the fender of a car, for example, indicates that "car" (the word you are teaching) and "fender" are synonyms. Many pictures of cars, or pens, or boys, or women, or whatever you are teaching and, in addition, a sweeping movement of your hand over the *entire* picture will ensure the proper association of word and object or person.

What criteria should guide us in choosing or drawing pictures? Pictures should be large enough to be seen by all students. The pictures of individual objects or people should be as simple as possible. Some of them should contain color for later use when adjectives of color are presented. The pictures should contain *no captions** of any kind since you will want to use them at times to have students *recall* the association of word and object. Situational pictures should not contain captions either. The same scene may serve as the basis for various oral discussions.

Some Uses

The pictures can be used in numerous ways. Individual pictures

* A caption, title, or brief description for your own use on the back of the picture will be helpful.

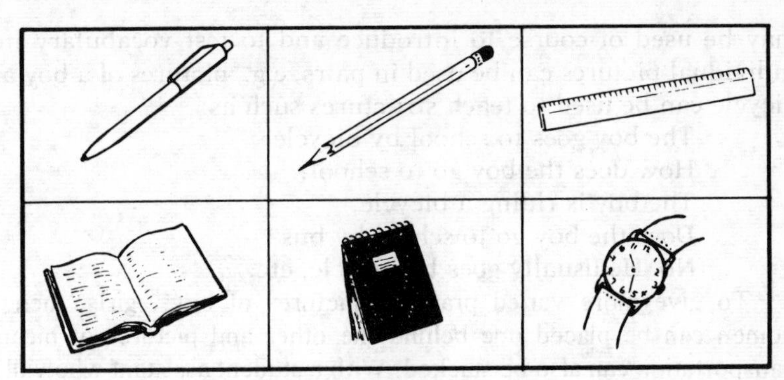

Count Nouns Chart

Mass Nouns Chart

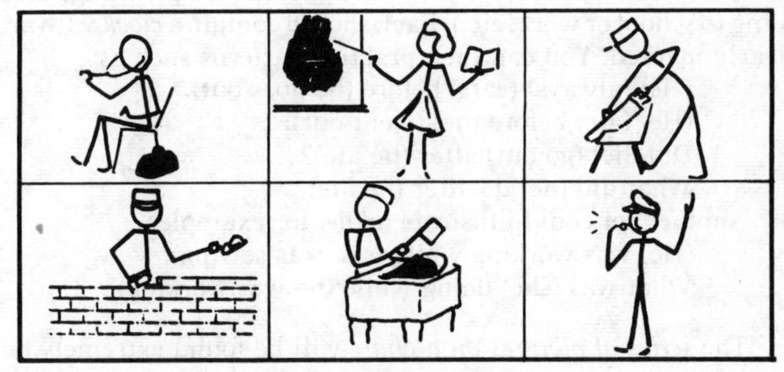

Work Activities Chart

may be used of course to introduce and to test vocabulary items. Individual pictures can be used in pairs, e.g., pictures of a boy and a bicycle can be used to teach structures such as:

The boy goes to school by bicycle.
How does the boy go to school?
The boy is riding a bicycle.
Does the boy go to school by bus?
No. He usually goes by bicycle, etc.

To give more varied practice, pictures of boys, girls, men, and women can be placed one behind the other and pictures of means of transportation can also be stacked. With a student assistant who will help you flip the pictures, *double* substitutions can be made; e.g.,

The girl goes by bus.
The woman goes by train, etc.

Three individual pictures (or stacked individual pictures on rings) can be used in the same fashion; e.g.,

The boy went to the library by bus.
The girl went to the hospital by car.
The man went to the United States by plane, etc.

The further use of individual pictures for testing purposes will be discussed in the next chapter.

The situational pictures are excellent for eliciting "real" language. "What do you see?" "What are they doing?" "Are they sad?" "Would you like to do that?" and any other structure (of age, weather, clothing, action) to which the picture lends itself can be practiced. If possible, situational pictures should be used to stimulate ideas for the "freer" compositions we discussed above.

Another very good use of situational pictures which you would have to create (very simple line drawings are all that is needed) would be the practice of complex sentences with *before, after,* and *while.* The pictures could show individuals doing something (eating, dressing, going to school or work, etc.). Each should contain a *clock* with an hour clearly marked. You can then practice patterns such as:

(He) (always) (eats) before (he goes out).*
(He) (ate) before (he) (went out).
Did (he) (go out) after (he ate)?
What did (he) do after (he ate)?

Another set could illustrate *while,* for example.

(He) was working while (she was sewing).
What was (she) doing while (he was working)?

The *series of pictures on a chart* will be found extremely helpful

* Notice that patterns indicating plurality, allow students to practice the three plural sounds: /z/, /s/, /ɪz/.

in giving extensive practice in numerous structures with a limited *known* vocabulary. You may add variety to the "sameness" of the chart by pointing to the pictures in the order in which they appear; by pointing to them at random; or by having a student point to them in sequence or at random and call on his classmates to respond. You may also add other appropriate utterances.

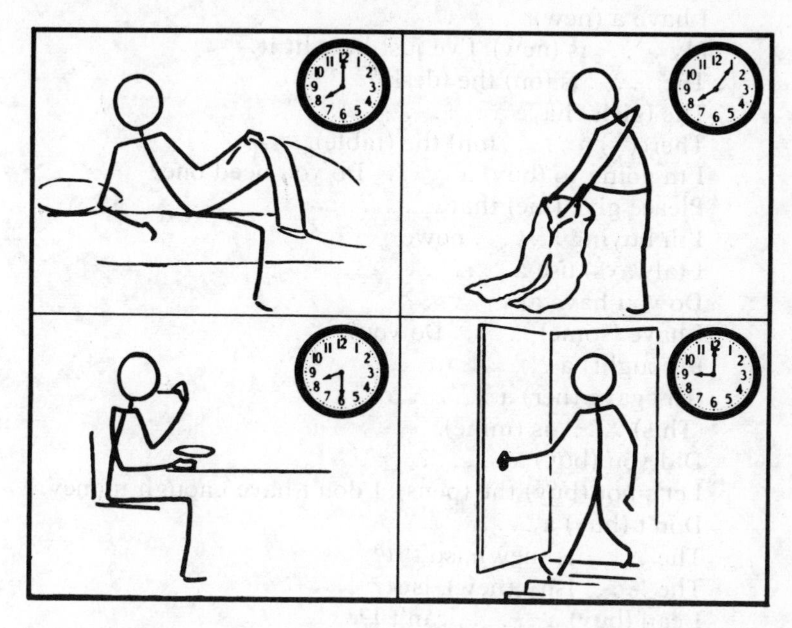

Let us take as an example a chart containing pictures of a pen, a pencil, a ruler, a book, a notebook, a watch.* Notice some of the possible patterns which can be practiced using the same chart at all levels of language learning. (Please remember that *you* always give the pattern sentence several times first.)**

What's this? It's a (pen)*
This is a . . . . . (If the students are *touching* the pictures.)
That's a . . . . .
Is this a . . . . . ? Yes, it is.
    No, it isn't. It's a . . . . .
What do you have?
    (I) (have) a . . . . .
(Do) (you) have a . . . . . ? Yes, I do.
    No, I don't.
I have a . . . . . , a . . . . . , and a . . . . .

---

* Parentheses indicate that other words may be substituted.
** The pattern should always be *one* which can be used logically with each picture on the chart.

Show us the . . . . . That's the . . . . .
May I have the (books)?
Where is the . . . . .?
Where are the . . . . .?
I'd like several . . . . . . I'm sorry. I don't have any.
How much is a . . . . . ? It's . . . . . cents.
I have a (new) . . . . .
My . . . . . is (new). I've just bought it.
The . . . . . is (on) the (desk).
The (girls) have a . . . . .
There('s) a . . . . . (on) the (table).
I'm going to (buy) a . . . . . . Do you need one?
Please give (me) that . . . . .
I'm buying a . . . . . now.
I (always) use a . . . . .
Do you have any . . . . . ?
I have (some) . . . . . . Do you?
I (bought) a . . . . . .
(He) gave (her) a . . . . .
(This) . . . . . is (mine).
Did you (buy) a . . . . . ?
Let's not (buy) the (pens). I don't have enough money.
Don't (buy) a . . . . .
The . . . . . is (new), isn't it?
The . . . . . isn't (new), is it?
I can (buy) a . . . . . , can't I?
I'm sure the . . . . . is (new).
If I had a . . . . . , I'd . . . . .
If I had had a . . . . . , I could have . . . . .
I'd like to (buy) a . . . . .
May I see a more expensive . . . . . ?
Thank you for (bringing) the . . . . .

And we could continue! Surprisingly enough, the students do *not* get bored with the same vocabulary. If the pace is brisk, if the procedures are varied, if they are saying correctly the new structures you are teaching, they will find pleasure and comfort in the familiar words.

Pictures can also be used to play games, to illustrate stories, and to do numerous other activities which will certainly occur to you as you use them.

2. Charts

Simple charts showing various grammatical relationships are

extremely valuable. The use of verb tenses and verb phrases can be illustrated graphically by simple lines on a chart as below:

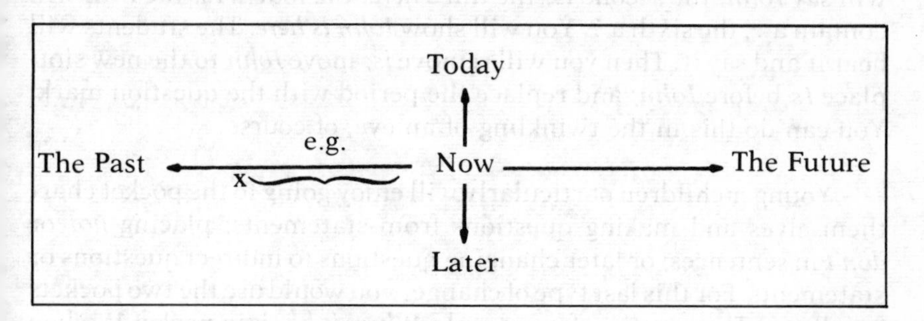

As you introduce a new verb phrase, you can point to a place or places on the chart in order to clarify the concept of time. You can also use lines, crosses, or any mark to show the time relationships involved; e.g., Did an action started in the past continue into the present? (A bracket ⏟ would be appropriate.)

You will find other charts useful adjuncts many times during the year. Among these could be charts containing question words, prefixes or suffixes, and the Viëtor triangle (See p. 25.)

3. Flash Cards or Word Cards

Cards with individual words (either printed or in manuscript) can be prepared and filed within the same categories and in the same order as the individual pictures. The cards should be about twelve inches long and four inches wide.

Younger children can be asked to match cards and pictures as soon as they can read. They can also match the cards with words written on the blackboard or on a large cardboard.

The cards can serve as word cues in the oral substitution drills outlined in the preceding chapter. They can be used for review purposes ("Make your own sentence using this word") or in playing games. Many other uses will occur to you as you use them.

4. The Pocket Chart

This simple teaching tool is an excellent device for dramatizing word order. It is easily made by taking a piece of cardboard or hard paper (about two feet in length by about one foot in height), and pinning (stapling or gluing) to it two narrow pockets about two inches high.

Let us assume that you want to teach inverted question word order with the sentence "John is here." You will need six cards. One will say *John;* the second *is;* the third *here;* the fourth *Is;* the fifth will contain a **.**; the sixth a **?**. You will show *John is here.* The students will hear it and say it. Then you will remove *is;* move *John* to the new slot; place *Is* before *John;* and replace the period with the question mark. You can do this in the twinkling of an eye, of course.

Younger children particularly will enjoy going to the pocket chart themselves and making questions from statements; placing *not* or *don't* in sentences; or later changing questions to indirect questions or statements. For this last type of change, you would use the two pockets as follows: The question, for example, *Where is he?* is in pocket 1. When you place or uncover *"Do you know" "I'm not sure,"* etc. in pocket 2, you will dramatize the change in word order in the second sentence by moving words from one slot to another.

It may be desirable to have younger students make small individual pocket charts so that they can "manipulate" sentences at their seats as you or a student do so at the large pocket chart in front of the room.

Basic words (forms of *be, do,* and *have,* frequency words, pronouns, names), punctuation marks, etc., can be kept on individual cards in clearly marked envelopes for easy reference and for quick changes.

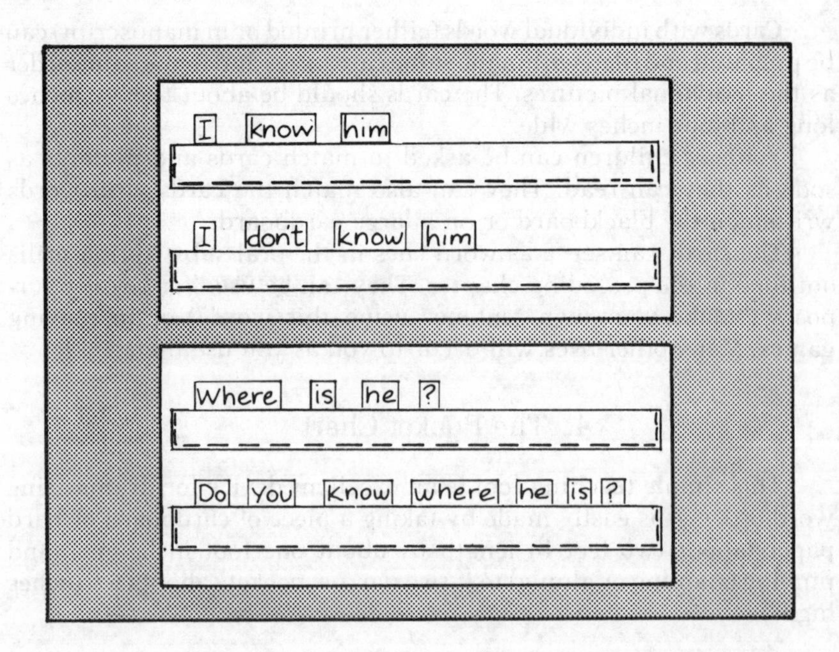

5. The Flannel Board*

This inexpensively made device is excellent as still another way of presenting and practicing vocabulary and structures—expressions of place, for example. With younger students, it is useful in playing games or in dramatizing stories. All that you need is a piece of the cheapest flannel glued, pinned, or thrown over a piece of wood or heavy cardboard about two feet long by two feet in height. (As a matter of fact, you may wish to make the pocket chart and flannel board of the same size placing one on each side of a board or cardboard.)

Pictures or cutouts with a small piece of flannel glued to the back adhere easily to the flannel and permit the illustration and teaching of many concepts or structures. Let us assume that you want to teach some prepositions. You may do this with cutouts of plates and utensils. You or a student may place a plate in the center, a fork to the left, and a knife and spoon to the right. You can teach many function words and structures, such as:

> The plate is in the center.
> Put the knife (above) the plate.
> Put the (plate) in the (upper) (righthand) corner.
> Please remove the (plate).

You may teach *on, next to, under, above,* etc., with a small piece of flannel cut out in the shape of a table and another piece of another color which can be placed *on, under,* etc., the table.

A use of the flannel board which has been popular in many countries is one in which I cut out the figure of a person from another piece of flannel; the head, ears, nose, mouth, eyes, neck, arms, body, legs. We've named it *Poor Jim.* Poor Jim serves to practice the names of parts of the body; words like *right* and *left*; names of illnesses. (When a student points to "Jim's" stomach, for example, a classmate could say, "Jim has a stomachache," if that is the pattern being practiced.) By pointing quickly to the figure, you can give students practice with contrasting expressions such as sore throat (arm, leg).

Fairy tales are more enjoyable to young students as some of the characters are placed dramatically on the flannel board and moved around as need be. (Try doing this with Goldilocks and The Three Bears some day even with adult students.)

Another amusing way in which the flannel board can be used is as follows: Make a cutout of a house or a room or anything which lends itself to this game. Let us assume you have made a house. Two students will go to the flannel board. One removes the window and says, "This is a funny (peculiar) house. It doesn't have a window." The next student quickly places the window back, removes the roof, and says,

* A *magnet board* can be used in the same way.

"Oh, yes, it has a window, but it doesn't have a roof," etc. Two or three pairs of students may play this game during a class period.

Poor Jim

6. Games and Songs

There are all kinds of language games and songs ranging from very simple to difficult ones which help give practice in language while keeping the class lively and interesting. The type of song you teach to your class will depend on the age, interests, and learning level of the students. Songs for children, for example, should contain a repetitive motif where possible. Songs for intermediate levels and/or older students may have love, patriotism, home, holidays, etc. as themes. Ideally, the songs should reflect the culture of English-speaking people both musically and thematically, but if you, someone in the music department of your school, or a creative student can put English words to favorite melodies from your students' countries, by all means, do so. These new English songs with melodies familiar to the students can be used most effectively.

Following are ten games which will start you on the road to collecting and adapting others for your classes: (See the Bibliography.)

The Curious Owl

Student 1 will ask student 2 a question; e.g., "How old are you?" Student 2 will answer. Student 3 will ask student 4, "How old is he (she)?" referring to Student 2. Student 4 will answer. Student 5 will begin again with "How old are you?" to Student 6.

I'm Thinking Of

The teacher or student (game leader) will choose an item (number, name, date, month, time, a sport, an activity, etc.) from among those items the class has been studying. The teacher or leader will whisper the item to another student so that there will be someone to verify the answer. The teacher or leader will call on individuals in the class to guess the correct item.

Individual—Is it . . . . . ?

Teacher or leader—No, it's not . . . .

Teacher or leader—Yes, it is. It's . . . .

Add-on

This is played with a *picture,* a *real object,* or *verbal* cues.

Student 1—I see a living room.

Student 2—I see a living room and a kitchen.

Student 3—I see a living room, a kitchen, and a bathroom.

or

Student 1—I like milk.

Student 2—I like milk and pie.

Student 3—I like milk, pie, and cake.

Oh, No; Not I

The teacher or a student makes a statement with such phrases as "I hear that," "I understand that," "I see that," "I have heard that," etc. What the teacher "heard" should be a statement which the student to whom it is made will want to deny. He will say that someone else is responsible. That student will say someone else is responsible, etc.

Teacher—I understand you came late this morning.

Student 1—Oh, no; not I. I didn't come late. He did.

Notes:

1. Responses can be varied and expanded in many ways depending upon the knowledge of the students; e.g., "I always come early (on time)" or "I'm *never* late to school."

or

Teacher—You're very sad, aren't you?

Student—No, I'm not sad. I'm very happy, but I think . . . . . is sad.

2. Use your knowledge of the students to inject humor into the practice without hurting the sensibilities of anyone.

Simon Says

Directions are given by the teacher or a student leader; e.g., hands on your head; pencils in your desk; hands on your tie; hands behind your back; etc. When the directions are preceded by *Simon says,* the students are to carry them out. When *Simon says* does not precede the directions, the students remain motionless.

It's More (Less)

a. *It's More.* To a list of prices or hours, students will be expected to *add* an amount set by the teacher or a group leader. For example, write on the blackboard "7 A.M., 8 A.M., 9 A.M., etc." Have students add a quarter hour or a half an hour to a basic sentence such as "I usually leave home at seven." The students will change it to "I usually leave home at a quarter past seven."

b. *It's Less.* Same as above, except that students will deduct an amount.

Opposites

Two teams are formed. The first person in Team 1 says a word. The first person on Team 2 has to say the opposite word. If he cannot, his team loses a point. (The same can be done with synonyms and with words of the same family.)

What Is It? (or Who Am I?)

a. *What Is It?* A description is given, e.g., "It has four legs." "It's made of wood." Students on teams have to say, "It's a chair."

b. *Who Am I?* A job description is given: "I cut meat." A student has to say, "You are a butcher."

Twenty Questions

One student is sent out of the room while the others decide on an object, person, or animal. When the student returns, he asks questions such as "Is it in the room?" "Is it big?" "Is it red?"

Charades

A proverb or a familiar concept of some kind can be acted out by a member of one team. Members of the other team have to guess what the concept is. They make statements identifying the concept; for example, "The book is difficult." "The boy is tall and handsome." "A stitch in time saves nine."

7. Real Objects

A corner of the room and a large box on reserve should contain *anything* you can gather together to illustrate vocabulary items or cultural concepts. Newspapers, menus, flags, maps, ticket stubs, cans, bottles, boxes, pieces of different kinds of cloth (wool, silk, cotton, nylon), wax flowers, dishes, silverware, etc., all form part of the "baggage" of the interested and interesting teacher and contribute to the "cultural island" we will talk about below.

8. The Record Player

Songs, dances, stories, plays, and other language learning materials can be found on records. Newer English textbooks are often accompanied by recordings of dialogues and of many practice activities. Some include pauses for student repetition.

The record player may be used within the classroom lesson to accustom students to a voice other than yours, to provide concerted drill, and/or to introduce songs and dances. You may also wish to make provision to have the class or groups of students listen to a story or play or to portions of the English textbook *after* the regular English period.

9. The Language Laboratory

Where tape recorders exist, you should make every attempt to use them extensively. If tapes have been made of the textbook lesson, they will be invaluable in giving the *additional* practice needed to reinforce the material you are teaching in the classroom.

Tapes have the advantage of maintaining the same intonation, repeating endlessly without tiring, providing a uniform length of pause for student repetition, etc. These characteristics may not always be true of the teacher who has to teach many different classes a day.

Many kinds of supplementary materials can be placed on tapes: pronunciation drills where contrasts are featured, sentences of varying lengths to teach rhythm, sentences illustrating basic intonation patterns, dialogues and stories for listening and repeating, oral practice activities where students "manipulate" a sentence to create a new one, dictations, aural comprehension exercises, and tests.

In addition to tapes of the textbook lessons themselves, you can use commercially prepared taped stories, plays, dialogues, or drills to enrich the work you are doing.

You will find the tape recorder effective also in showing pupils the progress they are making in learning English. At the beginning of the semester you can ask intermediate students to record a small passage. At the end of the semester they can record the same passage again.

For easy identification, each student should give his name before he starts to read. The number on the tape counter should be noted in a book. Enough tape should be left after each student's reading to permit him to re-record next to his original performance. In this way, the progress or sometimes, unfortunately, the lack of it will easily be apparent.

Many excellent books have been written about language laboratories so that I will not duplicate here what has been said so eloquently elsewhere. Allow me to make several comments, however.

▶A language laboratory need not be an elaborate installation of twenty or more sound booths. One tape recorder, when properly used, may be considered a "laboratory."

▶It is not absolutely necessary to make provision for student playback. Recent experimentation and observation indicate that listening to a good model and repeating a correct response are generally more effective than listening to oneself. This is especially true at the beginning level.

▶The directions on the tape (if teacher made) may be in the language of the students followed immediately by the English equivalent unless the teacher has clarified the directions in class or is present to clarify them. Gradually, the directions in the native language may be omitted.

▶In general, unless you feel that your English is *not at all* adequate, *the initial presentation* of teaching material should be done *by you.* The tape recorder can give more intensive and extensive practice, but it cannot answer questions, indicate relationships, emphasize, underline, and detect problems by looking at the learners' faces.

▶If you are not a native English speaker and feel that the tape recorder is necessary for the "first" presentation of new material, you should make use of it. You and the students can listen to and repeat the dialogue or the conversation together. It is more desirable, however, if you have the time, for you to listen to the tape as close to coming into class as possible and to present it "live" first.

▶When students use the laboratory outside of class time, you should give them the opportunity to display their greater accuracy or fluency when they return to the classroom.

▶The laboratory or a tape recorder with additional jacks (needed for multiple headphones) is very valuable for individualizing instruction. Students who have lagged behind the other members of the class can gather around the recorder in a corner of the classroom and listen to tapes of the preceding lessons. By the same token, students who have completed the regular class work may listen to supplementary materials (dictation, listening comprehension, reading comprehension, plays, anecdotes) while you work with another group or with the class.

▶The tape recorder in the center of the classroom (about forty pupils can listen clearly) or the language laboratory can be effective for individual or group testing or for listening or reading comprehensions and dictations. You can give the students answer sheets on which they will indicate the correct responses which you can then flash on a screen by means of an opaque or overhead projector, or elicit orally, or reinforce in any feasible manner.

▶You can use the laboratory as a library, where students may go during a free hour. This necessitates materials, catalogues, and aides, of course.

▶Listening should NOT be a passive activity. While listening, you should ask students to look at slides or filmstrips, reading passages, dictations in which words have been omitted or at any other material which will insure attentive activity.

The tape recorder and/or a full scale laboratory should be used not only to reinforce drills done in class but also to broaden the horizons of the students. While some students express boredom when material done in class is reheard verbatim in the Lab, I find that they are all eager to listen and react to supplementary material. Such material should be prepared by a team of several people, whenever possible.

Cassettes, for those of us who are afraid of threading tape-recording machines, are now available with suitable equipment which permits the teacher to drop the cassette (a very small, thin box containing the tape) into a special slot. Cassettes can be made to serve the same purposes as a tape recorder.

10. Filmstrips, Films, Radio, Television

Filmstrips (slides which are combined in sequence and which can be projected with a filmstrip projector on a wall or on a screen) can be used effectively to practice vocabulary, structures, and real communication while taking the pupils out of the confines of the classroom. Filmstrips need not have been prepared specifically for English teaching. Any strip showing some aspect of life can be used.

The filmstrip has several advantages. It can be stopped at each frame for as long as the teacher desires. It can be turned back or pushed forward to any frame. Since it contains *no* sound, the teacher and later the students can create appropriate utterances for each frame within the ability of the students. In harmony with the "spiral" approach, the same filmstrip can be shown many times throughout the English course, each time with more complex structures, or in different "registers."

Films for the English class fall into two categories: 1) those which give insight into various cultural aspects of English-speaking countries; and 2) those which are designed to teach the language at various learning levels. In this latter type, simple situations sometimes related to English-speaking countries are portrayed.

All films have the disadvantage of not being able to be turned back easily and quickly to a scene or language exchange that the students did not grasp. The "culture" films, in addition, are often spoken in language far beyond the ability of our students. In most instances, therefore, they have to be used without the sound track.

Films, when used, should be carefully previewed; students should be motivated; appropriate follow-up activities should be planned; e.g., questions and answers, summaries, or descriptions. Language-oriented teaching films are in preparation and should be available in the near future to *supplement* the teacher and the simpler instructional materials he would generally use.

Loop films are available which keep turning automatically so that the students can see and hear the same material as often as the teacher deems it necessary. Rehearing the same material several times is an excellent way of increasing comprehension. As the material is heard several times, the students will *anticipate* what is about to be said. This anticipation (sometimes called "suppletion" in language teaching) is excellent for comprehension, for longer term retention of structures and vocabulary, and, of course, for communication.

The *radio* is good as an additional means of immersing our students in sound, but, for beginning students, general programs have the same disadvantages as films. Several programs especially prepared for language learners are now available in many countries. In addition, you may find it desirable to transcribe a radio program (speeches, news broadcasts, ceremonies, songs) on a tape for later use in your classes.

An excellent procedure is to retain the original tape but to prepare two other versions of it—one at the elementary level and one at an intermediate level. Whereas with the elementary level version, you (or the tape) can ask Yes/No or True/False questions, with the intermediate level tape, the questions can be inverted questions requiring short answers (Yes, it is; No, they didn't, etc.). With the regular tape, note-taking, "Wh" questions, summaries, outlines, or other activities would be desirable. Except at the university level, the three versions would not be studied in one semester. Several teachers at different levels can use the graded tapes if they are aware of their availability and if they are kept in a central office.

Television offers many possibilities as a learning medium. Several courses for teaching English from the beginning to more advanced levels already have been prepared. The television programs which have been designed especially for language learners try to duplicate the classroom situation. Dialogues or dramatic vignettes depicting some cultural situation are utilized; structures are repeated and "manipulated"; some descriptions of word order and forms are given. The camera can come close up to the teacher's mouth to show lip position, mouth movements, or gestures. There are pauses for student repetition.

Television programs, however, cannot do the whole job. The majority of programs may be of only twenty minutes' duration. Much more time is needed to learn a slice of language, as we know. If programs are used *in conjunction with* the regular curriculum, they add spice and pleasurable variety to learning. They provide reinforcement, change of pace, different voices, and wider vistas than the teacher can provide. It is important, however, that additional explanations and practice be given by you. The television teacher cannot hear students' difficulties and errors; "free" answers are impossible; many oral activities cannot be done.

As with any other tool or technique, it is your use of it that determines its efficacy.

11. Programmed Instruction (Teaching Machines)

The last several years have seen the wider use of so-called teaching machines. This is a misnomer because they are not, in fact, machines. A "teaching machine" may consist of a simple box with an opening on top into which a program is inserted, and a knob on the side which a learner can turn. Some machines are much more complicated. They stop, turn back, or turn forward electronically depending on the student's response, which he indicates by making a mark on the program, or writing a number, a word, or a phrase.

The *program* (the term for the pages of learning material which are placed in the box) is the important part of the teaching machine. A good program is based on several principles: 1) It is very carefully graded. 2) Each item of learning is broken up into its smallest part and practiced in as many ways as possible. 3) It permits a student to work at his own speed. 4) It is self-teaching. 5) It gives immediate confirmation of the correctness of one's response. (If the mark on the paper is incorrect, the knob does not turn or a red light appears or some other signal is given.)

Because of the incontrovertible facts of which we are aware: that language is speech and that one learns a language first through the ear, "programs" for languages are, at this writing, not as successful as they are in other curriculum areas. The perfect synchronization of sound track and teaching machine which would permit the student to work at his own speed has not yet been devised. Since programmed instruction incorporates several basic premises of learning, it is to be hoped that further experimentation will permit the production of machines which will promote language learning.

Quite a number of programmed *textbooks* are now available. Generally, the correct responses are on the right side of a page (next to the corresponding frame). With a strip of cardboard supplied with the text which he can slide up or down, the student keeps uncovering or re-covering the response *after* he has tried to answer the question or complete the sentence.

For the reasons noted above, the material in such texts should be done orally, first by you or by a teacher aide. The programmed text can then serve to reinforce the material at the student's own pace.

12. Miscellaneous Materials

▶A cardboard clock with movable hands.

▶A puppet stage (made with an old crate or box).

▶Puppets (paper or rag), toy telephones.

▶Calendars (large ones showing days of the week and weather signals), maps, bulletin boards.

▶A large thermometer with a movable black or red strip to indicate the rise and fall of the mercury.

▶Books, magazines, and newspapers.

▶Last and *most* important, the blackboard or chalkboard and chalk. Use it to make quick sketches or stick figures, charts, diagrams, etc. If colored chalk is available, you may wish to use it to underline elements in words which will indicate structural relationships and forms.

I could mention many other materials, such as a camera, the opaque projector, the overhead projector, or the slide projector. *Any* of these machines and others which science will devise are good, but only in the hands of the efficient teacher who uses them judiciously *when* and *where* they can be most useful in bringing about the growth of listening, speaking, reading, or writing ability.

Some Teaching Techniques

In the next few pages, I plan to list some procedures and techniques which will help learners progress toward real control of the language items we are teaching while motivating them to continue their study of English. In our list, I will reinforce some of the pertinent suggestions given in the preceding pages.

1. Use the students and yourself (your clothing, the things you carry, etc.) to teach appropriate vocabulary *before* using pictures or other materials.

2. Start with the *known* environment of your students before fanning out to the wider English-speaking world. Relate your presentations to facets of language or of culture with which you can expect your students to be familiar. For example, if you are going to teach

vocabulary related to a beach scene in England, help the students recall a beach scene (or swimming, boating, or fishing) closer to their homes. Use many questions starting with "Do you" or "Have you."

3. Use dialogues wherever possible. Dialogues duplicate the communication situations in everyday life. Keep building on the same dialogue situation where possible. For example, with classroom objects:

A. Do you (have) a notebook?
Yes, I do.

B. Do you (have) your English notebook?
(No), I (don't).

C. 1. Do you want a notebook with lines?
2. Yes, please. How much is this one?
1. Twenty cents.
2. All right, I'll take it.

The possibilities for expanding the same dialogue situation are infinite. In addition to expanding the dialogue, you may want to give practice in *substituting* whole utterances in the responses. For example, the "response" in A above could be, "Yes. Do you want it?" or "Do you want to see it?" or "Do you need it?" The response in B could be "I'm sorry. I forgot it." or "Of course. I always have my English notebook."

Since dialogues appear more and more frequently in textbooks and since they are at the core of "situational" and "functional" teaching, let us take a few extra minutes to discuss their use.

A dialogue, as we learned on p. 54, may be used as the *"jumping off" focal point* for one or more lessons—as we present its structures, lexicon, or cultural situation. It may be used, however, as a *culminating* activity to demonstrate the use—in authentic communication—of structures and vocabulary items which have been presented in mini-situations, in narratives, or through other techniques; e.g., the mono-structural approach.

To help students *understand* the dialogue or the segment of a longer dialogue you are teaching, you may use any one or a combination of these procedures:

▶Give the situation of the entire dialogue simply and briefly in English, pointing to objects or pictures and *pointing to each of the figures* (stick figures drawn on the blackboard, drawings, flannel board cutouts, etc.) as you tell what each one is saying. *Students must be helped to relate the utterances to the appropriate speaker.*

▶Teach new words and expressions through association with pictures, real objects, pantomime, or gestures before saying the dialogue.

▶Give, where feasible, the native language *equivalent,* not word for word translations, of each utterance.

▶Explain the situation briefly in the native language.

To help students *say* the dialogue or the portion of that day's dialogue with reasonable fluency, you may wish to follow this procedure:

▶Have the students listen to it three or four times. The first two times stand at the board and *point to each figure as he or she speaks.* After that, particularly if the group is large, you may wish to stand in various parts of the room so that students can see your mouth and your gestures.

▶Say each utterance three or four times and engage the entire group in choral repetition.

▶Divide the group in half. Help each half of the group take one role in the dialogue.

▶Reverse the roles. (Repeat this procedure several times, if time permits.)

▶Ask a more able student to come to the front of the room to take one role of the dialogue. You will take the other. (Help him by standing behind him or next to him and whispering the utterance he has to produce.)

▶Follow this procedure with several individual students, depending on the complexity of the dialogue, the interest engendered, and the time available.

▶Help two students dramatize the utterances or ask one student to take one role *while the rest of the class takes the other.*

▶Help the students learn the dialogue by writing it on the chalkboard; gradually erasing more and more words from each utterance; and encouraging the students to reconstruct it.

To help make the dialogue a vehicle for teaching and reinforcing communication, you may ask, for example, that:

▶The dialogue itself be *read, copied, summarized,* or *adapted* (to indicate different speakers, a different time, or a different point of view), preceding and following such activity by dramatization and oral reading.

▶*Students answer questions* about it or that they *formulate questions* which their fellow students will answer. The questions are generally of *three* kinds:

a) Those which are based directly on the utterances, people, and situations in the dialogue being studied (often called Dialogue Variation);
b) Those in which the dialogue situation is related to the lives and experiences of the students. If, for example, the dialogue is about listening to records, the questions could elicit

the likes and dislikes of the students, their listening habits, etc. (called Dialogue Personalization);

c) Those which require the students to make inferences. ("How do we know?" "Why do you think?").

▶*Students change the dialogues.* You can ask more able students at the early levels or all the students at intermediate or advanced levels to suggest *alternative whole utterances* for a given utterance in the dialogue, without changing the situation. For example, a first sentence such as: "Let's study together tomorrow," may be changed to: "Would you like to study with me tomorrow?"

▶*Students create a dialogue.* As the students build up a repertoire of utterances from dialogues they have learned and as they gain insight into the conversational situations into which the utterances would be appropriate, they should be able to recombine these and create their own dialogues. (See p. 90.)

▶Students should be guided to *create* dialogues within *different* socio-cultural situations. For example, if they have learned to use the structure "How much" with relation to shopping for food, they should be guided to create dialogues using "How much" in buying a plane ticket or buying clothing. A dialogue about a visit to the doctor should lead to the preparation of another about a visit to the dentist. To illustrate further, a dialogue in which the ending of a business letter is discussed should lead them to write a dialogue about informal letters.

Activities such as these are particularly important if we wish to avoid the shock that language learners experience in speaking to native speakers when their stimulus sentence is not followed by the response they had been led to expect. This often happens, when a dialogue has been memorized without further study or creative recombination.

You may notice that I have not mentioned "memorizing" the dialogue. If a dialogue is memorized at all, it should be only by dint of its repetition, dramatization, and adaptation, and not because students have been asked to go home and memorize it. More important than memorizing a dialogue is to "exploit" it by adapting and varying it in ways suggested above.

▶*Students write narrative paragraphs* from the dialogue. You may wish to do this in two or three steps; e.g., Sentences (said by each speaker) will first be rewritten with verbs and names as, "No, I can't go," said Jane, and "I'm furious," shouted Donn. Then they can be written as: Jane said that she couldn't go. Donn shouted that he was furious. Later still, the sentences could be rewritten as: When Jane said she couldn't go, Donn became furious.

4. Plan as many different oral practice activities for each lesson as can be done briskly and with reasonable accuracy. As you write your

lesson plan, decide which of the drills outlined above are best suited to the item you are teaching.

5. Vary the type of student participation for the different parts of your lesson:

▶ Use chain drills, but break the chain after five or six students and start another chain in another part of the room.

▶ Call on students in order and then at random.

▶ Ask a question. Have *one* student answer. (It is *unwise* to ask for a choral answer to a question unless it has been thoroughly practiced immediately before.) It is also more desirable to ask the question, *then* to call on a student by name.

▶ Have a student or a group ask you a question. Answer it.

▶ Have a student ask another student a question.

▶ Have students manipulate the hands of the clock, the sentences in the pocket chart, or the material at the flannel board.

▶ Have students "shuffle" the pictures or the flash cards or touch the desired pictures in the picture series charts and ask questions about them.

▶ Have pairs of students come to the front of the room often to dramatize a dialogue—even if it is only two lines.

▶ Use games to reinforce structure and vocabulary.

▶ Use paired practice. (See p. 152.)

6. In drills, *always* give the model sentence or expression two or three times before asking the class or individuals to give it.

7. Call on your more able students *before* calling on the weaker ones. In this way, the latter group can practice responses which will be reasonably correct.

8. Use the students' native language *judiciously* when it will mean saving time or insuring comprehension.

9. Encourage your students to prepare materials (according to their ability, however). Ask your students to find pictures, to cut and mount them, to prepare flashcards, to draw pictures, and even to compose or build a dialogue with new words or structures they have learned. At the intermediate or advanced level, ask them to write short conversations and then plays which can later be dramatized.

10. Simplify and adapt stories which you can tell your students. If you have duplicating facilities, prepare simplified material for reading. I once saw the famous novel *Les Miserables* by Victor Hugo adapted and condensed most effectively into four double-spaced pages. Of course, it did not have the original "flavor," but the interest in the story line was very high, *and* it afforded excellent practice in "language."

11. Create a "cultural island" in your room. Do this by having pictures, maps, bulletin boards, proverbs, and labels in English. Use

English as much as possible during the hour. (You may want to set aside a few minutes at the *end* of the hour when students can ask questions or make comments in their native language. This is feasible *only* when all the students speak the same native language and when the language is familiar to you.) Classroom routines (taking attendance, describing materials) and recurring questions; e.g., "What does . . . . mean?" or "Who sees (hears) an error?" should be *in English*.

12. Utilize the community resources and bring the people in the community into your program. This is important not only because is provides additional stimulation for the students but also because it will foster interest in English language learning in the community. There are many ways of doing this.

▶ Ask English speakers to come to your classroom to speak about their trips, hobbies, interests, or jobs. The preparation for the visit (social amenities, questions to be asked, etc.), listening to the speech, and writing the letter of thanks to the visitor lead naturally to language learning.

▶ Start an English club to which community members may be invited. Plan topics for discussion or games, songs, etc., around the interests of the students.

▶ Ask the local printer (if possible) to help you print an English (or bilingual) newspaper.

▶ Prepare simple plays to which you can invite parents and other lay people in the community.

13. Utilize the incidental happenings in the school or the immediate community to teach or to review language items. Although I believe firmly in lesson planning, *no* plan should be so rigid that it cannot include references to unusual occurrences (if these are of interest to your students). The use of special events and incidental happenings not only extends knowledge but also illustrates that the structures or vocabulary practiced within one situation can be used to talk about another one.

14. Give your students the feeling and the assurance that English is a vehicle of communication which serves exactly the same purposes as does their native tongue. What do people all over the world generally talk about? The daily routine of sleeping, eating, shopping, working, and playing; age; births; marriages; illnesses, etc. Although it is true that we use different words or expressions, there are *equivalent* expressions to discuss equivalent events in *any* culture.

15. Provide opportunities for students to act as listeners and as speakers. Students should be able not only to make statements but also to make comments or responses, to ask questions, and to answer questions.

16. Use authentic language at *normal* speed in the classroom. Often, in the desire to simplify language for our students, we give expressions or words which we consider easier simply because they are shorter. Try to remember that sometimes the longer word may be more similar to a cognate in your students' language. Also, since everything is different for learners, they may just as well learn the expressions or words that native speakers of their age would generally employ in similar circumstances.

17. Spur your students to greater effort by training them to give long responses or multiple responses to a question or to a statement. The ability to sustain a longer conversation which duplicates real speech will give them a feeling of success and achievement.

Use "connecting" words (*and, but*) and formulas. Let us consider some brief examples of increasingly longer answers:

A. Using a picture series chart of "mass" nouns, for example, on which you or a student indicates the appropriate pictures, notice the possible progression:

I see milk; I see bread; etc.
I see a bottle of milk.
I see a loaf of bread.
I see a bottle of milk and a loaf of bread.
I see the bottle of milk, but I don't see the loaf of bread.
I don't see the bottle of milk, and I don't see the loaf of bread either.

B. Notice the exchanges possible in talking about an article of clothing:

a) 1 —I like your dress.
2 —Thank you.

b) 1 —I like your dress.
2 —Thank you. I made it myself.

c) 1 —I like your dress. Blue is my favorite color.
2 —Thank you. It's my favorite color, too.
1 —Where did you get it?
2 —My mother made it.
1 —Is it new?
2 —Yes, it is. This is the second time I'm wearing it.

You tell your students *how* you want them to respond; that is, tell them that you want them to make a response and then a statement; or that you want them to respond and ask a question, etc. When they have learned the appropriate expressions, you may also encourage them to agree, to disagree, to express surprise, to express pleasure, etc. as creatively as they wish.

18. Summarize what has been done at various times during the lesson. Make sure, through questions, charts, diagrams and as a last

resort through translation, that students *understand* what they are repeating.

19. *Teach. Don't test.* This does *not* mean that you should not give quizzes, tests, and examinations. (Testing will be the subject of our next chapter.) In presenting new material, give numerous examples so that students "see" the word order or new form. Don't try to elicit an "original" sentence after one or two examples.

Practice activities immediately following the presentation of new material should be confined to repetition after the teacher (class, groups, and individuals) and to simple substitution of *one* item only. The kind of problem-solving exercises where students have to make four or five changes in a sentence should have no place in a beginning language program.

20. Tailor your course to your students. Their interests, their environment, their abilities should be kept constantly in mind as you plan the content and activities of your lessons.

The last few years have seen a renewal of interest in the individualization of instruction. An entire volume can be written on this topic, but I will limit myself to a few remarks.

The principles on which the desire for individualized instruction are based are sound and ideal. The diagrams in professional journals which show a classroom with about twenty-five students engaged in about fifteen different (excellent) learning activities embody the dream of every teacher who knows that 1) each of his pupils is a unique human being who has a different pace and rhythm of learning and 2) the learner must be considered the primary person or factor in the learning process.

Individualized instruction must be considered, however, from several vantage points; e.g., in situations such as those in the United States, Great Britain, and other countries where immigrants or migrants enter schools at varying stages of literacy; where fifteen-year-old newcomers may be completely illiterate; or where they register for school at any time during the school semester, individualized instruction is the only feasible means of enabling students to 1) learn the language and 2) make a personal–social adjustment to the school and community. In this situation, groups of teachers or special bureaus of the school system should prepare individualized work sheets for *every facet* of language at *different maturity* and *learning levels.* (Not enough of this type of material is available unfortunately.) Paraprofessionals (teacher aides) or student helpers generally assist teachers in helping the newcomers.

In teaching situations like those of the above, individualized instruction* for the greater part of the school day is the only viable, feasible procedure.

Then my thoughts turn to schools in other countries in which I have worked where 1) the teacher has 70-100 learners in one class (so that he might have as many as 400 per day!!) and 2) where the ministry of education insists on uniform examinations given at one time. Teachers, although willing, devoted, and dedicated, do not have the physical time nor the resources to prepare materials for individual learners. They *do* individualize by asking different oral questions of their slower and more able pupils; by encouraging supplementary reading; by engaging students in group activities, and by stimulating teaching in pairs. But they would find it unrealistic to give examinations at different times or to prepare varied work sheets for individual learners.

Ideally, individualized instruction is possible *and* desirable in situations where the entire school and the school system will cooperate on the preparation of different programs—either within the school or within a classroom—which will take into consideration the age; personal, vocational, or professional interests of the students; and their pace *and* method of learning. Some concrete suggestions which appear in the literature include:

1) scheduling learning modules in which the English learner can be assigned to a teacher for different amounts of time each day and to a resource center where he will find assistants and materials to help him pursue his goals; (Obviously the cooperation of all the other departments is necessary and the principal or headmaster must also be committed to the idea.)

2) preparing a copy of a "contract" for each student (based on grades at previous levels, diagnostic tests, non-completed work to be covered, individual interests, etc.) which would include a list of resources; a schedule for group work and for tests; the goals he would be expected to achieve; an answer key; flexible materials (programmed or textbook);

3) giving students more responsibility for their own learning;

4) encouraging them to talk freely to each other about their work and to teach each other (setting up a system of student buddies).

Certainly, the best thinking of educators, psychologists, and linguists should be brought to bear on this challenging question of individualizing instruction to the fullest degree possible. Testing of student progress through sociograms, observation, and questionnaires by teachers and others; of heightened or lessened student motivation should be included in any survey.

---

*See p. 112 re: individualized instruction through tape recorders or the lab.

V. Testing and Evaluation

Provision for evaluation should be an integral part of the English curriculum. Indeed, criteria and measures for judging its efficacy should be "built into" the program from the very outset. The curriculum, in turn, should be revised and revitalized continuously in light of the findings of a valid, reliable, and comprehensive testing program.

The term "evaluation" in the title is broader than the traditional term, "testing." Evaluation would include assessing the student's progress toward the linguistic objectives of the course, determining his attitude not only toward English language learning but also toward native English speakers, judging the results of the methodology and the materials in use, and appraising the effectiveness of the total English program in serving the needs of the learners for whom it is intended.

In this section, we will consider four major questions with relation to testing. In as succinct a fashion as possible, the following questions: 1) Why do we test? 2) When do we test? 3) How do we test? 4) What do we test? will be discussed. These are the questions of primary interest to teachers.

Before proceeding to a statement of some basic premises under each of these questions, I would like to make a few comments about two tests which are often mentioned with relation to language study. The use of written "attitude" tests to judge cultural appreciation and understanding (and here we are using "cultural" in the broad anthropological sense) is still in the experimental stage. At the present time, therefore, the more satisfactory way to judge attitude is through observation of a student's reaction to reading material, to native English visitors, and to questions about English-speaking countries. His interest in language is easily judged through his participation in class. Does he volunteer? Does he give sustained answers? (Of course, lack of response may indicate timidity rather than apathy!) Does he prepare his work? A perceptive teacher is usually the best judge of desirable attitudes.

The other type of test to which I referred is the so-called "prognostic" test. In many school systems, students are tested *before* being admitted to a language program in order to determine whether they have the capacity to learn a language successfully. In the considered judgment of many teachers, results of the prognostic tests available at this time are not reliable or conclusive. The score on the tests would have to be studied with additional extensive data about each student before an accurate determination of future success could be made. Experiments have demonstrated clearly that motivation and perseverance on the part of the normal student and good planning on the part of a competent and sympathetic teacher are more reliable criteria of success in language learning than a score on a prognostic test.

We will confine our discussion, therefore, to diagnostic and achievement testing or, to put it in another way, to testing in order to discover our students' problems, weaknesses, or strengths and to ascertain their progress toward the goals of the English program.

Why Do We Test?

There are several reasons—some of which have broad implications, as you will see:

1. The obvious reason is that we have to grade students so that we can move them forward to the next higher class or retain them at their present level. They can derive the greatest benefit only from classes working at their level.

2. Another reason is that through appropriate tests, we can set realistic standards of achievement for groups or individuals. By comparing our test results with results in *similar* classes or communities teaching under similar conditions, we can judge whether we are setting our standards too high or too low.

3. Tests can also help us assess the effects of experimentation. For example, through a carefully controlled experiment, we may wish to determine whether the use of the students' native language in the classroom retards or increases their progress. Only a reliable and valid testing instrument will provide the answer.

4. The three most important reasons for testing as far as classroom teachers are concerned are: a) to diagnose the specific features of

the language in which individual students or groups are having difficulties; b) to help us gauge our ability as teachers; c) to find out how much our students have learned or achieved.

A few parenthetical remarks particularly with relation to "b" above may be pertinent at this point. Failure on the part of a few students does not necessarily mean that *we* have not planned or taught well. We are all aware that many factors (intellectual, physical, emotional, social) within an individual student may be at the root of the failure.

On the other hand, if the majority of the students fail a test, it would be desirable for us to review critically our presentation and the practice activities which we used in teaching the language item we are testing. It is only to the extent that the classroom teacher *translates the results of tests into more effective teaching procedures* that students will derive any benefit from a testing program. It goes without saying that poor grades by the majority should signal *reteaching* and retesting of the item or items involved.

When Do We Test?

In any school system, there are usually mid-term or end-term examinations in which the proficiency of pupils is tested. These examinations are very often school-wide or community-wide tests which include the language items covered in a prescribed number of units of work.

In addition to these tests, you will find it desirable to give a long comprehensive examination at the end of each unit of work and, at the beginning levels of language learning, a brief quiz daily or as many times as feasible each week.

The brief quiz is an excellent teaching device and can serve many purposes:

1. If the correct answers are given immediately after the test (as should be done), the knowledge of the correctness or lack of correctness of their responses will reinforce the students' learning of the response.

2. It gives the students a sense of achievement if they've done well. (Below we will indicate some techniques for insuring success.)

3. It gives you insight into students' difficulties and into segments of the unit which may have to be retaught *before* you proceed to new material.

4. It may be used as the springboard for the new lesson to be presented that day.

5. It gives you and the students a frequent "barometer" reading of progress.

6. An average of the many grades accumulated through this process does away with the unfortunate practice of giving a student a final grade which is based primarily on one or at most two examinations. An able student, prevented by illness or some other cause from doing well on one examination, may be saved from end-term or end-year failure by a consideration of the grades on the daily quizzes.

In schools or classes where students work individually under "contracts" which list *performance objectives,* tests are generally given when the learner feels he has fulfilled his contract to his satisfaction and is thus ready to take the test.

In stating performance objectives, several criteria are generally noted: 1) the structure or category to be studied; e.g., the simple past tense of regular verbs; 2) the number of practice sentences the learner is to do; 3) the time he should take to do them in; and 4) the degree of mastery (e.g., 24 out of 25 must be grammatically correct, said without false starts and unnecessary pauses, etc.).

I should add that some educators are beginning to question the advisability of using "performance objectives" in many situations. While it is true that students should know what is expected of them, factors such as strict attention to time, degree of mastery expected, and other motivational problems have made psychologists and others pause in their advocacy of "performance objectives." They feel that many learners would suffer under such pressure.

How Do We Test?

Today's accepted principles of language teaching demand that we emphasize oral tests as well as written tests. Let us consider written tests first.*

These, as we know, are of two types—short answer tests and essay tests. Short answer tests may duplicate the practice activities outlined in Chapter III. They may be of the multiple choice, completion, substitution, or transformation type. They have several advantages: They are *objective;* they can be *scored easily* and *quickly;* they permit the testing of a *wider area* of knowledge.

Essay tests have no part in a *beginning* language program. They are useful and desirable at the more advanced levels, however. Only through essay tests can we judge the students' use of varied structures, the richness of their vocabulary, and their ability to express ideas with clarity and precision. In other words, the longer essay tests permit us

* It goes without saying that written tests can be used to test understanding (recognition) and oral production.

to judge the ability of the students to use language as a tool for written communication.

From the teacher's point of view, essay tests are difficult to grade. (A scheme such as the one given for grading compositions will be found useful.) From the student's point of view, the subjective elements in the essay test may cause apprehension.

Oral tests are indispensable for judging oral production of sounds, stress, rhythm, and intonation patterns; fluency; and "automatic" responses to oral or written stimuli. Oral tests may be time-consuming, however. Several time-saving techniques you may wish to consider follow:

1. Make a chart of five or six points you wish to grade. Each day, for a week or two, call several students to your desk individually. Ask each to repeat, read, follow directions, etc., as indicated below. (Give only as much material as is needed to ascertain their knowledge of the language items you are testing.) Grade them only on the key points on which you had decided to grade them. Ignore (although it will be painful for you to do so in many cases) all other incorrect features.

2. If you have one, use a tape recorder on which directions or stimuli are given. Have the students record their responses on a tape. (Each student will be asked to start at a different number on the counter and to give his name at the *end* of the test.)

3. Use the tape recorder to give directions and cues. Have the students write their responses (cross or check) on an answer sheet. (This would test *aural* comprehension only.)

Combinations of aural and written tests would include those in which students take a dictation (full or spot as explained above) or a comprehension exercise, in which they answer, in writing, questions (given orally or in writing) on a dialogue or narrative paragraph they have heard.

What Do We Test?

Simply stated, we should test everything we consider important enough in language learning to teach. That means we should test the students' knowledge of the phonemic, structural, and lexical systems as well as their insight into any cultural aspects we have given them.

We should test the students' ability to understand, to speak, and—as soon as feasible—to read and to write. Within these listening and speaking skills, we should judge their ability to understand the formulas of the language, to ask and to answer questions, to make the normal responses which a situation demands, to start a conversation, or to narrate an event.

As I noted above, there is bound to be overlapping in many tests. For example, taking a dictation tests listening and writing skills and enables us to consider the students' grasp of the sound, structure, and vocabulary features contained in the passage.

The test stimuli or cues should be varied just as they are in the classroom practice activities. The stimuli might include, therefore, 1) hearing spoken words or utterances (live or on tape); 2) looking at a picture or several pictures; 3) looking at real objects; 4) reading a word, an utterance, or a passage.

Let us consider some simple tests which can be given in the classroom. Whether some of these are done orally or in writing (or by placing a correct symbol or letter on an answer sheet) will depend not only on the nature of the test but also on the age of your students. For these reasons, test suggestions are listed in no particular order.

Testing the Features of Language

To test their knowledge of the sound system
Have students:

1. Indicate whether two sounds—given orally or in writing, isolated or in words—are the same or different.
2. Indicate which pairs of words rhyme (e.g., a) send/lend; b) friend/fiend; c) enough/through).
3. Mark the syllable having the loudest stress (e.g., again, never, turn on, apple tree).
4. Indicate (by prearranged code) rising or falling intonation (e.g., "Did you go to school? Where did you go?").
5. Indicate from which column of words or pictures you (or a tape) are pronouncing a word or an entire utterance (e.g., think/thing; I saw the ship/I saw the sheep.).
6. Imitate sentences of varying lengths (e.g., I want a dress. I want a pretty red dress. I want that pretty red dress.).
7. Indicate stress and juncture in pairs of sentences (e.g., I saw him by the tree. I saw him buy the tree.).

To test their grasp of grammatical items
Have students:

1. Select the appropriate word from two or three words by underlining, numbering, or filling a blank on an answer sheet (e.g., The [boy, boys] usually walk to the door slowly.).
2. Perform any of the transformation exercises indicated in Chapter III, (e.g., "Make this a question: 'He went to the door.' " "Say you have *two:* 'I have a box.' " "Ask a question with 'Who': 'Mr. X is a mailman.' ").

3. Use the words "get up" (for example) in these sentences (e.g., It's seven o'clock in the morning. I'm . . . . now. Yesterday I . . . . at seven o'clock too. I usually . . . . at seven every day.).
4. Answer questions in the negative using a full sentence (e.g., Do you have some bread? Did you find someone there?).
5. Ask direct questions based on indirect questions (e.g., Ask X how old he is. Ask someone whether he knows Mr. . . . .).
6. Give the paired sentence (e.g., Mary is going to read later. The boys are going to study later. Mary reads every day. The boys . . . .).
7. Make all changes required by a cue (e.g., [These] This boy is tall.).
8. Indicate which pictures you are mentioning (e.g., This is a foot long. This is a long foot. This is a station wagon. This is a wagon station.).
9. Complete sentences:
   I. . . . . thirsty. (am, 's, have)
   I'd go if I . . . . time. (have, were, had)
10. Answer questions of various types (cf. Chapter III). Indicate whether you want a Yes or No answer; whether you want a short answer or a long answer; whether you want a combination short and long answer; whether you want them to agree, disagree, express surprise, sympathy, anger, etc.
11. Choose the correct form (e.g., The woman's name is . . . . [Peter, Mrs. Jones, Miss].).
12. Combine sentences (e.g., She's a student. She's very good. That man is my father. He's talking to Mr. Brown.).
13. Match the stimuli and responses. Have one additional response so that guessing will be minimized; e.g.:

I	II
1) Thank you.	a) Better.
2) How old is he?	b) He's twelve.
3) When are you leaving?	c) Of course.
4) How are you feeling?	d) You're welcome.
5) May I go out?	e) Tomorrow.
	f) In school.

14. Rewrite the sentence placing the adjectives in the correct position (e.g., [small, four] I have puppies.).
15. Indicate where a word belongs (e.g., "usually"—He *A* goes *B* to the park *C*.).
16. Select the appropriate coordinating conjunction when two are given (e.g., [and, but]; I'd go . . . . I'm tired.).

17. Select the appropriate subordinating conjunction when two are given (e.g., [while, unless]; He went to work . . . . she took care of the house.).
18. Select the appropriate connector (e.g., It was freezing. [However, Otherwise] we went out.).

To test their knowledge of vocabulary
Have students:

1. Indicate whether a statement is true or false (e.g., Spring comes before summer.).
2. Complete a sentence (e.g., The cow [barks, moos, shrieks].).
3. Select an unrelated word from a group of words (e.g., meat, soup, eraser, peas).
4. Give a synonym or choose one from a list (e.g., start [begin]).
5. Give an antonym or choose one from a list (e.g., finish [start]).
6. Give two other words from the same family (e.g., jewel [jewelry, jeweler]).
7. Make nouns from the following verbs (e.g., arrive, deny, permit).
8. Make adjectives from the following nouns (e.g., man, child).
9. Use the prefix meaning "not" in these words (e.g., ability, able, rational).
10. Use the suffix meaning "pertaining to" in words such as region, nature.
11. Select the appropriate word (e.g., [in, on] The picture is . . . . the wall.).
12. Select the appropriate word (e.g., [too, very] I can't drink the tea. It's . . . . hot.).
13. Choose the word(s) with the same meaning as the underlined word(s) (e.g., [must, should] I have to leave now.).
14. Choose the appropriate word (e.g., [breakfast, lunch, dinner, supper] We always have . . . . at seven in the morning.).
15. Paraphrase a sentence (using the same structure but different vocabulary).
16. Write three or more sentences using *different* meanings of a word (e.g., He *got* an A. He *got* the book. He *got* worried.).

Testing the Communication Abilities

To test their listening comprehension
Have students:

1. Carry out a request. Use one utterance with beginners and more than one with more advanced students (e.g., Go to the board. Go to the board and write your name. Go to the board, write your name, and then erase it.).

2. Take a spot dictation.* Distribute a sheet with a passage containing some missing words. As you dictate, students will write the missing words on the answer sheet.
3. Take an aural comprehension exercise.**
4. Complete the sentence when a choice is given (e.g., It's raining. I'll have to take an .... [examination, umbrella, envelope].).
5. Tell whether the items they hear are singular or plural, present or past, present or future.
6. Answer questions according to the cue or direction (e.g., [movies] Where did you go last evening?).
7. Select an appropriate rejoinder (when several choices are given) to a statement or request (e.g., May I smoke ? [Not at all; Of course.]).
8. Identify the central theme or the nature of a talk when listening to a news broadcast (e.g., social, political, artistic, educational).
9. Tell which statement (given orally or in writing) embodies the main idea of a passage they hear.
10. Give a summary of a talk they have listened to—live or on tape.
11. Take the role of listener or speaker in a dialogue.
12. Engage in role-playing exercises.

To test their speaking ability
Have students:
1. Repeat sentences of varying lengths.
2. Say a passage, poem, or dialogue they have learned.
3. Take one of the roles in a dialogue.
4. Answer questions either when specific instructions are given or without a cue.
5. Make a rejoinder to a statement or request.
6. Read aloud a passage of familiar material.
7. Read aloud a passage containing new material.
8. Ask direct questions when an indirect statement is given (e.g., Ask me how I got to school this morning.).
9. Transform sentences according to the direction given. (See p. 66.)
10. Give the equivalent of a short native language utterance. (Exercise caution.)
11. Formulate questions on a passage.
12. Tell what they would say (or do) in a certain situation. They would hear (or read) one or more sentences describing a situation, and they would tell what they would respond (e.g., You

*See p. 88 for procedures.
**See p. 84 for procedures.

know it's a friend's birthday. You meet her (him) on the street. What would you say? Someone tells you his mother is ill. What would you say?).

13. Describe what they see in a picture.
14. Tell about something they did at some particular time (before coming to school, perhaps), something that happened, or something that is going to happen.
15. Give a summary of something they are asked to read at the examination or that they have read at some time before.

*To test their reading ability**

Have students:

1. Complete sentences based on a passage read when a choice is given.
2. Complete sentences when a choice is not given.
3. Complete a logical inference (e.g., He had worked eighteen hours without stopping. He was .... [rich, tired, stupid].).
4. Read an unfamiliar passage aloud and answer questions on it.
5. Formulate questions on a passage.
6. Answer several questions on a passage read silently.
7. Give definitions of selected words in a passage. (The ability to use contextual clues would be apparent.)
8. Outline a paragraph.
9. Summarize a passage.
10. Indicate a possible rejoinder or sequence utterance to a statement or a series of statements.
11. Say whether a statement is true or false.
12. Indicate the characters in a story who had expressed a point of view or performed some actions.
13. Read a passage crossing out irrelevant words.
14. Read a passage silently within a limited time and answer questions on it. (This would enable you to test fluency and speed as well as comprehension.)
15. Discuss the cultural allusions in a poem or passage.
16. Give synonyms, antonyms, or paraphrases of certain words or expressions.

To test their writing ability

Have students:**

1. Insert punctuation marks and capital letters in a paragraph.

---

*Since the ability to read requires a knowledge of structure and vocabulary, many of the tests already suggested will also serve to judge reading power.

**Systematic sound-spelling correspondences should be tested, of course. In addition, any of the drills on pp. 66-70 can be written.

2. Write out in full the words for symbols or abbreviations (e.g., +, %, Mr., Inc., etc.).
3. Reconstruct a sentence from several words (e.g., boys/movies/yesterday).
4. Complete a sentence using the same verb in both spaces (e.g., [eat] He . . . . as he had never . . . . before.).
5. Expand several sentences into a letter, dialogue, or story.
6. Add details to a topic sentence.
7. Answer questions about themselves or some material they have studied.
8. Answer questions substituting pronouns for all nouns.
9. Take a dictation—spot or regular—or do a dicto-comp.
10. Do an aural comprehension exercise.
11. Rewrite a passage or story from their point of view, or in the past or future.
12. Write what they would say or do in a situation.
13. Write what they see in a scene.
14. Summarize a passage.
15. Formulate questions on a passage.
16. Write an essay on one of three topics you indicate (based on their interests, their reading, a cultural topic, a news item, etc.). You may wish, at times, to include some of the ideas they are to treat.
17. Rewrite a paragraph using a more casual (or a more formal) style.
18. Complete a dialogue when *words* are omitted from each utterance or when entire utterances are omitted, or write an original one.
19. Give the English equivalent of a passage in the native language or vice versa.
20. Write a story based on a series of related pictures.
21. Write a letter—business; personal.

Testing Cultural Understanding

Objective tests and essay tests may be used to test knowledge of facts and insight into cultural behavior.

Following are some examples:
Students may be asked to:

a) Complete a sentence (e.g., In [country], there is no school on . . . . and . . . . ; the . . . . is the center of social life.).

b) State which is true or false:
Most (Americans) have lunch at noon.
X was written by Y.
c) Choose (by circling, underlining, or writing on a separate sheet*) the correct answer: Americans belong to unions.
Some, All, None
d) Identify people or places:
All of the following are poets except:
Keats, Browning, Eliot, Damrosch
e) Define or identify by completing a sentence:
Mardi Gras celebrates . . . .
f) Explain a situation in a brief statement:
The shop will be closed on Boxing Day.
g) Indicate which behavior may be considered typical, A or B:
A—In (   ) people go to the theater at 2 P.M.
B—People go to the theater at 9:30 P.M.
h) Write a brief paragraph when a topic sentence is given:
Children and adults always look forward to New Year's Day.
i) Write an essay on any pertinent topic.

Testing Literary Appreciation

Both objective tests and essays will be useful. The objective tests can be of the types indicated above under Cultural Understanding. Students may be asked to *complete* sentences when a choice is given or when no choice is given, to *identify*, to *match*, to *define*, to *give an explanation*.

The knowledge tested will depend on the material taught. It may be related, for example, to:

1. Authors and the names of their works.
2. Literary movements: time and milieu. (The Romantic movement flourished in . . . . during the . . . . part of the . . . . Century.)
3. Story line or plot.
4. Works in which certain characters appeared (e.g., Portia and Shylock are characters in . . . .).
5. The main theme of a poem, play, or novel (e.g., ... is at the root of the tragedy of *Othello*.).
6. Cultural allusions in a poem, play, or novel.

*The possible choices can be labeled A, B, C.

7. The use and meaning of certain words or expressions in a literary work.
8. The form of a poem (e.g., ...is a(n) sonnet, ode.).

Essay tests should be required at advanced levels. If we feel that the student has the necessary ability to read a literary work in the original, we must also assume that his writing ability has kept pace. Only through an essay can we judge the students' ability to analyze a literary work; to discuss the differences between the techniques of Shaw and O'Neill, for example, or the differences or similarities between the philosophical theories of a Dewey and a Russell. In the majority of secondary schools, however, such abilities cannot be assumed even if the study of English was started in the elementary school. Again, each school will have to decide whether such tests are possible with its particular student population and resources.

Further Comments on Testing

In order to eliminate the fear of testing from the minds of your students and in order to make sure the results have validity, it is desirable to follow several elementary principles of test construction and procedure:

1. Announce your tests in advance.
2. Tell students exactly what you will hold them responsible for. (Students will study for the kind of test they know they will be given.)
3. Test only what you have taught thoroughly.
4. Make sure the directions are clear and familiar to the students. Use their native language if necessary. (You should use the *native* language when feasible when you are giving an unfamiliar type of question or test.)
5. Give an example, if possible, of the response you are seeking.
6. Start with the simplest items first.
7. Test their knowledge of English and not their memory of facts (unless it is a test of cultural understanding). A question such as "Marconi invented the . . . . ." is *not* a test of English.
8. Make aural comprehension exercises short and relatively simple—at the beginning stages particularly—so that again responses do not become solely a test of memory.

As our knowledge about language and the learning process increases, changes in classroom organization, in methods, and in testing are bound to emerge. Two new trends in the field of testing bear further study and examination:

1. Rather than *norm-referenced* tests in which a student's performance is compared with that of other students, some scholars recom-

mend the use of *criterion-referenced* tests which assess and report the student's performance in *absolute* terms; e.g., the student reads well enough to read recombined passages with familiar vocabulary. According to Valette, a true achievement test must by its very definition be a criterion-referenced test.

2. Mastery of clearly specified performance objectives should be promoted for all students and *formative evaluation* tests should be given to judge the degree of mastery attained. Such tests cover a unit of instruction and are graded on a mastery-non-mastery basis. A student is given as many chances as he needs to attain the mastery level. Since these tests are also designed to diagnose a student's weaknesses, the student is told what he should do to remedy the problems revealed by the testing instrument before he is encouraged to take the test again.

The measurement of students' progress toward the goal of creative communication is a vitally important facet of the language program. Testing should be a continuous process which will help reinforce our students' interests. Knowledge of one's progress and success, as we all know, acts as a powerful stimulant to learning. The cliché "Nothing succeeds like success" is never truer than in a language classroom.

In addition, test results which point up serious difficulty in some aspect of the curriculum will enable us to apply remedial measures quickly. Since language is a cumulative subject, it would be unwise to attempt to build a second or third story when the building blocks of our foundation are not well cemented.

In judging achievement, we should use our observation of students' performance as well as scores on more formal instruments of evaluation. For example, the preparation of assignments, participation in classroom activities, and the "carry-over" of language in clubs or after-school experiences also demonstrate interest and growth.

While good testing is essential, good teaching is infinitely more so. As a colleague remarked not long ago, "Let's stop weighing the baby all the time. Let's feed it instead."

VI. What If----? Some Dos and Don'ts

Although I hope you will agree that the material in the preceding pages is practical and generally applicable to a variety of teaching situations, it would be presumptuous to assume that all questions with relation to the teaching of English have been answered. Many others sometimes arise in the minds of teachers, particularly of new teachers, who find themselves in what they consider unusual teaching situations.

Before attempting to deal with some situations which some teachers deem unusual, let me state for whatever solace it may offer that teaching situations are surprisingly similar in most corners of the globe. This can be deduced from the fact that the same questions recur wherever I have lectured or worked. The conscientious teachers usually start with, "Yes, but, what if . . . ." I have thought, therefore, that it might be worthwhile to list some of the most frequent questions and to answer them briefly by giving some dos and don'ts where they are pertinent. This procedure will serve also to summarize or recapitulate what has been said in preceding chapters.

For the sake of convenience, the questions will be listed under several categories: the students, teaching colleagues, the school, materials, and methods.

Each of the following statements should be prefaced by "WHAT IF . . . . ?"

The Students

1. *There are over 65 students in each class.*

   a. Devise a set of hand signals and gestures to elicit various types of student participation (chorus, half class, groups, rows, individuals).

b. Divide the class into four groups for purposes of choral repetition. You may want to give each group a name for easy reference.

c. Use choral repetition and group repetition techniques.

d. Train student leaders to help check homework and correct short quizzes.

e. Establish routines of classroom procedure from the first day (e.g., for taking attendance, distributing and collecting materials).

f. Seat students in alphabetical order or in an order which they will maintain each day.

g. Prepare a seating plan which you will keep in front of you at all times.

h. Walk to various parts of the room as you model sentences and as you conduct various portions of the lesson so that all of the students can see you.

i. Change the students' seats in the middle of the semester so that those who had been sitting in the back will move forward. (Make a new seating plan.)

j. Engage in many chain drills but break them after six to eight people have recited. Start a new chain in another part of the room.

k. Call on individual students from various parts of the room to insure attention.

2. *Some students are very able; others are quite "slow."*

a. Make use of the abilities of your students. For example, have the more able students go to the blackboard for writing dictations and the answers to aural comprehensions. Have them recite first after you give the model so that other students will be exposed to reasonably correct answers. If you also provide activities in which the less able students can achieve success (doing the simpler pattern practice exercises on the board, coming to the front of the room, indicating pictures or objects and calling on a classmate, helping to grade papers based on a model), there will be no question of lowered morale on their part.

b. Ask the more able students to help the less able students in such activities as preparing assignments or writing compositions.

c. Seat able students next to "weaker" ones so that the latter will be sure to hear more reasonably accurate pronunciation.

d. Gear your lessons to the "average" students. Move forward to another unit of work as soon as the majority of students have grasped the content of the one you are teaching. Do not slow down for the less able students but make provision for giving them help at their stage of language learning in order that they may catch up to their classmates.

Since language learning is cumulative and since the reintroduction of learned material is a basic principle of current teaching practice, the less able students will have many opportunities to learn—with ever-increasing thoroughness—some language item they may not have grasped fully the first time.

e. Differentiate your assignments. The "slower" students should write out many pattern practice exercises; the more able students can answer questions, formulate questions to be asked of their classmates, write summaries, prepare dialogues, or write creative essays.

f. Don't expect all students to reach the same level of comprehension and of oral production in the same length of time. Some will have to stay at the repetition and pattern practice stages longer than will others.

3. *The students do not appear interested.*

a. Plan lessons in which there is a great deal of variety. Devote the longest time span in each lesson to the oral practice activities. Subdivide these activities into four or five different types to avoid boredom.

b. Insure wide student participation. Let students formulate questions, prepare pictures or other instructional materials, give cues for oral activities, lead games and songs, dramatize conversations, or help prepare a student publication.

c. Keep the pace of the lesson very brisk. Give the students the feeling that they're moving ahead all the time. When a student cannot answer a question, give the correct answer quickly or ask a more able student to give it. (Give a student reasonable time to answer; then move on to someone else and come back to the first student a little later in the lesson.)

d. Don't correct every mistake that students make. During the warm-up and motivation segments of the lesson especially, correct only those errors which impede understanding. Make a mental note of minor errors and give practice in their correction later in the hour or in a future lesson.

e. Don't strive for immediate "mastery." Accept reasonable fluency and reasonable accuracy (particularly of difficult sounds) since you will reintroduce all language items many times during the course.

f. Encourage your students by making it possible for them to enjoy many small successes frequently. Do this by announcing tests, differentiating assignments, and creating an audience situation when they have done supplementary outside reading or when they have learned the lines of a poem or a play.

g. Praise them—judiciously of course—but don't wait for them to give a perfect response before you do so. If their response today (although still poor) is better than yesterday's, it is reason enough for praise.

h. Make it possible for them to talk, as quickly as feasible, about the things they would talk about in their native tongue. Demonstrate that English is another mode of communication which permits them to say anything they can say in their language.

i. Utilize the people or places in the community to reinforce the students' knowledge of English while lending interest and variety to your lessons.

j. Plan a little more than you think you can cover in an hour. Plan for the slow and for the gifted.

k. Be flexible in your planning. If something of interest happens in your school or community and if you can use the happening to reinforce or to teach language items or an aspect of the culture—or, just as important, to strengthen your rapport with your students—put aside the lesson you had planned and "discuss" the interesting occurrence.

4. *Their native language is completely different from English.*

a. Give many examples of new structures. Engage in extensive choral repetition and in intensive practice activities.

b. Point out the contrasts and help students arrive at workable descriptions of the function and use of language items they are learning.

c. Introduce difficult items early in the program and reintroduce them as often as possible—in different situations and with other language items.

d. Teach vocabulary items around a center of interest (buying food or clothing or transportation) so that students can learn to remember words and concepts through association.

e. Teach word families, prefixes, suffixes, roots.

f. Show students how to find the meaning of long English words from the smaller words they contain (provided the root meanings are the same).

g. Grade the material you teach very carefully, building always on known language items *in English*. For example, teach "What do you eat at noon?" *after* you have taught "Do you eat at noon?"

h. Teach and, in the initial stages, practice words or structures with other words which serve as clues. For example, use *now* with the "ing" present; *yesterday* with the simple past.

i. Use many devices (chalkboard, charts, diagrams, pictures) to insure understanding.

j. Again, don't expect mastery or complete accuracy too soon. Practice the same material at ever-increasing intervals. Teach something on Monday, for example; review it on Tuesday; practice it again on Wednesday; then on Friday; then on the following Friday. Keep all the language items worth knowing "alive" by reintroducing them constantly with newly acquired items in new cultural contexts.

5. *There is a wide age span in my class. Some of my students are children; others are adults.*

a. *All* students will require the same kind of initial presentation. *All* will need to 1) understand what they are going to repeat; 2) repeat an utterance many times based on your model; 3) practice language items in a variety of drill types.

b. Divide your class into two groups *after* these three steps. Children will continue practicing by means of games, puppets, dramatizations. Adults will gain insight into the description of the grammatical phenomenon, will read and write, perhaps, and will engage in more complex drills.

c. Train group leaders for each group. For example, a very able adult can help you with the younger students a few minutes during each lesson.

6. *Students have different native language backgrounds.*

a. Prepare a brief chart of the English phonemes and structures you plan to teach in the early stages of your beginning level course.

b. Ask teachers or bilingual members of the community to indicate which of the phonemes and structures exist in the language backgrounds of your pupils. List these on your chart. Plan more repetition drills for those which do *not* exist in one or more native languages. *All* students will profit from the additional drills if you present the drills briskly and in an interesting manner. Those for whom the drills present no serious conflict will learn to say them more accurately and with more fluency.

c. Give very simple directions in English which you will illustrate and practice many times. At the beginning you will need only a few: *Listen* (place your hand behind your ear). *Repeat* (indicate through gestures that you will say something and they will say it after you). *Say. Ask. Answer.*

d. Start teaching those structures and words which you can easily demonstrate.

e. Use numerous pictures and real objects.

f. *All* students will have to learn the same sounds and structural features of English, the common core of the language. You will teach these through the techniques indicated above and any other that works with you. You will be able to note, after the very first repetition, problems caused by conflicts with a particular native language. If you feel that your normal plans for teaching particular items to the entire class need to be supplemented for students of a special native language background, assign some meaningful work to the group that does not need the practice (using pattern practice with a student leader, listening to a tape or record, preparing picture cards, etc.), and work intensively on the elimination of the problem(s) with the students who are experiencing difficulties.

g. It is desirable not to use *any* native language in the class (even if you are familiar with one) so that *all* students will have the feeling that they are members of a group and that no one group has special advantages over the other.

7. *Some students are "discipline" problems.*

a. Attention to some of the points made up to now will minimize discipline problems.

b. Keep the students busy with interesting work in which all participate. Establish routines. Change seats where necessary to separate the problem students.

c. Make *few* and very *reasonable* demands but insist that they be carried out when you *do* make them.

d. Accept reasonable excuses for nonpreparedness.

e. Excuse them from examinations when they have been absent.

f. Praise them!

g. Keep your expectations for them within their ability levels. Challenge the brighter ones, for example, by giving them more difficult assignments or by asking them to help their less able friends.

h. Make sure they understand exactly what you expect of them. Give directions in their native tongue if necessary. Give several illustrations of the response you desire.

i. Don't ask for a choral response to a question, unless you are specifically practicing that question and answer. In that way, *you* will model the answer just prior to their giving it, avoiding the confusion caused by students calling out different responses.

j. Train students, patiently, to keep together in choral repetition.

k. Don't raise your voice or continue to work when students are talking. Just stop and stand quietly. They will soon become attentive.

l. Don't penalize the wrong-doers! *Reward,* with praise, those who are attentive. The other group will soon be seeking your praise too.

8. *Adult students have varied interests and specializations.*

a. All students at the beginning level need to learn the same sounds, the same structures, and much of the common vocabulary which underlies our language.

b. At intermediate and advanced levels, suggest magazines for them in their specialties. Help them read them. Give them the specialized vocabulary in their field and show them where and how to insert it in the language pattern you are teaching.

c. Have them prepare brief talks about their interests for other class members.

d. Encourage students to ask each other questions about their interests.

e. At the advanced level, give individual reading assignments based on their interests.

Our Colleagues

1. *Each person in the school (or department) teaches another facet of the English course.*

a. Arrange for frequent meetings so that you can correlate your work. The person in charge of teaching pronunciation and intonation, for example, should give practice in the patterns which have been learned in the structure class. The teacher of reading should be aware of the vocabulary and the structure patterns which have been taught, etc.

b. Plan jointly sponsored activities in which students see and appreciate the fact that any utterance or any conversational exchange includes features of the sound, structure, and vocabulary systems as well as aspects of culture.

2. *The other teachers haven't used my methods, materials, etc. Students have never . . . .*

a. Spend the first few days training your students to respond to *your* hand signals or gestures; to engage in chain drills; to ask and answer questions; to dramatize dialogues; to keep together in choral work, etc. Establish types of and standards for student participation.

b. Find out how much your students *know* by asking many questions in English the first few days. Don't ask them what they learned, but elicit the information by asking questions which incorporate the structures and vocabulary you might assume they have learned. Start teaching them from *that point.*

The School

1. *We must use the syllabus supplied by the school.*

Use it, by all means. Within the items or skills listed in the syllabus, prepare a variety of activities; engage in oral work; follow the six steps in language learning; change the order of presentation of material if the order in the syllabus is not in harmony with some of the principles we have discussed and with which you may agree. You will find it possible to cover the same amount of material prescribed for you but in a manner which may be more interesting to you and to your students.

2. *The school (or the Ministry or the Education Department) prepares the examinations.*

Everything that has been mentioned above can be repeated in answer to this question. One word must be added, however. If the examination also includes translation of unrelated sentences (as may be the case), help your students prepare for such translations. Do so by taking typical sentences from translations and by giving *pattern practice* of each type as explained under Translation in Chapter III.

The Materials of Instruction

1. *The textbooks are traditional.*

a. Examine each unit carefully. Regroup the structure points for presentation; prepare interesting oral practice drills; practice only the logical and authentic sentences in the text; prepare question-answer drills and dialogues; present and practice everything *orally* in mini-situations before assigning writing exercises.

b. Don't use the textbook entirely as it is. For example, do not emphasize words and sentences which are not of high frequency. Formulate (or have the students formulate) interesting questions on the reading material.

c. Choose a limited amount of material for each lesson and build interesting exercises around that limited material.

d. Prepare or help your able students prepare two or three dialogues using the structural items and vocabulary found in the textbooks. Help the students understand, dramatize, and perhaps read and write the dialogues.

2. *The school has no money or limited money for equipment.*

a. Chalkboards and chalk are found in nearly every school. Things like pictures can be made on any paper, with pencil, pen, or crayon.

b. No one would deny that record players and tape recorders could enrich a teaching presentation, but electronic equipment should always be considered *supplementary* equipment. You alone can create a pleasant and productive language class by your enthusiasm, your attitude toward your students, and your careful attention to lesson planning.

Methods

1. *The students cannot understand a dialogue or a reading passage.*

Help them to understand by showing pictures, dramatizing the material, giving cognates, and even by giving the native language equivalent (if all speak the same native language and you are familiar with it).

2. *The students have trouble making the . . . . . . sound even after I have taught it.*

a. Reteach it and practice it whenever you can do so. Use diagrams, descriptions of vocal organs, phonetic symbols, and reminders of other sounds they know in their native tongue or in English to help them hear and produce the sound.

b. Reintroduce it whenever possible. Don't expect mastery too soon!

c. Make sure it appears frequently in some of the pattern practice exercises and conversations.

3. *The students get bored with (forty) repetitions.*

a. No one says that everything should be repeated (forty) times! If ten repetitions are enough to insure reasonably good pronunciation and accuracy, go on to the next phase of learning.

b. Strike a happy medium between giving enough repetitions to form the correct habit and avoiding boredom. As soon as you note a slackening of interest, proceed to something else but make a note to reintroduce the material which may not have been learned to your complete satisfaction.

4. *Students are afraid to speak in class.*

a. Start with choral repetition, followed by group repetition.

b. Call on the more able or less timid students first.

c. Be patient with the really timid persons. In the beginning stage, have them come to your desk and repeat things after you. (The other students can be busily engaged in another type of language work.)

d. Praise them for any effort, no matter how slight.

e. If they are young, use puppets to give them the feeling they are not seen as they speak.

f. Use paired activities. (See p. 152.)

5. *Students want to know why things are said the way they are.*

a. Help them answer their own questions about "grammar" by saying and showing numerous examples of any structural item.

b. Prove to them that the knowledge of the "rule" will not help them to create sentences or to communicate. Demonstrate the value of a statement which describes what actually happens in saying an utterance.

c. If they are adults and if you know their native language, show them that there may be no reason or logic behind a word or utterance in their language.

d. Discuss with them the nature and function of language.

6. *Students want to keep their books open when reading.*

a. Although some educators consider it desirable for students to keep their books closed during the teacher's initial oral reading, this need not be a "hard and fast" rule. If you have an English I course, you should be able to train students from the outset to keep their books closed and to listen to you with understanding (if your principal or supervisor insists on this). (See p. 84.)

b. If they have not received training in listening with books closed, you may prepare them for closed book reading by using very simple material, by reading very short segments at a time, and by asking simple questions.

c. Encourage them to try to understand with books closed. Read the same sentence several times, if necessary, until they develop confidence.

d. *Vary* your procedures. Have "open book" reading sometimes and "closed book" reading other times.

e. Remember that reading means looking at written words.

7. *The school wants us to start reading very soon in our program.*

a. Introduce reading if your syllabus requires it but make sure your students can say with reasonable fluency the words and sentences they are going to see.

b. Clear all difficulties *first*—of pronunciation, of structure, of vocabulary—before reading.

c. Read the passage orally for them several times.

In Conclusion

Other questions and problems will undoubtedly arise as you teach various groups of students or as you move from one school or community to another. No two individual students, no two schools, no two communities, no two teachers are exactly alike.

All any book can do or *should* do is set down the principles and practices which have been found effective by a representative group of teachers in representative communities throughout the world.

A grave injustice would have been done you if I had led you to believe that there existed only one acceptable method or only one set of materials or techniques. While it is true that our current knowledge of the nature of language and of language learning makes certain principles of teaching more desirable and effective than others adhered to in the past, it is also true that within those principles there is ample opportunity for teacher creativity and for flexibility of procedure and activities. While it is also true that we are teaching English as a second language, we cannot lose sight of the fact that we are teaching it to human beings. As teachers we are, in effect, attempting to graft new habits and new behavior patterns on individuals who come to our classroom with highly diverse backgrounds of ability and of experience.

Moreover, advances in many branches of science may require you to modify or add to your store of knowledge or skills of teaching English at any time in the future. It is my hope that some of the guidelines I have indicated will prepare you to adapt your teaching to any situation in which you may find yourselves and to accept new ideas in the context in which you know they will be most helpful to you and to your students.

The suggestions in this book have been so briefly stated, constituting as they do a synthesis of observation, interviews, and workshop experiences that a concluding statement becomes exceedingly difficult to write. Nevertheless, it may be desirable to reaffirm several comments and principles which have been scattered throughout this text:

1. You, the teacher, are more important than any method or material. It is what you do with any method or with any piece of material which will determine its effectiveness in helping your students learn. Student growth should be judged not only in terms of number of language items acquired or increased fluency but also in

terms of attitude toward English-speaking peoples and toward the continued study of English.

2. Student growth depends to a large extent upon your own professional growth. In a dynamic field such as ours, no teacher can afford to remain at a standstill. We should keep up with new findings, with new materials, and with the reports of teaching and learning experiences of our colleagues. This is possible by subscribing to journals in the field, attending conferences where possible, becoming members of professional organizations, and doing extensive reading. You should conduct experiments of your own. Many facets of theory and practice are still in need of further research. Your contribution, added to that of others, cannot help but be of value to many persons engaged in the field.

If English is not your native language, you may want to increase your competence in the language (or maintain it if you are not working in an English-speaking country) by taking advantage of the numerous seminars which are organized for teachers of English. If possible, you should arrange visits to English-speaking countries.

3. Under professional growth should be included a knowledge of many other areas of learning. The interested and interesting teacher constantly enriches his personality and hence his teaching through the study of aspects of method or knowledge culled from other subjects in the school curriculum and from other sciences.

4. You should learn to blend many ingredients together in order to give students the kind of learning experiences which contribute to the development of correct habits, broad interests and knowledge, basic skills, and desirable attitudes. Every learning experience should be carefully planned. It should have well-defined, carefully circumscribed objectives; it should be made interesting to the students because it uses *them, their* interests and ability, and *their* environment as a starting point; it should insure the active participation of all the students; it should utilize varied materials and activities; it should look back on what has been learned and lead to further language growth. Every segment of newly acquired language should be skillfully woven into the existing fabric of communication.

5. In addition, participation in each class hour should give the students the conviction that they are moving ahead. That does not mean that they have to learn a new large body of material each time or that they have to begin a completely new unit. It may mean that they acquire a little more accuracy in producing a sound; a little more fluency in saying a familiar sentence, a new word; a new way of doing a drill through a different use of material or a different type of student participation. Our goal should be continuous and gradual progress rather than immediate "mastery."

6. In the philosophy underlying today's language learning program, great emphasis is placed on the ability of the teacher to detect errors in pronunciation (even in choral recitation), to identify and diagnose speech problems of students, and to model new structures. In short, it is considered important that the teacher develop what is generally called a "listening ear." I would like to suggest that a "listening heart" is of equal importance.

The teacher who can give each student the feeling that he is an important part of a group, that he is capable of learning, and that he can achieve success; the teacher who can demonstrate an understanding of conflict—both environmental and linguistic; the teacher who, through his enthusiasm, his art, and his skill, makes language learning a subject to be looked forward to—will in the final analysis be the one who will forge ahead of his less perceptive colleague in promoting the desirable habits and attitudes needed for language learning. Teachers who embody the personal and professional characteristics outlined here cannot help but push aside the language barriers which impede communication among men.

Appendix I
Practice in Pairs

The article by Professor Geoffrey Broughton written for the Brazilian journal "English Teaching" and reproduced in the Italian journal LEND in cooperation with the British Council of Italy is so valuable that I have decided—with Professor Broughton's permission—to use it exactly as I found it. I am sure you will find the suggestions as practical and realistic as I have found them.

Practice In Pairs

by Geoffrey Broughton

The teacher of English is often faced with the conflicting problems of teaching large classes and the need to give them massive practice in the structures of the language. What is more, few course books, if any, give sufficient practice material to insure controlled oral drill to the point of saturation in the patterns that have been taught. Understandably, many teachers take the line of least resistance to these difficulties, and limit their oral work to a minimum of class repetition and a few scattered questions.

Yet massive oral practice is possible with large numbers of learners and one device open to the teacher in such a situation is to set the students working orally in pairs. This article is an attempt to suggest how it may best be done.

After all, the essence of language is communication, at its simplest meaningful verbal intercourse between two people. Common patterns are found in seeking information (by question and answer), seeking confirmation (by affirmation and agreement), eliciting disagreement (by affirmation and negation), or eliciting verbal action (by command and obeying). And these are some of the modes that the teacher can readily harness to paired language practice. This, at the reinforcement stage of language learning, gives a communication situation in its simplest form, yet with an optimum control over the resulting dialogue.

Perhaps an example will best illustrate the advantages and potential of oral practice in pairs. Imagine the situation where the teacher has introduced defining relative clauses—with *who* and *whose* (e.g., The man who brings the milk; The man whose car is outside; etc.). The learners have met and understood examples and seen how they work in context. Now is the time for practicing them and the "line-of-least-resistance" teacher sets a written exercise from the book. But this can hardly be called massive practice, and the ten or fifteen sentences each student writes (even if correct) can hardly be sufficient to drive home the new patterns to the point where they are integrated with the general body of his language mastery. The written exercise certainly has its place as a slightly different kind of reinforcement, but it should be preceded by oral drill.

The paired practice is introduced by the teacher putting on the blackboard:

a nurse

a librarian

and asking: *"Where does a nurse work?"* ("A nurse works in a hospital.") and *"Where does a librarian work?"* ("A librarian works in a library.") Then comes the new pattern in the questions: *"Which one is the person who works in a hospital?"* ("A nurse.") and *"Which one is the person who works in a library?"* ("A librarian.")

Now the teacher adds to the blackboard list familiar nouns which fit the pattern: a waiter, a secretary, a cashier, a shop assistant, a bus driver, a teacher, an actor, a hairdresser. Then he asks the class, *"Which one is the person who works in a ______?"* He asks five or six questions, if necessary writing up the place of work opposite each noun:

a nurse	*a hospital*
a librarian	*a library*
a waiter	*a restaurant (a café)*
a secretary	*an office*
a cashier	*a bank*
a shop assistant	*a shop*

a bus driver	*a bus*
a teacher	*a school (a college)*
an actor	*a theater*
a hairdresser	*a hairdresser's*

Now the class is able to do its first piece of work in pairs. "Practice in pairs," the teacher says, "the person on the left asks the questions; the person on the right answers." Notice that there is no problem for the learners as to what to ask and what to answer. Notice also that the teacher has made things easy for the weaker and less enterprising students who will ask the questions they have heard the teacher ask; but the more enterprising will want to start with the questions the teacher deliberately left out.

Watching and listening carefully, the teacher decides when to change the questioners and, when he judges that the material has nearly been used up, instructs the persons on the right to ask the questions and those on the left to answer.

After a suitable time for this practice, the teacher stops the activity and prepares the class for the development of the activity. So far, all the questions have started, *"Which is the person who works in a______?"* But we can make the question more general by adding more nouns to the blackboard and giving more choice in the question, though still practicing the same pattern.

So a new blackboard list is begun alongside the first, starting with:

a postman
a pilot

As before, the teacher puts the first questions to the class: *"Which one is the person who brings our letters?" "Which one is the person who flies planes?"* Now this second list is developed on the blackboard by the addition of familiar nouns, and these are used to frame questions. Again, if necessary, a brief help towards the answer may be added:

a postman	*brings letters*
a pilot	*flies planes*
a farmer	*grows food*
an author	*writes books*
a musician	*makes music*
a window cleaner	*cleans windows*
a dentist	*looks after teeth*
a florist	*sells flowers*
a tennis player	*plays tennis*
an architect	*designs houses (buildings)*

After five or six questions to the class, they are told for the second time, "Practice in pairs," with one member of each pair being the questioner to start with, and later the other. This practice continues for a suitable period—up to two minutes—before the teacher brings it to a stop and introduces a related pattern. As a reminder, he puts part of the familiar pattern on the board—"The person who works in a hospital." Now he asks: *"What's a librarian?"*, eliciting the answer "A person who works in a library" and *"What's a postman?"* ("A person who brings letters.") Two or three other examples show the class the new, related pattern of question and answer. *("What's a ______?"* "A person who______.")

And the learners are ready for the third short session of work in pairs.

This particular set of twenty nouns has been selected to be used with other related patterns, using *whose.* So, after the third paired practice, the teacher reminds the class of one of the *whose* patterns. *"Which one is the person whose work is in a hospital?"* (A nurse.) *"Which one is the person whose work is bringing letters?"* (A postman.) A fourth paired practice follows, and the fifth, using the same lists and a *whose* answer, is started by sample questions and answers like: *"What's a waiter?"* ("A man whose work is in a restaurant.") *"What's a farmer?"* ("A man whose work is growing food.")

Set out like this, such an activity appears to be more tedious than it is. Notice that all the sentences are meaningful to the learners, that they are being drilled in making correct sentences, and that the periods of paired practice are broken up by the teacher's exposition and questions. So that, in fact, the learners here have done a total of some eight or ten minutes of very solid practice in two kinds of defining relative clauses and during that time have personally either asked or answered up to a hundred questions using the relevant patterns. This is the kind of massive practice which reinforces the active handling of structures in preparation for the written exercise.

The experienced teacher will soon recognize what a wide range of patterns can be practiced in this way. There is the obvious range of structures which involve direct questions—What's that? Is that a NOUN? Is that an ADJECTIVE?, Where is the NOUN? and many others. Question tags, using the anomalous finites (*can, must, may, will,* etc.) are a very profitable area—You can swim/run/drive/dance, etc., can't you? You can't fly/walk on your hands/see an elephant, etc., can you?

Rather less obvious, however, is a range of traditional exercises, which may easily be converted to oral practice in pairs. For example, one coursebook, practicing *used to,* gives an old school timetable, followed by this substitution table:

How many sentences can you make?

The class
The boys

used to

do
have
study
learn

play football

French, German, English,
History, Geography,
Math, Science, Music

on

Monday.
Tuesday.
Wednesday.
Thursday.
Friday.

For practice in pairs, the teacher need only start asking, *"When did the boys use to have French?"* and so on. Then, with the school timetable on the blackboard, the learners can continue in pairs asking each other similar questions. The related pattern *"What did they use to do on ______?"* follows naturally.

Some traditional exercises are more difficult to turn into question and answer, but can be rephrased to give a challenge and its reply. The familiar conversion exercise where direct speech is to be reported can be handled in this way. For example, the following sentences might be set for reporting:

> *She said, "I want to see that film."*
> *She said, "I'll go tonight."*
> *She told him, "I think I'll get the best seats."*

A way of working these in pairs would be like this:

A. *She said, "I want to see that film."*
B. *Yes, I know. She said she wanted to see that film.*
A. *She said, "I'll go tonight."*
B. *Yes, I know. She said she would go tonight.*
A. *She told him, "I think I'll get the best seats."*
B. *Yes, I know. She told him she thought she would get the best seats.*

These short periods of oral work, of course, are intended to give maximum practice for the class and are certainly more demanding on the teacher. Not only must he plan the sequence of the drills with great care, but while the pairs are working, he should move around the class to make sure that mistakes are not being made, and generally keeping his finger on the pulse of the class. In this way he knows when to stop the activity as the students are reaching the last examples, or in the rare cases where individuals have not properly understood the procedures. Another advantage of the teacher moving about is that he can control the noise level. Though if he is firmly in control of the learners he can usually make sure that the general noise level does not rise above an acceptable hum of interested conversation.

Perhaps these considerations suggest the fundamental secret of the success of this kind of oral activity. It depends completely on the willingness of the class to participate (a matter of discipline) and their understanding of what they are expected to do (a matter of organization). The young or inexperienced teacher may be chary of letting control go out of his own hands and may even encounter difficulties when he tries paired practice for the first time. But its advantages repay the organizational efforts involved. It is worth spending extra time in getting the pairs working well on the first occasion. The earliest drills should be straight repetitions of class practice. It helps when learners always work with the same partner, so that a routine is established for the activity.

Notice too, how the use of the blackboard as a focal point gives each pair something external to themselves to concentrate on. Not only does it keep them working, but it also discourages them from drifting into a non-English private conversation. But perhaps most important is the challenge of running correctly through an interesting and meaningful exercise: once it becomes meaningless or tedious it loses interest.

Here, then, is an activity method which the teacher of the largest class can use; one in which no learner need leave his seat; one in which the maximum use is made of the learners' time; and if it is devised with a little imagination from the teacher, one which the learners will enjoy whenever the teacher says—"Practice in pairs."

Appendix II Picture Compositions

This stimulating article by Donn Byrne, English Language Officer of the British Council of Italy, will undoubtedly open up new vistas to many readers. I had the privilege of seeing Mr. Byrne demonstrate the use of the pictures with a large group of learners. The language he elicited—at various levels and in different varieties—was indeed amazing and the interest engendered, even more so.

Visual Sequences for the Production of Dialogue

by Donn Byrne

Visual sequences of the kind depicted below, where the dialogue is implicit in the situations, have to be interpreted rather than described. There are two main ways in which the dialogue element may be 'extracted':

(1) The students may first be asked to say what they think the pictures are about. For example, in Picture A, Mrs. (Ball) wants some sugar. She asks her husband to go and get it. Perhaps at the start her husband is reluctant to go (Why?).
So she has to persuade him (How?). In Picture B she offers him a list because there are other things which she needs (What are they?), but

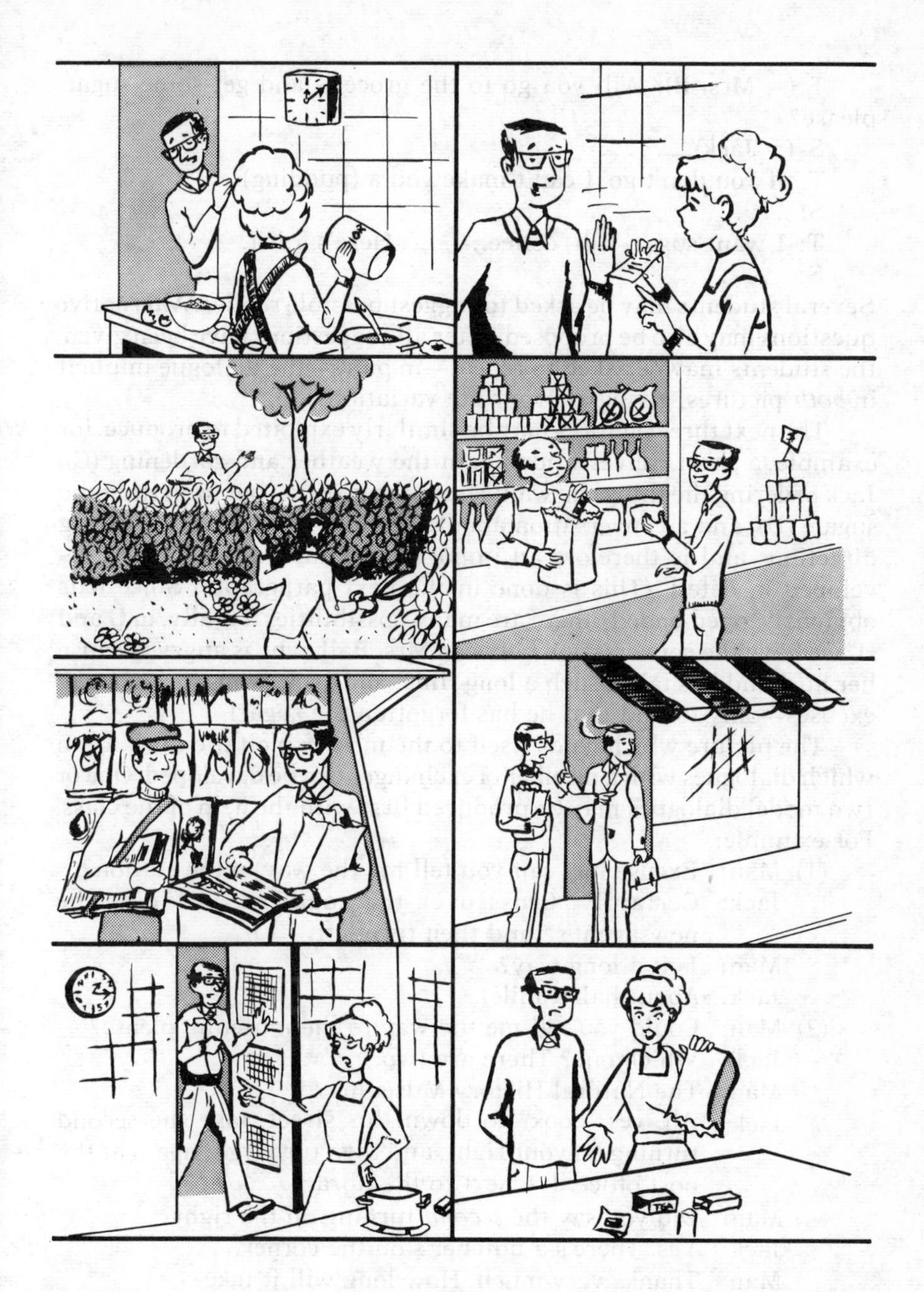

he refuses to take it. The students are then asked to devise appropriate dialogue to fit these statements. All this may be done as a group activity.

(2) Alternatively, the dialogue may be cued directly by providing the first line of the exchange. For example:

T (= Mrs. B): Will you go to the grocer's and get some sugar, please?

S (= Jack): . . . . . .

T: If you don't go, I can't make you a (pudding).

S: . . . . . .

T: I want sugar, salt, coffee . . . . . . Here's a list.

S: . . . . . .

Several students may be asked to suggest possible replies. Alternative questions may also be proposed. After all suggestions have been given, the students may be asked to repeat—in pairs—the dialogue implicit in *both* pictures, giving appropriate variations.

The next three pictures may be similarly exploited to produce, for example, a short conversation about the weather and gardening (C), Jack ordering the things he wants from the grocer—but forgetting the sugar! (D), and a conversation about the news (E). F involves giving directions and is therefore an important picture which can be developed in detail. (This is done in the next paragraph.) Since it is obviously 'open-ended,' there are many possibilities. Finally, in G and H, we have the conversation between Mrs. Ball, who is angry because her husband has taken such a long time, and Jack, who tries to make excuses—only to find that he has forgotten the sugar!

The picture which lends itself to the most exploitation is F, from which dialogues with a number of exchanges can be developed. One or two model dialogues may be produced first with the help of the class. For example:

(1) Man: Excuse me, can you tell me the way to the station?
Jack: Certainly. Cross over the road, go as far as the newsagent's* and then turn left.
Man: Is it a long way?
Jack: About half a mile.

(2) Man: Could you tell me the way to the museum, please?
Jack: Which one? There are two.
Man: The Natural History Museum.
Jack: Ah, yes. Look, go down this street, take the second turning on your right, and then turn right again at the post office. It's next to the library.
Man: Did you say the *second* turning on the right?
Jack: Yes. There's a butcher's on the corner.
Man: Thanks very much. How long will it take?
Jack: Oh, about fifteen minutes.

The class can then be divided into groups to produce other dialogues, which can be acted out in front of the class.

Further work can also be done. For example, a set of questions

* "Newsstand" in American English.

which might be asked about Picture A could run as follows:

(A) Where was Mrs. Ball? What was she doing? Why did she call her husband? What did she want him to buy? Did he want to go to the grocer's? What did she say to him?

Similarly a true/false drill can be carried out. For example:

Ask the students to say whether the following statements are true. If they are false, get them to give the correct ones.

(1) Mrs. Ball was reading the paper in the kitchen.
(2) Mrs. Ball asked her husband to go to the grocer's.
(3) Jack wanted to go to the grocer's.
(4) Jack took the list which his wife offered him.

Finally, the students may be asked to reconstruct the entire story, using suitable dialogue, with minimum cues from the teacher. At this stage it should be sufficient to say: *Picture A - Mrs. Ball* to elicit a whole series of statements:

Mrs. Ball was in the kitchen.
She was cooking.
She found that she did not have any sugar, so she called her husband.
"Jack!" she said ...... etc.

Similarly the callword *Jack* should elicit:

Jack was (watching TV).
He came into the kitchen ...... etc.

Numerous composition exercises can be based on this oral preparatory stage, including of course the writing up of dialogues. An interesting group project would be to ask the students to write in the form of a short play, divided into scenes and with appropriate stage directions, an account of what the various people in the story did and said. For example:

Scene 1—Mrs. Ball is cooking in the kitchen. She finds that she did not have any sugar.

Mrs. Ball (calling her husband): Jack!

There is no answer.

Mrs. Ball: JACK!

Jack (coming into the kitchen): Yes, dear! What is it?

Mrs. Ball: I've run out of sugar. Run along to the grocer's and get me some, please.

Jack: But I wanted to watch TV ...... etc.

Appendix III
Situational Topics

The list below will be useful to you in planning numerous types of language activities. It may suggest 1) possible themes for a dialogue, a dictation, a listening comprehension exercise, a reading passage, some directed dialogue, a discussion, a written composition; 2) topics for cross-cultural research; or 3) situations around which to present and practice language items and structures.

Addresses
Addressing people
Age
Appointments, making
Art
Banking services
Barber shop, going to a
Beauty shop, going to a
Clothing (see also Shopping):
- altering
- buying
- cleaning
- describing
- making
- taking care of
- wearing

Dancing
Dates
Days of the week
Dentist, seeing a

- homework
- materials and objects used in
- subjects studied
- teachers
- transportation to

Seasons

Shopping for:
- clothing
- food
- household supplies
- medicines
- toilet articles

Sizes (See also Clothing, Shopping)

Sports (See also Recreation)

Telephoning:
- getting information
- leaving messages
- long distance
- public booths
- saying phone numbers

Television

Telling time

Theater

Time, expressions of

Transportation:
- buying tickets
- means of
- schedules
- terminals
- timetables
- using a car

Visiting, people and places

Weather

Work:
- aspiring to certain kinds of
- hours of
- laws related to
- looking for
- payment received for
- preparing for

Worshipping

Appendix IV
Myth and Reality in TESOL: A Plea for a Broader View

The following article will not be new to some of you. It has appeared in the *TESOL Quarterly* and in the *English Teaching Forum*. It is an adapted version of a paper given by me at the Lackland Air Base in 1970. It incorporates, however, some of the answers inspired by the excellent questions asked by the superb group of teachers and administrators at Lackland who are dedicated to teaching English to adults from over forty countries.

I offer it here as another "summing up" of some of the ideas expressed in this Guide. Although it is concerned primarily with adult learners, you will note that the principles and many of the techniques are as applicable to young learners.

The version appearing here is from *The English Teaching Forum*, Volume X, March-April 1972, Number 2, pp. 2-9.

* * *

While there is consensus about the two desired terminal objectives of most language courses—bilingualism and biculturalism—discussions about other facets of language teaching are characterized by vigorous claims and counterclaims. The areas of dispute are many—unfortunately—and range from important considerations such as the selection of students to trivia about the number of repetitions needed to learn a word. The heat generated by the thousands of words written and spoken about comparatively unimportant issues often prevents teachers, administrators, and curriculum writers from finding the key to the more efficient and productive presentation of language that would indeed produce the world-minded citizens so desperately needed.

Before discussing the realities that teachers of English must deal with daily—that is, language-teaching techniques—I would like to share with you some of the concern I have felt as I have listened to several unsubstantiated myths that have sprung up around our profession. My concern has been reinforced by articles on teaching that keep appearing in many respectable language journals, which tend to encourage a feverish advocacy of *one* theory, *one* method, or *one* set of techniques.

In the last decade especially, it has been disheartening and frustrating to hear language-teaching specialists talk as if God had called to Moses as he was hurrying down the mountain with the tablet containing the Ten Commandments and said "Moses! Moses! Come back. I forgot the most important commandment—number eleven: Thou shalt teach language in only one way." Interested, conscientious teachers and other educators concerned with learning theories and teaching practices have always realized, in all eras and in all countries, that there is never an "either/or" answer to any facet of educational theory or practice. They have always known that an eclectic, integrated approach—one that combines nonconflicting and mutually supporting theories from several disciplines—is generally the most productive. They know, too, that even when experiments have proved that premise X is incontestably true and that practice Y should flow naturally from it, they must not lose sight of the individual differences that exist in the school community, and among teachers and learners—differences that will require modification or adaptation of the practice.

I am afraid that, in formulating a methodology of language teaching, we have leaned too heavily on the science of linguistics and have drawn insufficiently from the related sciences of psychology, anthropology, and sociology. Let me hasten to say, in defense of the linguists, that the majority of them, alternately blamed and praised for the misnamed "linguistic approach," never intended to address themselves to the problems of *teaching* language. (At a recent conference of language teachers Noam Chomsky, author of the currently popular generative-transformational grammar theory, reiterated that point.) The linguists' main interest has been to analyze and describe languages. They can give us—and have given us—the content of our discipline. Many of their principles and analytical procedures can point the way to methodological changes—as, for example, in grading linguistic material or in preparing drills—but the majority of linguists do not even pretend that they can tell us how to transmit that linguistic material most effectively.

Some Language-Teaching Myths

I will discuss briefly a few of the misconceptions about language learning and teaching that, unfortunately, have had an overwhelming influence on classroom teaching techniques and materials of instruction during the last two decades. I do not give them here in order of importance; they strike me as all equally reprehensible.

The "deferment of reading" myth

The first myth is that a long aural-oral period should precede the students' introduction to the printed word. To my knowledge, no experiment has ever been performed that would justify a long, rigidly-adhered-to time lag between the students' reasonably good oral production of an utterance and their seeing it in print. Common sense would indicate that factors such as the age of the students, their native-language reading background, the length of the course, and the use to which they will need to put their English in the immediately foreseeable future—all these factors should be considered in determining the period of deferment of reading.

A long aural-oral period has been found to create tension in students who find it difficult to retain a stream of speech in their minds and who cannot turn back to a printed word to verify a bit of language they may not have grasped the first time. Furthermore, it discounts the fact that in most countries the textbook carries prestige, the fact that individuals learn in different ways, and that some may learn best by using their eyes and ears at the same time. Also, it is simply not true to say that many more oral repetitions are possible when students do not see the printed page. If the instructor models the written utterance orally with normal speed and rhythm—as he should do, since reading is related to speech—the same number of student repetitions is possible with as without the printed page.

The "dialogue memorization" myth

The second misconception is that long dialogues should be learned by heart and that their meaning is not of primary importance. I will discuss the teaching of dialogues later in this article, but let me say here that if the students memorize dialogues at all they should accomplish this feat by frequent dramatization, role playing, questions of all kinds, and especially by the study of alternate words and utterances appropriate in the context of the particular dialogue. For example, in a dialogue set in an automobile repair shop a possible stimulus sentence such as *May I have a hub cap?* might elicit not only the response *Yes, here's one* but also such utterances as *For what kind of car?* or *We're out of them right now* or *Aluminum or chromium?* Since each native speaker of English uses the language code in a personal, individual manner, it is unrealistic to expect that the students will ever hear again the exact response utterance contained even in the most authentic dialogue.

More importantly, the teacher should make the total meaning of the dialogue clear to the students before having them repeat or dramatize it. He should help them relate the dialogue situation to a situation familiar to them in their own experience. He must help them to become aware of who is speaking each utterance of the dialogue and to grasp at least the general meaning of the structures and words in the conversation through the use of pictures, real objects, pantomime, or other techniques. The meaning of the language items should be further clarified and impressed on the students through word and structure drills conducted after the presentation and dramatization of the dialogue. Nothing is more frustrating than to hear someone recite or be forced to parrot meaningless noise, no matter how well organized it may be.

The question of whether to use the dialogue for the presentation of new grammatical and lexical material or whether to teach the dialogue after the structures have been learned must also take into account such factors as the students' immediate need for the sociocultural concepts in the dialogue and the number of fixed high-frequency expressions or formulas that it contains. (Expressions such as *Please, How do you do?* and *How much does it cost?* may be considered fixed expressions of high frequency.) There should be no hard-and-fast rule about the placement of dialogue study in the lesson unless all the subsequent text material in the unit is based on it.

The "vocabulary restriction" myth

Another myth arises from statements that vocabulary is not as important as grammatical structure. While no one would deny the importance of the systematic teaching of structure, we should take into account the students' interests, motivations, and sometimes even their personal welfare, before placing unrealistic restrictions on vocabulary growth. The ability to talk about a number of everyday things—even with poor pronunciation and, yes, even with "grammatical errors"—will give students a feeling of success and achievement. It will make them realize quickly that they are learning an instrument of communication that enables them to say in another tongue the things they say in their own. For many adults, especially, it is demoralizing to revert to a stage of speaking similar to that of a two- or three-year-old.

The "no equivalent" myth

A more irritating misconception holds that there is no one-to-one equivalent in any two languages for any word or expression. This is not really true. A study by Eaton reported in John Carroll's text *Language and Thought* indicates that there are at least 600 words for which one could find equivalents in every known language. We exaggerate when we say, for example, that *I have breakfast* has no equivalent. While breakfast may consist of different foods, eaten at different hours—even among persons in one community or members of one's own family—the basic concept of "having breakfast" is generally familiar to all people.

The "no native language" myth

Although I realize that my next item—the ban on using the students' native language—is controversial, I would recommend that *on occasion* you help the students, or permit them to help one another, with a few words in the native language to clarify something they may not have comprehended in English.

I am not advocating the widespread use of the students' native language. What I am suggesting is that we should allow the judicious use of the native language when needed. It is difficult to sustain the motivation of students who are forced to sit through a class or a laboratory session when they have not understood what the lesson is about or what they are expected to do. Moreover, we delude ourselves if we think the student is not translating each new English item into his native tongue when he first meets it. The art of the teacher lies in helping the student eliminate the intermediate translation step as quickly as possible through a variety of carefully planned and briskly conducted drills.

Let me make it clear that I am not advocating the return to the traditional grammar-translation method, particularly as it was practiced by poor teachers. But it might be valuable and desirable to reevaluate the limited, judicious use of the students' native language on the sentence level, particularly when we are dealing with motivated adults in intensive programs.

The "no grammar" myth

Perhaps the most counter-productive fiction of all has been the one concerning the teaching of grammar—what has been called "teaching *about* the language." Research studies and education texts such as Jerome Bruner's *The Process of Education* (Cambridge: Harvard University Press, 1960) emphasize the fact that a conscious awareness of structure should precede drills and activities of any kind.

The two theories that should guide our presentation and practice of language material—as far as our present knowledge of language-learning theory can help us—are the habit-formation and the cognitive-code theories. In the former, as we know, students, through constant repetition of a model and through pattern manipulation, develop the habit of forming and arranging words in utterances in certain ways as they hear or see a stimulus or cue.

In the cognitive-code theory, students are guided to observe and to note the recurring elements in language items and are then helped to make a generalization about them. The generalization and the practice stemming from it enable them to use the items in other similar utterances and in other situations where they are appropriate.

We should apply *both* theories, not one or the other, in the language classroom. Certainly students will need to make the forms of words and their arrangement matters of habit, so they can give their attention to the expression of ideas. On the other hand, the *guided* perception of the system inherent in the forms and arrangements will enable them not only to make correct analogies but also to become competent in recognizing and, hopefully, in producing similar utterances without the constant guidance of the teacher. The rule or generalization should be based on several examples of structural arrangements and sentence patterns whose meaning has been clarified through their use in relevant situations. Simply-worded questions related to the structures and patterns should lead students to gain insight into the sound, form, position, and function of every grammatical item.

Pattern practice will acquire more meaning for students if they are aware of the language items that are being drilled. Adults, in particular, need initial intellectual understanding, which will then be reinforced through various drill activities. Well-formed utterances on the adult level are generally the result of concise analysis and extensive practice.

The "manipulation phase" myth

Another myth is related to pattern practice. Some texts and some teachers spend an inordinate amount of time on the manipulation phase of language activities. While pattern-practice drills are necessary and helpful, they should not be used exclusively even on the first day of a beginning-level class. The teachers should ask the students questions such as "What would you say?" as, through pictures and situations created in the classroom, he encourages them to use the new language items in normal, relevant activities. Only if this is done will students believe that the manipulation and repetition phase of learning has merit. They need to feel that what they are learning is valuable to them not only in a foreseeable future when they can "communicate" but also at the present moment.

Automatic responses and habit formation need not necessarily *precede* communication; *both* should be written into the daily lesson plans. Indeed, the teaching of any grammatical item or skill— listening, speaking, reading, or writing—should generally proceed in two parallel streams. In order to engender and sustain motivation, the teacher should, for example, help his students understand and read natural, stimulating, interesting material they can use immediately. At the same time, of course, the individual sounds, grammatical items, or sound-symbol relationships needed for reading should be presented systematically. It is imperative, however, that the normal use of language should not "wait on" the mastery of any individual item.

The "mastery" myth

The last of the myths I should like to touch on is the concept of "mastery." Instead of concentrating on mastery or perfection of any sound, form, or expression within a delimited time span, I would urge that we aim toward the more reasonable concept of the *gradual* shaping of these items toward the desired terminal behavior. While mastery is an ideal to which we all aspire, the too early insistence on it may discourage students unnecessarily. Such insistence discounts the fact that in the learning of any subject—not language alone—plateaus may be reached, particularly in the early stages of learning where little progress is made. It also loses sight of the fact that language learning is a cumulative matter which permits the reintroduction and integration of previously learned material in subsequent lessons.

Moreover, we should accept the fact that some students will never be able to eliminate a foreign accent. To spend hours of time perfecting a speech sound that does not make a difference in the meaning of a word or an utterance is basically nonproductive for many adult learners. Our aim, of course, is to make the students' speech comprehensible, not only during the segments of the lesson devoted to systematic pronunciation practice, but throughout the entire lesson.

Some Important Teaching Factors

Let us now turn from exploding myths—a necessary preliminary exercise—to examining some factors in our students and in ourselves, and some techniques that you may wish to consider in planning your teaching program. These will be related to: (a) the knowledge and skills needed by the teacher; (b) the importance of gaining insights into the characteristics of our students; (c) the selection, gradation, and presentation of material; and (d) some techniques of instruction.

The teacher's skills

There can be no doubt that the single most important factor in the instructional process—the important variable—is the teacher. It is what the teacher does to create a desirable classroom climate, to plan a variety of learning activities, to use materials of instruction effectively, and, most important, to try to identify with the needs and aspirations of students. It is these things that will determine, in the final analysis, whether learning will take place. I do not believe at all that teachers are "born"—although I would admit that genes and early environmental influences have an effect on personality and character—but I am convinced that everyone who is willing and interested can hope to become a skilled and effective teacher. In addition to attitude traits such as a sense of justice, an abiding desire to grow professionally, fairness, tact, humility, intellectual curiosity, and enthusiasm for teaching—either simulated, on occasion, or real—the teacher needs to develop certain knowledge, skills, and insights. He should, for example:

1. Study the educational backgrounds of his students as a springboard for planning varied group or individual activities.
2. Gain conscious familiarity with features of the English sound, grammar, vocabulary, and cultural systems. He should make an inventory of the pronunciation and grammatical items that cause his students difficulty.
3. Learn methods and techniques of teaching English as a second language.
4. Integrate principles and/or procedures of related disciplines (linguistics, psychology, sociology, and anthropology) in the teaching of English.
5. Understand the dynamics and techniques of grouping. These are crucial in providing for the wide ranges in ability and the varied interests of the students.
6. Learn how to utilize the course textbooks and/or develop supplementary instructional materials in harmony with program objectives and students' goals and learning problems.
7. Learn the science and art of evaluation. Not only should he judge his own teaching skill, but he should also assess the students' progress in order to plan for possible "remedial" teaching, for regrouping in the classroom, and for recommending placement in other more appropriate classes provided by the school.
8. Create a warm, "accepting" classroom environment conducive to successful learning and ego enhancement.

Characteristics of the students

Now let us turn to some factors in the students. We must realize, first of all, that each of our students is a highly individual human being. Each of them has developed different strategies for learning —strategies that we may be completely unaware of. Each will restructure the material we are teaching, integrating it with elements from previously learned items, translating to or from his native tongue, or taking personal shorthand notes. From his earlier educational experience he will have developed various strategies for assimilating material. Hopefully, these strategies will facilitate his learning; but often poor learning habits or poor study habits may retard language development, and new study habits will have to be gradually substituted through continuous teacher guidance and encouragement. The student will substitute new strategies for old only if he is convinced that the new ones will help him attain the goals set by the teacher or himself.

Each of the students will be at a different point on the continua of listening, speaking, reading, and writing abilities, not only in his native language but also in English, from the very first day of the language program. Each student will come to class with deeply ingrained values and with an experiential backgound that may color his acceptance or rejection of the linguistic or cultural material we may be trying to inculcate.

Each student, of course, may have not only a different learning style but also greater or lesser aptitude for learning a language. As we know, there is some agreement as to the innate capacities that may enhance language learning. These innate capacities, studied extensively by John Carroll and other psychologists, include phonetic coding, grammatical sensitivity, rote-memorization ability, and inductive language-learning ability. Recent research has indicated that the factor of time is also critical in the acquisition of knowledge. People learn not only in different ways but at different rates. In the light of such differences, it behooves us as teachers to help students maintain initial positive motivation by making it possible for them to satisfy goals—both long-range and immediate—that *they* consider important: of reading, perhaps, in their field of interest; of creating and dramatizing conversations they feel they will need in order to function effectively; of learning to guess meaning from an oral or written context; of accumulating lexical items that they want to learn; of using a dictionary efficiently.

We will have to plan for group-learning activities and for individuated instruction, for the reasonable shaping of the students' behavior toward intermediate and final course objectives, and for their gradual understanding of English speakers' habits and customs. It is imperative as we do this that we help the students retain pride in their own way of life and that we do not create stereotypes of American or British speakers of English in their minds.

It is essential that we avoid reinforcing the students' natural but traumatic feeling of "anomie." This phenomenon of language learners, in which they feel they are living in a no-man's land, where they no longer feel free to use their native language and yet are not ready to use the new tongue, has been studied extensively by sociologists such as Lambert and Gardner.

Lambert and Gardner and their associates have also considered the types of learner orientation that enhance motivation: *instrumental* and *integrative*. We should foster both types of motivation in our classes.

We can achieve *instrumental* orientation through numerous activities in which students use language as a tool of communication to express, meaningfully and authentically, their needs, desires, concerns, and aspirations. We can, moreover, design practical activities and situations in which pairs of students face each other and engage in brief conversations.

In order to foster *integrative* orientation, we can plan such experiences for the students as meeting and talking to sensitive, empathetic native speakers of English.

Another characteristic we should be aware of is that the adult with clearly defined goals is more critical and questioning than the younger student. Whether right or wrong, he has ideas about how the lessons should be conducted. He needs the constant satisfaction of realizing progress toward his goals as he perceives them. He does not come to us as a *tabula rasa*. He has learned a perfectly adequate language; he has lived through numerous experiences. Far from ignoring these facts or trying to eradicate them, we should ask ourselves continuously how we can make the best of these two priceless assets that he brings with him to class.

Selection and presentation of material

Let us turn now to a brief listing of some aspects of methodology and some time-honored teaching techniques.

1. *Pronunciation*. You should choose for emphasis the pronunciation items that cause your students difficulty in comprehension and production. You should make an inventory of the troublesome features and give extensive practice in them. After conducting repetitive drills for individual sounds, you should have the students practice them in high-frequency words and utterances, with appropriate normal intonation and rhythm, within everyday situational contexts.

2. *Authentic, Natural Sentences.* You should clarify and drill grammatical items in authentic, natural sentences. Unless you provide additional words or use them in a meaningful context, you should not practice sentences such as *Don't I see the plane?* or *Does she speak to me every day?* since they would normally not be said by a native speaker.

3. *Situations.* You should teach grammatical items in situations, with lexical items that will help to clarify their meaning and would generally co-occur with them. For example, sentences such as *The coffee is too hot* and *The coffee is very hot* might well be meaningless to students if presented in isolation. But if, at the same time, they see a cup of coffee with curls of steam coming from it and hear you and see you dramatize the sentence *It will burn my tongue* (for the concept "too") and *I love hot coffee* (to convey the notion of "very"), the meaning of the sentences will come alive for them. Similarly, it would be helpful if when you first present utterances with the simple past you always include the word *yesterday,* and with utterances with the present perfect, the expression *many times.*

4. *The "Rule."* You should state the generalization, or "rule," for each grammatical item *simply* (after you give two or three examples of its use) in terms of its *sounds, form, position,* and *function.* You should write the examples of its use on the chalkboard, underlining the grammatical item you are stressing. Through asking simple questions such as "Where is the word X?" you should help the students "see" the grammatical relationships and you should elicit from them statements about the systematic features in sounds, position, and so on—in other words, you should *draw from the students* the "rule" underlying the use of the item.

5. *Six Sequential Steps.* In presenting any item, you should generally proceed in six sequential steps. (See pp. 54–55.)

6. *Verb Forms.* In teaching verb forms, you should concentrate on the pronouns *I* and *you* in questions and statements, since these will permit immediate, meaningful conversation.

7. *Vocabulary.* You should give priority to vocabulary items that students need in order to talk about themselves, their community, and matters of personal health and welfare—particularly if they are studying in an English-speaking community. You should teach vocabulary within categories or centers of interest—for example, food, transportation, recreation. If you use as illustrations real objects or *several* pictures of an item, this will help prevent the students from confusing the concept represented with some detail or background feature in a single picture.

There should be some system to the development of vocabulary. Students find it helpful, for example, to learn the noun, verb, adjective, and adverb forms of a content word wherever such forms exist. While the students may place these in lists for easy reference and perception of form, they should always learn and use each word in a clearly understood context. Whenever feasible, you should teach synonyms, antonyms, prefixes, and suffixes as well as other common words within the same category *(decade, century, era, period, etc.)*.

8. Cultural Background. You should use great sensitivity in developing in the students an awareness of and some insights into the culture of English-speaking people. I think it is better to concentrate on similarities rather than differences, emphasizing always the basic oneness of human nature and the role of geographical or historical factors to explain possible differences.

Further tips on techniques

1. Make every effort to help the students listen carefully and produce only correct responses. The trial-and-error method of learning, especially in an intensive course, is basically nonproductive and psychologically unsound.

2. Let the students know immediately that their responses are correct (when they are). You can achieve this simply by a nod, a sound of approval, a word of praise—or by asking other students to repeat the student's correct response. The knowledge that one's response is correct confirms the response and reinforces the learning process.

3. When a student is trying to express an idea during warm-up or "free" conversation periods, I would let some errors go by unless they impede comprehension. (I would make a mental note, however, and help the student with the item during a class break.)

If a student makes an error during a drill period, however, you might simply say "Listen" and give the correct form. It is undesirable to repeat the incorrect form, not only because the student who made the error will feel humiliated but also because your repetition of it might confirm the error in other students' minds.

4. Short daily quizzes on the previous day's presentation—which I highly recommend to you—should be corrected immediately. Since the new lesson is generally based on material learned during the preceding session, it is essential that you and the students be aware of any problem that may exist. There are two other immediate reasons for giving daily quizzes: a high score enhances the student's feeling of achievement, and the anxiety surrounding the taking of tests will diminish as students come to regard them as routine, nonthreatening activities.

5. Order all sentences within drills in such a way that they will provide practice in items that generally belong together and that are learned more quickly through association. I would drill together, for

example, sentences with *be* or *have* or *can*, even though the sentences on the laboratory tape will appear in another order. I would first drill the utterances around a particular verb form or item. You can do this by marking the sentences in your text in colored pencil or by renumbering them for the first round of practice. Then, after the students have gained some confidence in performing drills, you can give the utterances in the order in which they will be heard on the tape.

Another point I would like to make regarding drill sequences is this: For questions requiring Yes or No answers, I would conduct the drill so as to elicit first only responses beginning with *yes*. Then I would elicit all the *no* responses. Alternating *yes* and *no* is not only confusing to students, but it does not provide the kind of practice that reinforces realistic situations. A response such as *Are you a teacher?* answered alternately with *yes* and *no* violates basic principles of situational development. If the *no* responses are not authentic, you may introduce the drill by saying, "Now, let's pretend."

6. Before requiring students to engage in the more complex transformation drills, we should give them extensive practice in making substitutions in already-transformed sentences. For example, if our aim is to teach the students to transform direct speech into indirect speech, we would not immediately expect them to combine *he asked* and *What's the girl's name?* Intermediate steps, in my experience, would call for substitution drills in sentences such as *He asked what the girl's name was,* in which the students would substitute other pronouns or proper names for *he* and other words for *girl* and *name.* Several substitution drills, each with five or six examples, will help students internalize the word order and rhythm of the pattern and will reduce stumbling in the transformation exercise.

Another helpful drill for practicing indirect speech, and numerous other grammatical items, is the directed practice drill. You might want to engage in it in the three stages mentioned on pp. 66–67.

7. You should not only give clear instructions for every practice exercise but should also give examples of the changes or operations required. This becomes essential when, for example, you ask the students to change a statement to a question containing the pronoun *I* and the context does not make it clear whether they should retain the *I* in the response or use *you.*

8. By the same token, you should not as a rule ask the students to prepare any work at home or in the language laboratory unless you have first presented it and clarified it in class. For example, if the students "learn" pronunciation or meaning incorrectly, it will take more time to eradicate the errors than it would have taken to guide them in a brief oral "preview" of the new vocabulary. Of course, you should give the students guided practice in using a dictionary and in

utilizing contextual clues to help them select the most appropriate word from the numerous dictionary meanings. But how could they, without your guidance, decide which of the many meanings of words such as *time, give, run,* or *take* to select?

9. Especially at the elementary level, you should first go over in class all work assigned for the language laboratory. Moreover, at any level, the first part of the next class period should include activities that will permit the students to demonstrate the greater fluency and skill they have gained through work in the laboratory. Students will place more value on the laboratory session if you thus demonstrate that you consider it an integral and reinforcing part of their classroom work.

10. In order to develop reading comprehension, you should see that all reading is of the intensive type. After an appropriate stage-setting related to the students' experiences, you should clarify all difficulties in the reading passage: pronunciation, grammar, vocabulary, cultural allusions, situation. With the students' books open (since you are now emphasizing reading and not listening comprehension), you should read one or two sentences aloud and ask several types of questions about them (Yes-No questions and questions beginning with one of the *wh-* words). After you treat an entire portion in this way, you should ask for a summary—a sequential one—with each of several students contributing one idea and then one or two students giving the entire summary briefly. You should follow this with word-study exercises, other types of questions, paraphrases, and related activities that will contribute to the development of the total reading skill.

11. You should use dialogues for multiple purposes. In addition to using the utterances in them as models for grammatical or lexical study, you should also use dialogues extensively for question-and-answer practice. Some questions may be on the content of the dialogue itself; others may be of a personal nature but related to the theme of the dialogue. For example, if the dialogue is about movie-going, you might ask such personalized questions as *Do you like to go to the movies? What kind of movies do you like best? Do you ever see English films?*

The students should also practice entire alternative sentences that would be appropriate in the context of the dialogue. It goes without saying that you should encourage them to formulate their own questions on the dialogue, which they can then ask you or their fellow students.

12. Whenever possible, you should individualize your instruction, fitting it to the abilities and interests of the students. This is desirable even at beginning levels. For example, you can ask timid students or "late starters" questions that require only a Yes or No

response, while you ask more advanced extroverts to make a longer response or encourage them to formulate their own questions.

13. You might wish to try the following sequence of student participation:

a) You question individual students or give cues to which individual students will respond. (It is a good idea to prepare a small card, to fit in your left hand, on which you have written cue words or questions. This makes for a brisk, rhythmic drill.)

b) In directed practice, have individual students question each other or make statements in chain fashion as they sit in pairs facing each other.

More essential than anything I have said to this point is that you should give the students a constant feeling of success and of confidence in their ability to learn the language. Announcing all tests in advance; making sure that tests are based only on what has been taught *and learned;* individualizing instruction; providing many warm-up and summary periods; preparing all homework with the students except, perhaps, for those at advanced levels; planning for the inclusion of many audience situations in which more advanced students may tell you and their fellows about books they have read, things they have done, places they have visited, persons to whom they have talked—all these things will contribute to the feeling of security and accomplishment that students need to sustain motivation and enthusiasm.

Many other techniques could be noted, of course, but no article or book or form could ever hope to list them all. Only the teacher in the classroom can be fully cognizant of the problems and the joys, the frustrations and the satisfactions, the intuitive procedures that "work"—which are the very essence of teaching. The instructor with a sense of commitment to his profession, and with the conviction that people can learn, thinks primarily of the joys and satisfactions of teaching as he comes into contact with human beings whose futures he may help to mold.

The important moment of reality comes when the enthusiastic and well-prepared teacher is aware of his students' unspoken "well done" and when he sees the glint of comprehension and the smile of confidence on their faces. For those of us who have made teaching our life's work, all myths are dispelled and we are left at the end of each day with a sense of fulfillment and enrichment gained from the interaction with our students.

Appendix V
Definitions of Useful Terms

On the pages which follow, you will find, in alphabetical order, brief, simple definitions of terms as I have used them in the context of this book or of others you will find in reading.

ACCENT: 1) A synonym for *stress.* (See STRESS.) 2) Marks indicating the four word, phrase or sentence stresses: ʼ (primary); ^ (secondary); ˋ (tertiary); ∪ (weak). 3) A written mark over certain vowels of a word to differentiate it from another word spelled in the same way—Italian: e (and); è (is). 4) A written mark indicating syllabic stress—Spanish: está (he is); ésta (this one). 5) A written mark indicating vowel quality—French: père (father); allé (gone). 6) A "foreign" accent—a pronunciation deviation in the target language which identifies or marks the speaker as non-native. 7) Regional or dialectal accents.

ACHIEVEMENT TEST: One which measures how much of a body of language material taught has actually been learned by the student.

ACTION SERIES (also called the Gouin Series from the name of its originator): Utterances which verbalize a series of sequential actions being performed; e.g., I'm getting up; I'm going to the board; I'm writing my name; etc.

ACTIVATED HEADPHONES: Those which amplify a speaker's voice and permit him to hear himself as he speaks.

ACTIVE VOCABULARY: The content and function words of a language which are learned so thoroughly that they can be used in the performance of any communication act; the vocabulary which can be easily recalled for production. (See PASSIVE KNOWLEDGE.)

ALLOPHONE: One of the variant sounds of a phoneme. For example, the different *p* sounds in *pill, spill, cup* are all variants, or *allophones* of the phoneme /p/. Allophones do not differentiate meaning.

ANALOGY: The ability to form a word or pattern on the basis of knowledge of similar words or patterns. For example, if your students know the forms *boy/boys; girl/girls; ruler/rulers* they should by *analogy* be able to give the form *pencils* when you give the stimulus word *pencil.*

ANOMIE: A traumatic feeling experienced by learners who no longer identify with the native language community but who are not yet ready to "belong" to the English-speaking community.

ANTHROPOLOGY: One of the social sciences which studies all the features of the culture (including language) of a society.

ARTICULATION: 1) The smooth, continuous development from one level of language learning to the next. 2) The production of distinct sounds by the vocal organs—e.g., tongue between the teeth or tip of tongue against the tooth ridge.

AUDIO-LINGUAL: 1) A term used to indicate an approach to language learning—first by hearing, then by repeating. 2) Listening and speaking. (Another term for audio-lingual is aural-oral.)

BACKWARD BUILD-UP: The teaching technique whereby long sentences are divided and reconstructed from the end into small meaningful segments for ease in repetition. (See pp. 60–61.)

BEHAVIOR: 1) A way of doing something habitually as a result of the assimilated acquisition of a skill or a body of information or knowledge. 2) The visible activity displayed by a learner which can be observed and evaluated.

BICULTURALISM: The state of being able to operate comfortably and appropriately in two cultural settings.

BIDIALECTALISM: The state of being able to use two dialects (e.g., local, regional, standard). The level of competence will depend on such factors as environment, age, and use.

BILINGUALISM: The state of being able to use two languages with almost equal facility.

BRITISH TERMINOLOGY (linguistic)

class: sets of language elements; e.g., verbal, noun
form: grammar and lexis.
structure: the systematic relationship between classes.
substance: form and content.

system: a restricted group of items which provides a choice of possibilities for a particular function; e.g., person, number, demonstratives (this, that).

unit: any stretch of speech carrying grammatical pattern (morph, word, group, clause, sentence).

CATENATION: Combinations of sounds permitted in the language system.

CHAIN: The type of pupil activity in a classroom in which a student makes a statement, asks a question, or responds; then the student next to him or behind him makes a statement, responds, or asks a question. (See p. 68.)

CHORAL REPETITION: The imitation of spoken material by an entire class or by a group speaking together.

CLOZE TEST: One in which students are to restore words which have been systematically omitted.

CLUSTER: 1) The sequence or bunching together of consonants; e.g., wo*rks*, *spr*ing. 2) The sequence or bunching together of other language elements (vowels, nouns, verbs, etc.).

CODE: The total shared language system of a community. (See PAROLE.)

COGNATE: A word in one language which looks similar to and has a meaning equivalent to a word in another language; e.g., (Spanish/English) *nacional/national.* Beware of false cognates; that is, words which look the same but have different meanings; e.g., (Italian) *attualmente* = at the present time; (English) *actually* = really.

COGNITIVE CODE THEORY: One which holds that 1) the learner perceives (or is guided to discover) the "rule" or generalization underlying a feature of language from several examples of it; 2) language is rule-governed behavior.

COLLOCATION: The co-occurrences (of sounds, structures, or lexical items) permitted by the language system.

COMMUNICATIVE COMPETENCE: The ability to recognize and to produce authentic and appropriate language correctly and fluently in any social situation.

COMPETENCE: 1) In a psycholinguistic sense, the achieved ability of the speaker or listener to understand and produce language utterances. 2) In transformational theory, the ability to recognize well-formed sentences; deviant (non-grammatical) sentences; "look-alike" sentences which come from different deep structures; and synonymous sentences having different surface structures. (See PERFORMANCE.)

COMPOUND SYSTEM: One in which the foreign language is learned and used in relation to the native language. (See COORDINATE SYSTEM.)

CONFIRMATION: Knowledge given a learner—orally or through some other technique—that his response is correct.

CONFLICT: Interference or problem in learning a second or foreign language caused by the ingrained habit of saying something in a certain way in one's native tongue.

CONNOTATIVE: The personal meaning a word may have for individuals depending on their experiences with the word or its referent.

CONSCIOUS SELECTION: The step in the learning process in which students choose between two language items which are in contrast. (See p. 55.)

CONSOLE: The teacher's control center in a language laboratory.

CONSTITUENT: Any one of the smaller structural units linked together in a larger construction. For example in *The boys bought balls, the boys* (the NP or Noun Phrase) and *bought balls* (the VP or Verb Phrase) are the *immediate constituents* of the sentence. The *ultimate constituents* would be boy/s and ball/s which cannot be divided further.

CONSTITUENT THEORY: The binary division of an utterance into smaller and smaller constituents until ultimate constituents are identified. (These may be segments of words.) (See p. 8 and above.)

CONTENT WORDS: Vocabulary items that refer to *things, actions,* or *qualities.*

CONTEXT: The forms or words within any connected stretch of speech which surround other words and thus help to give them their particular meaning. (Often *context* and *situation* are used interchangeably but they should not be.) *Context* is *intralingual* whereas *situation* is *extralingual.* (See SITUATION.)

CONTINUANT: A sound which can be prolonged indefinitely like *m* or *f*.

CONTINUUM: An uninterrupted sequence of steps or phases in a process. In foreign language learning, we speak of the stages in acquiring full listening comprehension, for example, as points or steps on a "continuum."

CONTRASTIVE ANALYSIS: A comparison of all the features of the native language of a learner which differ from those of the target language.

CO-OCCURRENCE: 1) The normal, permitted combination of words in an utterance; e.g., we can say, *I watched a film,* but not *I watched a book.* (The British term for this is "collocation.") 2) The environment (the surrounding words) of a word or structure; e.g., The Queen *of* (England).

COORDINATE SYSTEM: One in which the target language is learned as a parallel, completely independent system, without relation to the native language. (See COMPOUND SYSTEM.)

CORRELATION: 1) The act of bringing together learnings from more than one subject area for their mutual enrichment. 2) A positive or negative relationship betweeen two tests or two abilities or factors; e.g., There is not necessarily a high (or positive) correlation between intelligence and the ability to learn the elementary mechanisms of foreign language.

COUNT NOUN: One that can be modified by a numeral; e.g., four *apples. Ink* on the other hand is called a *mass noun* since it cannot easily be modified by a numeral.

COVERAGE (in semantic theory) includes: definition (Does the replacing word define the other?); inclusion as in synonyms; extension of a meaning to cover another; power of combination to form other words.

CUE: A stimulus which is given to elicit a response. The cue may be a gesture, a picture, a word, a sentence, etc. which is used to call forth a desired response.

CULTURAL ISLAND: The total immersion of the foreign language learners into the foreign culture through the continuous use of the foreign language in class, the display of its authentic materials, the listening to its speakers, etc.

CULTURE: The language, customs, values, beliefs, art forms, and achievements of a society.

CURRICULUM: The knowledge, information, skills, abilities, activities, materials, etc. which are included in the teaching of any subject.

DECODE: The process by which a hearer derives the total meaning (linguistic and cultural) of a verbal message. (See ENCODE.)

DEDUCTIVE PROCESS: One in which a rule is formulated first and then followed by examples which conform to it. (See INDUCTIVE PROCESS.)

DENOTATIVE: The dictionary meaning of a word. (See CONNOTATIVE.)

DERIVED: An utterance, word, or expression produced by the application of a transformation rule to a basic word or utterance; e.g., *kindness* is derived from *kind; Hamlet was written by Shakespeare* is derived from *Shakespeare wrote Hamlet.*

DETERMINER: A word such as an article, a possessive adjective, a partitive, which marks a noun; e.g., *the, a, some, each, any.*

DIAGNOSTIC TEST: One which permits the examiner to judge the student's strengths or weaknesses, problems or difficulties.

DIALECT: A variety of the national language used by members of a speech community living in a given geographical area.

DIPHTHONG: A sound which combines two vowel sounds; e.g., /ɔɪ/, /aʊ/.

DISTRACTOR: An incorrect item given purposely by the examiner in a test.

ENCODE: The process through which a speaker conveys his thought by means of a verbal message; to put thought into linguistic form. (See DECODE.)

ENVIRONMENT: 1) The surrounding sounds, syllables, or words of any element of language. 2) The surrounding community.

EQUIVALENT: A word, expression, utterance, or sentence in one language which is not a word-for-word translation of a word, etc. in another language but which conveys the same meaning.

EVALUATION: Tests (oral, written, short answer, essay, etc.) and other measures such as observation and/or questionnaires to ascertain results being achieved, and progress being made toward objectives of language learning.

FADE: 1) In teaching, the gradual withdrawal of cues so that the student is required to produce utterances on his own. 2) In speech, the lowered volume at the end of an utterance.

FEEDBACK; the control of one's performance derived from the awareness of its effects; e.g., the speaker controls his flow of speech by hearing his own words, or by listening to or noting the reaction of others.

FIT: The relationship between the sounds of the oral language and the writing systems which represent it.

FORMAL: Pertaining to the arrangement of sounds, letters, or words in an utterance.

FORMULA: A fixed expression of greeting, thanks, agreement, etc. such as *Thank you, How do you do* which native speakers use habitually in communication.

FORMULATE: Verbalize; put into words.

FRAME: 1) In programmed instruction, a minimal unit of instruction. 2) A syntactic pattern, each slot of which would always contain words of the same class (determiner, noun, verb, etc.).

FUNCTION: The grammatical role of an item or structure; e.g., subject, object.

FUNCTIONAL: Pertaining to real use; communicative.

FUNCTION WORDS: Words which have little or no meaning by themselves but which are used in utterances to signal grammatical relationships (e.g., auxiliaries and prepositions). With *content words*, they constitute the vocabulary or lexicon of a language.

GENERALIZATION: The verbalized "rule" or description of a language item which results from the learner's perception of its recurring, consistent sound, form, position, function, and meaning.

GENERATE: 1) In generative-transformational grammar, to list the rules which account for the existence of all the acceptable (well-formed) sentences in the language. 2) To create or produce.

HABIT: A permanent ability to act in a particular manner.

IDIOLECT: The way the individual uses the language of the community; his "parole."

IDIOM: An expression whose total meaning cannot be derived from the meaning of each individual word within it; e.g., *I can't do without you.*

IMMEDIATE CONSTITUENTS: Two or more units on one level of structure which form a single unit on the next higher level; e.g., The subject and predicate are IC's of the sentence; the verb phrase and complement are IC's of the predicate.

INCREMENTAL LEARNING: Learning in small steps.

INDUCTIVE PROCESS: One in which a series of examples or model sentences are given in order to enable the learner to formulate a generalization, description, or "rule." (See DEDUCTIVE PROCESS.)

INFLECTION: A change in the form of a word to indicate plurality, possession, etc.

INFORMANT: A native speaker or one with near native ability who may be used as an authentic resource person with relation to his language or culture.

INTEGRATION: 1) The process of combining related material or elements which belong together. 2) The fusion of different elements into a coherent whole. 3) In discussing individuals, one speaks of a well-adjusted, or well-integrated, personality.

INTERACTION: The give and take of communication.

INTERCHANGE: A conversation of two or more utterances.

INTERFERENCE: A difficulty or problem in the learning of one habit because of the existence in the learner of a conflicting one; e.g., the difficulty of learning to produce a sound in the target language because it does not exist or exists in another position in the learner's native tongue.

INTERNALIZE: To understand and learn material so thoroughly that it can be produced at will.

INTERVOCALIC: Between two vowels.

JACK: A box or other piece of equipment for a tape recorder to which additional headphones can be attached.

JUNCTURE: A change in the quality of sounds and in the meaning of an utterance produced by pauses in speech; e.g., nitrate/night rate; I scream/ice cream.

KERNEL SENTENCE: A basic sentence in a language—usually simple, active, and without modifiers—which can undergo many transformations based on a series of rules. A kernel sentence has two parts or two constituents: a noun phrase (NP) and a verb phrase (VP). ("Base" sentence is being used more frequently.)

KINESICS: The study of the non-verbal motions used in communication; e.g., gestures, facial expressions.

LANGUAGE FEELING: (Sprachgefühl) The intuitive awareness, resulting from intensive practice in the foreign language, enabling the learner to recognize and to control his production of well-formed sentences.

LANGUE: The total language system—the code—of the community as compared to an individual's expression (his "parole"). Both terms, "langue" and "parole," originated with Ferdinand De Saussure, a Swiss linguist.

LEARNING: The process which leads to the acquisition of any form of behavior.

LEVEL: 1) The height to which the voice rises or falls in speaking. In English, for example, we distinguish four pitch levels. 2) The stage of learning—beginning, intermediate, advanced. 3) The degree of achievement toward a goal.

LEXICAL COMBINATION: Words which co-occur; e.g., part of.

LEXICON: The words or vocabulary of the language.

LINGUISTICS: A science which systematically analyzes and describes a language as it is used by its native speakers. There are several branches of linguistic science; e.g., historical, comparative, contrastive, psycholinguistics, sociolinguistics.

MACHINE TRANSLATION: The equivalent of a text in one language rendered in another language by means of a computer.

MARKER: A word or morpheme that helps identify the function of another word; e.g., *'s* added to a singular noun indicates possession; *the* before a word identifies it as a nominal.

MASTER: 1) (verb) to learn thoroughly. 2) (noun) an original recording from which copies can be made.

METALINGUISTICS: 1) The scientific study of linguistics and its relation to other cultural factors in a society. *Paralinguistics, kinesics, proxemics,* for example, are included in metalinguistics. 2) The study of the language used to talk about language.

MIM-MEM: Mimicry-memorization. A teaching technique in which students imitate a model and then repeat it to the point of memorization.

MINIMAL PAIR: Two words that sound alike except for one *phonemic* difference; e.g., bag/back; ship/sheep; bit/pit.

MODEL: 1) The perfect or near-perfect production of a sound, word, or utterance given by the teacher or a recording for imitation by the learners. 2) A tentative or hypothetical design or explanation for any phenomenon.

MONITOR: To listen to students through any inter-communication device as they record.

MONOSTRUCTURAL APPROACH: A teaching method in which individual structures are presented one at a time through several examples and not in a dialogue or reading passage.

MORPHEME: The smallest meaningful unit of language. It may be "free" (a word such as *girl* which can stand alone) or "bound" (the *s* of *girls* which indicates plurality but which cannot stand alone).

MORPHOLOGY: The study of the changes in forms of words produced by inflection or derivation.

MORPHOPHONEMICS: The study of the relationships and changes in phonemes because of their environment or position within a word (a morpheme) or before another word; e.g., in English, the plural morpheme changes its sound depending on the final letter of the word (/z/ in *boys* but /s/ in *books* and ɪz/ in *boxes*).

MULTIPLE CHOICE TEST: One in which the student is asked to select an answer to a question or problem from among several choices given.

OPERANT CONDITIONING: The shaping (reinforcing or extinguishing) of the learner's responses through the forging of a bond between stimulus and response and confirmation of the correct response (termed "reward").

PARADIGM: A complete systematic set of the forms of a word or of a verb conjugation; e.g., English: I, me, my, mine; Spanish: present of the verb *hablar* (to speak): habl*o*, habl*as*, habl*a*, etc.

PARALINGUISTICS: The study of tone of voice, tempo of voice, groans, sighs, and other non-articulated sounds which convey meaning to a listener.

PAROLE: The individual speaker's use of language to convey messages.

PASSIVE KNOWLEDGE: that which is needed for understanding or recognition only; "receptive" knowledge as opposed to "active."

PATTERN: 1) An arrangement of sounds or words which recurs systematically and is meaningful. 2) The basic design that underlies a sentence.

PATTERN PRACTICE: Drills and activities in which the patterns of a language are learned to the point where students can repeat, alter, or respond to them habitually and fluently.

PAUSE: Another word for JUNCTURE.

PEER TEACHING: Two or more students helping each other to learn by practicing and engaging in communication activities with each other.

PERFORMANCE (in Generative-Transformational Theory): 1) The overt verbal behavior of a speaker. 2) An instance of a speaker's competence.

PERFORMANCE OBJECTIVE: The degree of learning of an item or a skill which a student is expected to achieve under certain well-defined, clearly specified conditions.

PERSONALIZATION: Relating dialogues, readings, etc. to the learners' lives and experiential background through questions.

PHATIC FUNCTION OF LANGUAGE: The ability of a speaker to start, interrupt, or discontinue a conversation.

PHONEMICS: The systematic study of the meaningful sounds of language.

PHONETICS: The study of the sounds of speech—the phonemes and the allophones—and the way they are produced, transmitted, and received by the listener.

PHONOTACTICS: The arrangement of sounds in a language; the study of the restrictions (inappropriate combinations) or arrangements of sounds.

PHRASE STRUCTURE RULE: One which governs the construction of the two basic parts of utterances: the noun phrase (NP) and the verb phrase (VP) of kernel (or base) sentences.

PITCH: A voice tone which distinguishes meaning.

PRAGMATICS: The study of the correlation of linguistic forms to situational settings.

PROFICIENCY TEST: One which permits the measurement of a person's knowledge and ability in a foreign language without regard to formal study or text used.

PROGNOSTIC TEST: One which permits the making of hypotheses about a person's possible success in language study. Synonym = APTITUDE TEST.

PROGRAMMED LEARNING: The systematic grading and sequencing of language material and its presentation in the smallest possible segments, generally in frames. The material to be learned (the program) is generally placed in a "teaching machine" or in a text. Since this is often used without an instructor, the device or text directs the student to proceed to the next step when his response has been correct; to go back to a previous step or engage in related drills if the response has been incorrect. It is generally self-pacing; that is, a student can work at his own speed.

PROMPT: To whisper a word or expression to the learner in order to help him produce an utterance.

PROP: A real object (a flag, a flower, a piece of bread) or any device used in teaching to simulate reality and to elicit student response.

PROXEMICS: The study of distances maintained by speakers of different languages as they speak to each other or to others.

PSYCHOLINGUISTICS: The scientific study of the relationships between linguistic data and psychological processes.

RECOMBINE: To bring together familiar sentences, dialogues, or reading passages in order to create new dialogues, etc. in which all the elements are familiar to the learners.

REDUNDANCY: The multiple clues in language, some of which could be eliminated without loss of essential information; e.g., in *The boys are wearing their coats,* the /z/ sound, the verb *are,* the possessive *their,* and the /s/ sound in *coats* all indicate plurality.

REENTRY: The systematic reuse or reintroduction of words and structures which have been learned with newly acquired language items (in dialogues, readings, etc.) in order to 1) keep them alive in the learners' minds, and 2) demonstrate that a word or pattern can be used in many different situations.

REFERENT: The actual object or situation in the real world to which a word is related or to which it refers.

REGISTER: The variation in language (in pronunciation, grammar, or vocabulary) as used by persons in different *jobs* or *professions,* in different *situations (formal* or *informal)* and in different *modes (speaking* or *writing).*

REINFORCEMENT: 1) The consolidation or further learning of material. 2) The confirmation or reward which increases the likelihood of a student's giving a correct response again at another time.

REJOINDER: An emphatic response given to a statement or question. The rejoinder may be a formula, another question, or another statement which reiterates or emphasizes the initial utterance.

RELIABILITY: The degree to which a test is consistent in measuring what it is supposed to measure.

RHETORIC: The method and study of the organization of syntactic units into larger patterns.

RHYTHM: The regularity of speech sequences.

RULE: 1) The description of the form, function, and position of a recurring systematic feature of language. 2) In transformation theory, the instructions or directions which account for the existence of kernel (base) sentences (Phrase Structure Rules) and derived sentences (Transformation Rules).

SEGMENT: A syllable of a word or a group of words in an utterance.

SEGMENTAL PHONEMES: The vowels and consonants.

SEMANTICS: The study of word meanings and their effect on communication, interaction, and interpersonal relationships.

SEMIOTICS: The study of the exchange of any messages whatsoever and of the signs which underlie them.

SHAPE: To lead the learner gradually to a closer approximation of the desired terminal behavior through successive listening and speaking experiences.

SIGN: The general term which designates anything which stands for or represents something else.

SITUATION: The relationship between the elements, events, or things present in the environment and the language used in talking about them; e.g., buying groceries in a market, going to a doctor's office, watching a television program.

SITUATIONAL TEACHING: A method in which the new structures or words for presentation *and* practice are embedded in an authentic conversation or in a narrative event, or in which they are taught in a context of situation.

SLOT: The position of a word or phrase in a sentence which can be occupied by other words or expressions of the same class; e.g., in "I went to the store," the slot *I* can be occupied by *He, Mary, The boys,* etc.

SPEECH: The oral expression of verbal behavior.

SPIRAL APPROACH: A method of presentation of material in which the same language item or cultural topic is taught in increasingly greater depth at each succeeding level of learning.

STIMULUS: Any signal (manual, oral, visual) to which a person responds or reacts. Also called a "cue."

STOP: A consonant which is made with a momentary stoppage of breath; e.g., /p/, /t/.

STRESS: The prominence of syllables or words in speech.

STRING: A sequence of language items. In transformational theory, the terminal string, for example, is the final sequence of words in an utterance that may have undergone one or more transformations.

STRUCTURE: 1) The recurring patterns of language elements as they occur in forms of words and in arrangements of words in utterances. 2) The grammar of the language. 3) A grammatical item that contains more than one word; e.g., *may have gone.* 4) Any organized, systematic item of language.

STRUCTURE DRILL: An exercise or oral activity in which patterns or structures are practiced.

STRUCTURE WORD: A synonym for FUNCTION WORD.

STYLISTICS: The study of the use of the most appropriate expression available, both connotatively and denotatively, to convey any idea.

SUPRASEGMENTAL PHONEMES: Pronunciation features of pitch, stress, and juncture which co-occur with or are superimposed on the vowels and consonants.

SYMBOL: A meaningful sign which is consciously produced; e.g., a word or a phonetic symbol.

SYNTAX: The arrangement of words in utterances and sentences.

SYSTEM: Sets of recurring combinations and sequences of sounds and words into patterns which signal meaning.

TAGMEME: 1) The slot and its filler. 2) A significant unit of syntax.

TARGET LANGUAGE: The foreign language that is being learned.

TAXONOMIC: Pertaining to the description and classification of structures of language.

TEACHING MACHINE: A mechanical device used in some forms of programmed instruction (See p. 115.)

TENSE: The *formal* categories of verb inflections; e.g., in English, we speak of the simple present and past tenses only: walk*s*; walk*ed*.

TERMINAL BEHAVIOR: The desired outcome that a learner should achieve in terms of the acquisition of some habit, skill, knowledge, or attitude.

TERMINAL CONTOUR: The intonation patterns at the end of an utterance. In English, for example, there are three: rising, falling, and sustained.

TRACK: 1) A pattern of subject or course organization in a school or school system. For example, in the first year of the secondary school, there may be two language tracks, one for students who had studied English in the elementary school and one for beginners. 2) A stretch or path along a tape on which a recording can be made.

TRANSFER: The ability to use knowledge about a feature of one's native language or of the target language in learning another related feature. (Negative transfer implies the making of false analogies.) (See p. 14.)

TRANSFER RULES (in Generative-Transformational Theory): These consist of two parts: 1) The phrase structure that base sentences must have before transfer rules can be applied. 2) The operation or sequence of operations producting a new sentence.

TRANSFORMATION THEORY: A theory of language analysis which assumes 1) that all utterances, the surface structure of the language, are derived from basic sentences—the deep structure of the language—by a series of rules; 2) that all native speakers have competence in recognizing well-formed sentences but cannot necessarily produce them; 3) that language is creative and stimulus-free. (See the Bibliography, p. 195, for further study.)

UNCONSCIOUS SELECTION: The habitual, fluent use of the correct sound, word form, or word arrangement in "free" communication.

USAGE: The selection by a speaker of a certain language variety or register.

UTTERANCE: A word, a fixed expression, or a sentence said by a speaker which has meaning, and before which and after which there is silence on his part.

VALIDITY: The degree to which a test measures what it is supposed to measure.

VARIATION: 1) A change of some kind. 2) In audio-lingual methodology, the asking of questions on the dialogue itself.

VARIETY OF LANGUAGE: Changes (phonological, syntactic, or lexical) within the *code* brought about by such factors as geography (in the case of dialects), social or professional role, situation (formal or informal), and mode (oral or written).

VERBAL BEHAVIOR: 1) Language. 2) Any manifestation of self-expression and/or communication.

VOICED SOUND: A sound made with the vocal cords vibrating; e.g., /b/, vowels.

VOICELESS SOUND: A sound made while the vocal cords are not vibrating; e.g., /p/.

Appendix VI
Bibliography

Following is a selected list of books for further reading. For your convenience, you will find them under the major topics treated in this Guide: Foundations—Structure—Methodology—Materials and Equipment—Testing and Evaluation. There will be some overlapping; e.g., some books listed under Foundations also contain material on Structure. Although you will find that some excellent materials (books and especially articles) are not mentioned, there are many helpful resources listed in the Bibliographies below and in the end Bibliographies of other texts listed in Section 2.

Bibliographies

AARONS, A. "TESOL Bibliography" in *Florida Foreign Language Reporter,* January 1965.

ALLEN, H. *Linguistics and English Linguistics.* New York: Appleton-Century-Crofts, 1966.

ALLEN, V. F. and S. FORMAN. *English as a Second Language.* New York: Teachers College Press, 1967.

BAKER, H. *A Checklist of Books and Articles for Teachers of English as a Foreign Language.* NAFSA. New York: 1959.

BIRKMAIER, E. and D. LANGE. "A Selective Bibliography on the Teaching of Foreign Languages 1920-1966" in *Foreign Language Annals I.* New York: Modern Language Association (MLA), May 1968.

BROZ, J. and A. HAYES. *Linguistics and Reading.* Arlington, Va.: Center for Applied Linguistics (CAL), 1966.

CHAMBERLAIN, J. *Source Materials for Teachers of Foreign Languages.* Washington, D.C.: National Education Assoc. (NEA), 1968.

DINGWALL, W. O. *Transformational Generative Grammar.* Arlington, Va.: CAL, 1965.

EATON, E., M. HAYES and H. O'LEARY. *Source Materials for Secondary School Teachers of Foreign Languages.* Washington, D. C.: USOE, 1966.

English as a Second Language in Elementary Schools: Background and Text Materials. Arlington, Va.: CAL, 1966.

English Teaching Bibliography. The British Council, London, England.

FRANK, M. *Annotated Bibliography of Materials for English as a Second Language.* New York: NAFSA, 1962.

HAMMER, J. and F. RICE. *A Bibliography of Contrastive Linguistics.* Arlington, Va.: CAL, 1965.

JOHNSTON, M. and A. JEWETT. *Resources for Teaching English. References for Teachers of English as a Foreign Language.* Washington, D. C.: USOE, 1956.

KEESEE, E. *References of Foreign Languages in the Elementary Schools.* Washington, D. C.: USOE, 1963.

LADO, R. *Annotated Bibliography for Teachers of English as a Foreign Language.* Washington, D. C.: U. S. Government Printing Office, 1955.

Language Teaching Bibliography. London: Center for Information on Language Teaching, 1968.

MALKOC, A. *TESOL Bibliography:* Abstracts of ERIC Publications and Research Reports. Washington, D. C. TESOL: Georgetown University Press, 1971.

NOSTRAND, H. L. (ed.). *Research on Language Teaching. An Annotated International Bibliography.* Seattle, Wash.: U. of Washington Press, 1965.

O'HANESSIAN, S. *Interim Bibliography on the Teaching of English to Speakers of Other Languages.* Arlington, Va.: CAL, 1963

_______. *30 Books for Teachers of English as a Foreign Language.* Arlington, Va.: CAL, 1967.

_______ and R. WINEBERG. *TESOL in Adult Education Programs: An Annotated Bibliography.* Arlington, Va.: CAL, 1966.

OLLMAN, M. J. *MLA Selective List of Materials for Use by Teachers of Modern Foreign Languages in Elementary and Secondary Schools.* New York: MLA, 1965.

PEDTKE, D. et al. *Reference List of Materials for English as a Second Language.* Arlington, Va.: CAL, 1969.

RICE, F. and A. GUSS. *Information Sources in Linguistics.* Arlington, Va.: CAL, 1965.

ROBINSON, J. (comp.). *An Annotated Bibliography of Modern Language Teaching (1946-67).* London: Oxford U. Press, 1969.

RUTHERFORD, P. *A Bibliography of American Doctoral Dissertations in Linguistics*. Washington, D. C.: CAL, 1968.

SABLESKI, J. (ed.). "A Selected Annotated Bibliography on Child Language" in *Linguistic Reporter*. Washington, D. C.: CAL, Vol. 7, No. 2, April 1966.

SHEN, Y. and R. CRYMES. *Teaching English as a Second Language*. Honolulu: East-West Center Press, 1965.

STEHLIK, V. *An International Bibliography of Foreign Language Teaching Methods for 1967*. Prague: Academy of Sciences, 1969.

SVOBODNY, D. *Research and Studies about the Use of Television and Films in Foreign Language Instruction: A Bibliography with Abstracts*. New York: MLA, 1969.

UNESCO. *A Bibliography on the Teaching of Foreign Languages*. Paris, 1955.

WALTERS, T. *The Georgetown Bibliography of Studies Contributing to the Psycho-Linguistics of Language Learning*. Washington, D.C.: Georgetown U. Press, 1965.

WYLIE, L. et al. *Six Cultures. Selected and Annotated Bibliographies*. New York: MLA, 1961.

Books

Foundations

(Linguistics, Psychology, Anthropology, Psycholinguistics, Sociolinguistics, Educational Theory.)

AGARD, F. B. and H. DUNKEL. *An Investigation of Second Language Teaching*. Boston: Ginn, 1948.

ALATIS, J. (ed.). *Bilingualism and Language Contact: Anthropological, Linguistic, Psychological, and Sociological Aspects*. Washington, D. C.: Georgetown University Press, 1971.

ALLEN, H. B. (ed.). *Readings in Applied English Linguistics* (second edition). Appleton-Century-Crofts, 1972.

ANDERSON, J. *The Grammar of Case*. Cambridge, England: Cambridge University Press, 1971.

ANDERSON, W. and N. STAGEBERG. *Introductory Readings on Language*. New York: Holt, Rinehart and Winston, (rev.) 1966.

AUSUBEL, D. *Educational Psychology: A Cognitive View*. New York: Holt, Rinehart and Winston, 1968.

BACH, E. *An Introduction to Transformational Grammar*. New York: Holt, Rinehart and Winston, 1963.

——— and R. HARMS (eds.). *Universals in Linguistic Theory*. New York: Holt, Rinehart and Winston, 1968.

BARRUTIA, R. *Linguistic Theory of Language Learning as Related to Machine Teaching.* Heidelberg: Verlag, 1969.
BELYAVEV, B. L. *The Psychology of Teaching Foreign Languages.* New York: Macmillan, 1964.
BENEDICT, R. *Patterns of Culture.* Boston: Houghton Mifflin, 1934.
BLOOMFIELD, L. *Language.* New York: Henry Holt, 1933.
BOAS, F. *Race, Language and Culture.* New York: Macmillan, 1940.
BOLINGER, D. *Aspects of Language.* New York: Harcourt Brace Jovanovich, 1968.
BRUNER, J. *The Process of Education.* Cambridge, Mass.: Harvard University Press, 1961.
______, R. OLIVER, and M. GREENFIELD. *Studies in Cognitive Growth.* New York: John Wiley and Sons, 1966.
BURLING, R. *Man's Many Voices. Language in its Cultural Context.* New York: Holt, Rinehart and Winston, 1970.
CARROLL, J. B. *Research on Teaching Foreign Languages.* Cambridge, Mass., Harvard University Press, 1960.
______. *The Study of Language.* Cambridge, Mass.: Harvard University Press, 1953.
______. *Language and Thought.* Englewood Cliffs, New Jersey: Prentice Hall, (new ed.) 1965.
CHERRY, C. *On Human Communication.* New York: Wiley, 1961.
CHOMSKY, N. *Aspects of the Theory of Syntax.* Cambridge, Mass.: M.I.T. Press, 1965.
______. *Language and Mind.* New York: Harcourt Brace Jovanovich, 1968.
______. *Syntactic Structures.* Gravenhage, The Netherlands: Mouton, 1957.
______. *Studies on Semantics in Generative Grammar.* The Hague: Mouton, 1972.
CRYSTAL, D. *Linguistics.* London, England: Penguin, 1971.
DE CECCO, J. (ed.). *The Psychology of Language, Thought and Instruction.* New York: Holt, Rinehart and Winston, 1967.
DE SAUSSURE, F. *Course in General Linguistics.* New York: Philosophical Library, 1959.
DINEEN, F. *An Introduction to General Linguistics.* New York: Holt, Rinehart and Winston, 1966.
DI PIETRO, R. *Language Structures in Contrast.* Rowley, Mass.: Newbury House, 1971.
DUNKEL, H. *Second Language Learning.* Boston: Ginn, 1948.
EMIG, J. A. et al. *Language and Learning.* New York: Harcourt Brace Jovanovich, 1966.
FERGUSON, C. A. and W. A. STEWART (eds.). *Linguistic Reading Lists for Teachers of Modern Languages.* Arlington, Va.: CAL, 1963.

FILLMORE, C. J. "The Case for Case" in E. BACH and R. T. HARMS (eds.) *Universals in Linguistic Theory.* New York: Holt, Rinehart and Winston, 1968.

FIRTH, J. R. *The Tongues of Men and Speech.* London: Oxford University Press, 1964.

FISHMAN, J. *Readings in the Sociology of Language.* The Hague: Mouton, 1969.

———. *Sociolinguistics.* Rowley, Mass.: Newbury House, 1970.

FODOR, J. and J. KATZ (eds.). *The Structure of Language: Readings in the Philosophy of Language.* Englewood Cliffs, New Jersey: Prentice Hall, 1964.

GREENBERG, J. *Anthropological Linguistics: An Introduction.* New York: Random House, 1968.

———. *Language, Culture and Communication.* Stanford, California: Stanford University Press, 1971.

———, (ed.). *Universals of Language.* Cambridge, Mass.: M.I.T. Press, 1966.

HALL, E. T. *The Hidden Dimension.* Garden City, N. Y.: Doubleday, 1966.

———. *The Silent Language.* Garden City, N. Y.: Doubleday, 1959.

HALL, R. *An Introduction to Linguistics.* Phila., Pa.: Chilton 1965.

———. *Linguistics and Your Language.* Garden City, N. Y.: Doubleday, 1960.

HALLIDAY, M., A. MCINTOSH, A. and P. STEVENS. *The Linguistic Sciences and Language Teaching.* London: Longmans Green, 1964.

HARMS, R. T. *Introduction to Phonological Theory.* Englewood Cliffs, New Jersey: Prentice Hall, 1968.

HARRIS, Z. S. *Structural Linguistics.* Chicago: University of Chicago Press, 1963.

HARSH, W. *Grammar Instruction Today.* Davis, California: Davis Publications in English, No. 1, 1965.

HAYAKAWA. S. I. *Language in Thought and Action.* New York: Harcourt Brace Jovanovich, 1964.

———. *Symbol, Status and Personality.* New York: Harcourt Brace Jovanovich, 1958.

HJELMSLEV, L. *Prolegomena to a Theory of Language.* Madison, Wisconsin: Wisconsin University Press, 1961.

HOIJER, H. (ed.). *Language in Culture.* Chicago: University of Chicago Press, 1954.

HORNBY, A. S. *Essential Linguistic Foundations of Foreign Language Teaching.* London, England: Oxford University Press, 1962.

HUGHES, J. *The Science of Language.* New York: Random House, 1962.

HYMES, D. (ed.). *Language in Culture and Society. A Reader in Linguistics and Anthropology.* New York: Harper and Row, 1964.

JACOBOVITS, L. *Foreign Language Learning: A Psycholinguistic Analysis of the Issues.* Rowley, Mass.: Newbury House, 1970.

______ and M. MIRON. *Readings in the Psychology of Language.* Englewood Cliffs, New Jersey: Prentice Hall, 1967.

JACOBS, R. and P. ROSENBAUM. *English Transformational Grammar.* Waltham, Mass.: Blaisdell Publishing Co., 1968.

JACOBSON, R. and M. HALLE. *Fundamentals of Language.* The Hague: Mouton, 1956.

JESPERSEN, O. *Language: Its Nature, Development and Origin.* London: Allen and Unwin, 1922.

______. *The Philosophy of Grammar.* London: Allen and Unwin, 1958.

JOOS, M. (ed.). *Readings in Linguistics: The Development of Descriptive Linguistics in America.* Chicago: University of Chicago Press, 1966.

______. *The Five Clocks.* New York: Harcourt Brace Jovanovich, 1967.

KANSLER, D. H. *Readings in Verbal Learning.* New York: John Wiley and Sons, 1966.

KATZ, J. *The Philosophy of Language.* New York: Harper and Row, 1966.

______. and P. POSTAL. *An Integrated Theory of Linguistic Descriptions.* Cambridge, Mass.: M.I.T. Press, 1964.

KELLY, L. *25 Centuries of Language Teaching.* Rowley, Mass.: Newbury House, 1969.

KLUCKHOHN C. *Culture and Behavior.* New York: The Free Press, 1962.

______. *Mirror for Man.* New York: McGraw Hill, 1949.

KROEBER, A. L. (ed.). *Anthropology Today.* Chicago: University of Chicago Press, 1953.

LADO, R. *Linguistics Across Cultures.* Ann Arbor, Mich.: University of Michigan Press, 1957.

LAMBERT, W. and R. GARDNER. *Attitudes and Motivation in Second Language Learning.* Rowley, Mass.: Newbury House, 1972

______ and O. KLINEBERG. *Children's Views of Foreign Peoples.* New York: Appleton-Century-Crofts, 1967.

______. "Psychological Approaches to the Study of Language" in the *Modern Language Journal.* March 1963.

______. "A Study of the Relationship of Attitudes and Motivation in Second Language Learning" in the *Modern Language Journal,* 47, pp. 114-121.

LANDAR, H. *Language and Culture.* New York: Oxford University Press, 1965.

LENNEBERG, E. *Biological Foundations of Language.* New York: John Wiley, 1967.

LEOPOLD, W. F. *Speech Development of a Bilingual Child.* Evanston, Ill.: Northwestern University Press, 1949.

LUGTON, R. (ed.). *English as a Second Language: Current Issues.* Philadelphia, Pa.: The Center for Current Development, Inc., 1970.

LYONS, J. *Introduction to General Linguistics.* Cambridge, England: Cambridge University Press, 1968.

MALINOWSKI, B. *A Scientific Theory of Culture and Other Essays.* New York: Oxford University Press, 1960.

MALSTROM, J. *Language in Society.* New York: Hayden, 1965.

MARCKWARDT, A. *Linguistics and the Teaching of English.* Bloomington, Ind.: University of Indiana Press, 1966.

________. *Studies in Languages and Linguistics in Honor of Charles Fries.* Ann Arbor, Mich.: English Language Institute, 1964.

MARTINET, A. *Elements of General Linguistics.* London: Faber, 1964 and University of Chicago Press, 1964.

________. *A Functional View of Language.* Oxford, England: The Clarendon Press, 1962.

MCINTOSH A. and M. HALLIDAY. *Patterns of Language: Papers in General, Descriptive and Applied Linguistics.* London: Longmans Green, 1966.

MEAD, M. *Continuity in Cultural Evolution.* New Haven, Conn.: Yale University Press, 1964.

The Meaning and Role of Culture in Foreign Language Teaching. Washington, D.C.: Georgetown University, School of Languages and Linguistics, 1961.

MILLER, G. A. *Language and Communication.* New York: McGraw Hill, 1963.

MONTAGU, A. *The Cultured Man.* New York: World Publishing Co., 1958.

MOULTON, W. *A Linguistic Guide to Language Learning.* New York: (MLA), 1966.

NAJAN, E. (ed.). *Language Learning: The Individual and the Process.* Bloomington, Ind.: Indiana University Press, 1966.

NILSEN, D. "The Use of Case Grammar in Teaching English as a Foreign Language" in *TESOL Quarterly,* Vol. 5, pp. 293-301, December 1971.

ORNSTEIN, J. and W. GAGE. *The ABC's of Languages and Linguistics.* Philadelphia, Pa.: Chilton, 1964.

OSGOOD, C. and T. SEBEOK. *Psycholinguistics: A Survey of Theory and Research Problems.* Bloomington, Ind.: Indiana University Press, 1965.

PALMER, F. R. *Grammar*. London, England: Penguin, 1971.
PAST, R. *Language as a Lively Art*. Dubuque, Iowa: Brown, 1970.
PEAL, E. and W. LAMBERT. "The Relation of Bilingualism to Intelligence" in *Foreign Language Teaching* (J. Michel, ed.). New York: Macmillan, 1967.
PEI, M. *Glossary of Linguistic Terminology*. New York: Doubleday, 1966.
________. *An Invitation to Linguistics*. New York: Doubleday, 1965.
PIAGET, J. *The Language and Thought of the Child*. New York: Humanities Press, 1959.
PIKE, K. *Language in Relation to a Unified Theory of the Structure of Human Behavior*. The Hague: Mouton (second revised ed.) 1967.
PIMSLEUR, P. and T. QUINN (eds.). *The Psychology of Second Language Learning*. Cambridge, England: The Cambridge University Press, 1972.
POLITZER, R. *Linguistics and Applied Linguistics: Aims and Methods*. Philadelphia, Pa.: The Center for Curriculum Development, Inc., 1972.
POSTAL, P. *Aspects of Phonological Theory*. New York: Harper, 1968.
POSTMAN, N. and C. WEINGARTNER. *Linguistics: A Revolution in Teaching*. New York: Dell, 1967.
POTTER, S. *Modern Linguistics*. New York: Norton, 1964.
REIBEL, D. and S. SCHANE (eds.). *Modern Studies in English: Readings in Transformational Grammar*. Englewood Cliffs, New Jersey: Prentice Hall, 1970.
RIVERS, W. *The Psychologist and the Foreign Language Teacher*. Chicago: University of Chicago Press, 1964.
ROBINS, R. H. *General Linguistics: An Introductory Survey*. London: Longmans Green, 1964 and Indiana University, 1965.
ROSENBERG, S. (ed.). *Directions in Psycholinguistics*. New York: Macmillan, 1965.
________ and J. H. KOPLIN. *Developments in Applied Psycholinguistic Research*. New York: Macmillan, 1968.
SAMARIN, W. *Field Linguistics: A Guide*. New York: Holt, Rinehart and Winston, 1967.
SAPIR, E. *Culture, Language and Personality*. Berkeley, Calif.: University of California Press, 1956.
________. *Language: An Introduction to the Study of Speech*. New York: Harcourt Brace Jovanovich, 1921.
SAPORTA, S. and J. R. BASTMAN (eds.). *Psycholinguistics: A Book of Readings*. New York: Holt, Rinehart and Winston, 1961.
SEBEOK, T. (ed.). *Current Trends in Linguistics*. The Hague: Mouton, 1968.

SKINNER, B. *Verbal Behavior.* New York: Appleton, 1957.
SMITH, D. and R. SHUY. *Sociolinguistics in Cross-Cultural Perspective.* Washington, D.C.: Georgetown University Press, 1972.
STERN, H. (ed.). *Languages and the Young Child.* London: Oxford University Press, 1969.
STREVENS, P. D. *Papers in Language and Language Teaching.* London: Oxford University Press, 1965.
STURTEVANT, E. *An Introduction to Linguistic Science.* New Haven, Conn.: Yale University Press, 1947.
TITONE, R. *Studies in the Psychology of Language Learning.* Zurich, Switzerland: P.A.S., 1964.
———. *Teaching Foreign Languages: An Historical Sketch.* Washington, D.C.: Georgetown University Press, 1968.
ULLMANN, S. *Semantics: An Introduction to the Science of Meaning.* Oxford, England: Blackwell, 1962.
VYGOTSKY, L. *Thought and Language.* New York: John Wiley and Sons, 1961.
WALLWORD, J. *Language and Linguistics.* London, England: Heinemann, 1969.
WARDHAUGH, R. *Topics in Applied Linguistics.* Rowley, Mass.: Newbury House, 1973.
WEINREICH, U. *Languages in Contact.* New York: Linguistic Circle of New York, 1953.
WHORF, B. *Language, Thought, and Reality.* Cambridge, Mass.: M.I.T., 1956.
WILSON, G. (ed.). *A Linguistics Reader.* New York: Harper and Row, 1967.

Structure
(Phonetics, Phonemics, Morphology, Syntax, Vocabulary.)

ALLEN, R. et al. *English Sounds and their Spellings.* New York: Crowell, 1966.
———. *A Modern Grammar of Written English.* New York: Macmillan, 1965.
BALL, W. *A Practical Guide to Colloquial Idioms.* London: Longmans Green, 1958.
BLOCK, B. and G. TRAGER. *Outline of Linguistic Analysis.* Baltimore: Linguistic Society of America, 1942
BOLINGER, D. *Interrogative Structures of American English.* Alabama: The University of Alabama Press, 1957.
BRENGELMAN, F. *The English Language: An Introduction for Teachers.* Englewood Cliffs, N.J.: Prentice Hall, 1970.

BRONSTEIN, A. *The Pronunciation of American English.* New York: Appleton-Century-Crofts, 1960.

BUCHANAN, C. *A Programmed Introduction to Linguistics–Phonetics–Phonemics.* Boston, Mass.: D.C. Heath, 1963.

CALFORD, J. and C. OGDEN. *Word-Stress and Sentence-Stress.* London: Basic English Publishing Co., 1956.

CAMPBELL, R. N. and J. W. LINDFORS. *Insights into English Structure: A Programmed Course.* Englewood Cliffs, N.J.: Prentice Hall, 1969.

CATTELL, N. *The New English Grammar: A Descriptive Introduction.* Cambridge, Mass.: M.I.T. Press, 1969.

CHAFE, W. *Meaning and Structure of Language.* Chicago, Ill.: University of Chicago Press, 1970.

CHOMSKY, N. and M. HALLE. *The Sound Patterns of English.* New York: Harper and Row, 1968.

CROWELL, T. *Modern Spoken English.* New York: McGraw Hill, 1961.

English Pronunciation: A Manual for Teachers. New York: Collier Macmillan International (English Language Services, Inc.), 1968.

FERGUSON, C. (Gen. ed.). *Contrastive Structure Series.* Chicago, Ill.: University of Chicago Press, 1960-1965.

______. *Essays: Language Structure and Language Use.* Stanford, Calif.: Stanford University Press, 1971.

FRANCIS, N. *The Structure of American English.* New York: Ronald Press, 1958.

FRIES, C. *The Structure of English.* New York: Harcourt Brace Jovanovich, 1952.

______ and R. LADO. *English Pronunciation.* Ann Arbor, Mich.: University of Michigan Press, 1954.

________________. *English Sentence Patterns.* Ann Arbor, Mich.: University of Michigan Press, 1954.

________________. *Lessons in Vocabulary.* Ann Arbor, Mich.: University of Michigan Press, 1956.

GLEASON, H. *An Introduction to Descriptive Linguistics.* New York: Holt, Rinehart and Winston, 1961.

______. *Linguistics and English Grammar.* New York: Holt, Rinehart and Winston, 1965.

HERNDON, J. *A Survey of Modern Grammars.* New York: Holt, Rinehart and Winston, 1970.

HILL, A. *Introduction to Linguistic Structures.* New York: Harcourt Brace Jovanovich, 1958.

HOCKETT, C. F. *A Course in Modern Linguistics.* New York: Macmillan, 1958.

HORNBY, A. S. *A Guide to Patterns and Usage in English.* London: Oxford University Press, 1954.

JESPERSEN, O. *Essentials of English Grammar*. New York: Holt, Rinehart and Winston, 1933.

JONES, D. *An Outline of English Phonetics*. Cambridge, England: Heffer, 1960.

JONES, L. and J. WEPMAN. *A Spoken Word Count*. Chicago: Language Research Associates, 1966.

KING, H. *English Phonology: Guide and Workbook*. Ann Arbor, Mich.: Ann Arbor Publishers, 1961.

______. *Guide and Workbook in the Structure of English*. Englewood Cliffs, N.J.: Prentice Hall, 1967.

______. *The Verb Forms of English*. New York: Longmans Green, 1957.

KINGDON, R. *The Groundwork of English Intonation*. London: Longmans Green, 1958.

KRUISINGA, E. *An Introduction to the Study of English Sounds*. Groningen, The Netherlands: Noordhoff, 1960.

KUFNER, H. *The Grammatical Structure of English and German*. Chicago, Ill.: University of Chicago Press, 1963.

LAKOFF, G. *Irregularity in Syntax*. New York: Holt, Rinehart and Winston, 1970.

LANGACKER, R. *Language and its Structure*. New York: Harcourt Brace Jovanovich, 1968.

LEES, R. *The Grammar of English Nominalizations*. Bloomington, Ind.: Indiana University Press, 1968.

LONG, R. *The Sentence and Its Parts*. Chicago, Ill.: University of Chicago Press, 1961.

MARCKWARDT, A. *American English*. New York: Oxford University Press, 1958.

______ and R. QUIRK. *A Common Language*. New York: MLA, 1964.

PIKE, K. *The Intonation of American English*. Ann Arbor, Mich.: University of Michigan Press, 1953.

______. *Phonemics*. Ann Arbor, Mich.: University of Michigan Press, 1947.

PRATOR, C. and B. ROBINETT. *A Manual of American English Pronunciation*. New York: Holt, Rinehart and Winston, 1972.

QUIRK, R. *The Use of English*. London: Longmans Green, 1962.

______, S. GREENBAUM, G. LEECH, and J. SVARTIK. *A Grammar of Contemporary English*. London: Longmans Green, 1972.

ROBERTS, P. *English Sentences*. New York: Harcourt Brace Jovanovich, 1962.

______. *English Syntax*. New York: Harcourt Brace Jovanovich, 1964.

______. *Understanding English*. New York: Harper and Row, 1958.

SHEN, Y. *Articulation Diagrams of English Vowels and English Consonants*. Ann Arbor, Mich.: Braun and Brumfield, 1965.

______. *English Phonetics (Especially for Teachers of English as a*

Foreign Language). Ann Arbor, Mich.: Braun and Brumfield, 1962.

______. *The Pronunciation of American English for Teachers of English as a Foreign Language*. Ann Arbor, Mich.: University of Michigan Press, 1964.

SLEDD, J. *A Short Introduction to English Grammar*. New York: Scott Foresman and Co., 1959.

STAGEBERG, N. *An Introduction to English Grammar*. New York: Holt, Rinehart and Winston, 1965.

STRANG, B. *Modern English Structure*. New York: St. Martin's Press, 1962.

THOMAS, O. (ed.). *The Structure of Language*. Indianapolis, Ind.: Bobbs-Merrill, 1967.

THORNDIKE, E. and I. LORGE. *The Teacher's Wordbook of 30,000 Words*. New York: Teachers College, Columbia University, 1944.

TRAGER, E. and S. HENDERSON. *The PD's: Pronunciation Drills for Learners of English*. Washington, D. C.: English Language Services, Inc., 1956.

TRAGER, G. and H. SMITH. *An Outline of English Structure*. Washington, D. C.: American Council of Learned Societies, 1957.

TROUBETZKOY, N. *Introduction to the Principles of Phonological Descriptions*. The Hague: Maritmes Nojhoff, 1968.

WEST, M. *A General Service List of English Words*. London: Longmans Green, 1953.

ZANDVOORT, R. *A Handbook of English Grammar*. Englewood Cliffs, N.J.: Prentice Hall, 1966.

Methodology

ABERCROMBIE, D. *Problems and Principals: Studies in the Teaching of English as a Second Language*. London: Longmans Green, 1964.

ALLEN, H. and R. CAMPBELL (eds.). *Teaching English as a Second Language: A Book of Readings*. New York: McGraw Hill, 1972.

ALTMAN, H. *Individualizing the Foreign Language Classroom*. Rowley, Mass.: Newbury House, 1972.

BENNETT, W. A. *Aspects of Language and Language Teaching*. Cambridge, England: Cambridge University Press, 1968.

BILLOWS, F. L. *The Techniques of Language Teaching*. London: Longmans Green, 1961.

BLOOMFIELD, L. *Outline Guide for the Practical Study of Foreign Languages*. Baltimore: Linguistic Society of America, 1942.

______ and C. BARNHART. *Let's Read, A Linguistic Approach*. Detroit: Wayne State University Press, 1961.

BROOKS, N. *Language and Language Learning*. New York: Harcourt Brace Jovanovich, 1964.

BUMPASS, F. *Teaching Young Students English as a Foreign Language.* New York: American Book Co., 1963.

CHAPMAN, L. R. *Teaching English to Beginners.* London: Longmans Green, 1966.

CLOSE, Q. *English as a Foreign Language.* London: Allen and Unwin, 1962.

CORNELIUS, E. *Language Teaching: A Guide for Teachers of Foreign Languages.* New York: Thomas Y. Crowell Co., 1953.

CROFT, K. (ed.). *Readings in English as a Second Language.* Cambridge, Mass.: Winthrop Publishers, 1972.

DACANAY, F. R. and D. BOWEN. *Techniques and Procedures in Second Language Teaching.* Dobbs Ferry, New York: Oceana, 1967.

DERRICK, J. *Teaching English to Immigrants.* London: Longmans Green, 1969.

DIXSON, R. J. *Practical Guide to the Teaching of English as a Foreign Language.* New York: Regents Publishing Co., 1960.

DODSON, C. J. *Language Teaching and the Bilingual Method.* London: Pitman & Sons, 1967.

FINOCCHIARO, M. *Teaching Children Foreign Languages.* New York: McGraw Hill, rev. ed. 1964.

———. *Teaching English as a Second Language.* New York: Harper and Row, rev. ed. 1969.

——— and M. BONOMO. *The Foreign Language Learner.* New York: Regents Publishing Co., 1973.

FRAZER, H. and W. R. O'DONNELL (eds.). *Applied Linguistics and the Teaching of English.* London: Longmans Green, 1969.

FRENCH, F. G. *Teaching English as an International Language.* London: Oxford University Press, 1965.

FRIES, C. *Linguistics and Reading.* New York: Holt, Rinehart and Winston, 1963.

———. *Teaching and Learning English as a Foreign Langauge.* Ann Arbor, Mich.: University of Michigan Press, 1948.

———, and A. FRIES. *Foundations for English Teaching.* Tokyo, Japan: Kenkynsha English Language Exploratory Committee, 1961.

FRISBY, A. *Teaching English. Notes and Comments on Teaching English Overseas.* London: Longmans Green, 1957.

GATENBY, E. V. *English as a Second Language.* London: Longmans Green, 1944.

GAUNTLETT, J. C. *Teaching English as a Foreign Language.* London: Macmillan, 1957.

GIRARD, D. *Linguistics and Foreign Language Teaching.* London: Longmans Green, 1972.

GOUIN, F. *The Art of Teaching and Studying Language.* London: G. Phillips and Son, 1912.

GRITTNER, F. *Foreign Language Teaching in America's Schools.* New York: Harper and Row, 1969.
GURREY, P. *Teaching English as a Foreign Language.* London: Longmans Green, 1955.
_______. *Teaching English Grammar.* London: Longmans Green, 1964.
HALL, R. A. *Sound and Spelling in English.* Phila., Pa.: Chilton, 1961.
HORNBY, A. *The Teaching of Structural Words and Phrases, Stages 1-2.* London: Oxford University Press, 1959-61.
_______. *The Teaching of Structural Words and Sentence Patterns.* London: Oxford University Press, 1959-62.
HUGHES, J. B. *Linguistics and Language Teaching.* New York; Random House, 1968.
JESPERSEN, O. *How to Teach a Foreign Language.* London: George Allen & Unwin Ltd., reissued 1961.
KARP, T., P. O'CONNOR, and B. W. ROBINETT. *Principles and Methods of Teaching a Second Language: A Motion Picture Series.* Washington, D.C.: CAL, 1963.
KEESEE, E. *Modern Foreign Languages in the Elementary School.* Washington, D.C.: U. S. Department of Health, Education and Welfare, Bulletin N. 29, 1960.
LADO, R. *Language Teaching.* New York: McGraw Hill, 1964.
LAWRENCE, N. *Writing as a Thinking Process.* Ann Arbor, Mich.: University of Michigan Press, 1972.
LEFEVRE, C. A. *Linguistics and the Teaching of Reading.* New York: McGraw Hill, 1964.
LEVENSON, S. and W. KENDRICK (eds.). *Readings in Foreign Languages for the Elementary School.* Waltham, Mass.: Blaisdell, 1967.
MACKEY, W. F. *Language Teaching Analysis.* London: Longmans Green, 1965.
MATHIEU, G. (ed.). *Advances in the Teaching of Modern Languages.* London: Pergamon Press, 1962.
MÉRAS, E. A. *A Language Teacher's Guide.* New York: Harper and Row, (second ed.), 1962.
MICHEL, J. (ed.). *Foreign Language Teaching: An Anthology.* New York: Macmillan, 1966.
MORRIS, I. *The Art of Teaching English as a Living Language.* London: Macmillan, 1954.
NIDA, E. *Learning a Foreign Language* (a handbook prepared especially for missionaries). New York: Free Press, 1960.
_______. *Toward a Science of Translating.* London: E. J. Brill, 1964.
O'CONNOR, P. *Modern Foreign Language in High School: Pre-reading Instruction.* Washington, D.C.: U.S.O.E., 1960.
OINAS, F. J. *Language Teaching Today.* Bloomington, Ind.: Indiana University Press, 1960.

Oral English: Planning and Conducting Conversation Classes and Discussion Groups. Washington, D.C.: Information Center Service, U.S.I.S., 1963.

PALMER, H. *Principles of Language Study.* London: Oxford University Press, 1964.

_______. *The Teaching of Oral English.* London: Longmans Green, 1940.

PIERCE, J. E. *A Bilingual Method of Teaching Second Languages.* New York: Pageant Press, 1968.

PIMSLEUR et al. *Under-Achievement in Foreign Language Learning.* New York: MLA, 1966.

POLITZER, R. *Foreign Language Learning.* Englewood Cliffs, N.J.: Prentice Hall, 1965.

_______. *Performance Criteria for Foreign Language Learners.* Stanford, Calif.: Stanford University Press, 1966.

_______ and F. POLITZER. *Teaching English as a Second Language.* Lexington, Mass.: Xerox College Publications, 1972.

Proceedings of Stanford Conferences on Individualizing of Instruction in Foreign Languages. Rowley, Mass.: Newbury House, 1971.

RICHARDS, J. *Language Learning and Language Teaching.* Rowley, Mass.: Newbury House, 1972.

RIVERS, W. *Teaching Foreign Language Skills.* Chicago: University of Chicago Press, 1968.

ROBINSON, L. *Guided Writing.* New York: Harper and Row, 1967.

RONCEK, J. (ed.). *The Study of Foreign Languages.* New York: Philosophical Library, 1968.

SCHERER, G. and M. WERTHEIMER. *A Psycholinguistic Experiment in Foreign Language Teaching.* New York: McGraw Hill, 1964.

SPOLSKY, B. *The Language Education of Minority Children.* Rowley, Mass.: Newbury House, 1972.

STEVICK, E. *Helping People Learn English.* Nashville, Tenn.: Abingdon Press, 1957.

_______. *A Workbook in Language Teaching.* (with special reference to English as a foreign language). Nashville, Tenn.: Abingdon Press, 1964.

STRYKER, S. *Teaching American English.* Rowley, Mass.: Newbury House, 1972.

SWEET, H. *The Practical Study of Language.* London: Oxford University Press, reprinted 1964.

VALDMAN, A. *Trends in Language Teaching.* New York: McGraw Hill, 1966.

WALLACE, B. *The Pronunciation of American English for Teachers of English as a Second Language.* Ann Arbor, Mich.: George Wahr, 1957.

WEST, M. *Learning to Read a Foreign Language.* London: Longmans Green, 1941.

________. *Teaching English in Difficult Circumstances: Teaching English as a Foreign Language.* London: Longmans Green, 1960.

WIDDOWSON, H. *Language Teaching Texts.* London: Oxford University Press, 1971.

WILKINS, D. *Linguistics in Language Teaching.* London: Arnold, 1972.

WISHON, G. and T. O'HARA (eds.). *Teaching English: A Collection of Readings.* New York: ABC, 1968.

Materials and Equipment

CARROLL, J. B. "A Primer of Programmed Instruction in Foreign Language Teaching." in *IRAL,* 1963.

CORDER, S. *The Visual Element in Language Teaching.* London: Longmans Green, 1966.

DETERLINE, W. *An Introduction to Programmed Instruction.* Englewood Cliffs, N. J.: Prentice Hall, 1962.

DEVEREUX, E. (ed.). *An Introduction to Visual Aids.* London: Matthews, Drew and Shelbourne, 1962.

DORRY, G. *Games for Second Language Learning.* New York: McGraw Hill, 1966.

GRAZIA, A. de and D. SOHN (eds.). *Programs, Teachers and Machines.* New York: Bantam Books, 1964.

HAYES, A. *Language Laboratory Facilities.* Washington, D. C.: U.S.O.E., 1963.

HIRSCH, R. *Audio-Visual Aids in Language Teaching.* Washington, D. C.: Georgetown University, 1954.

HOCKING, E. *Language Laboratory and Language Learning.* Washington, D. C.: N.E.A. Monograph N. 2, 1964.

HOWATT, A. *Programmed Learning and the Language Teacher.* London: Longmans Green, 1969.

HOLTON, J. S. (ed.). *Sound Language Teaching.* New York: University Publishers, 1962.

HUEBENER, T. *Audio-Visual Techniques in Teaching Foreign Languages.* New York: New York University Press, 1960.

HUTCHISON, J. *Modern Foreign Languages. The Language Laboratory.* Washington, D. C.: U.S. Government Printing Office, 1961.

IODICE, D. *Guidelines to Language Teaching in Class and the Laboratory.* Washington, D. C.: Electronic Teaching Laboratories, 1962.

JOHNSON, F. and L. *Stick Figure Drawings for Language Teachers.* Boston, Mass.: Ginn & Co., 1971.

JOHNSTON, M. and C. SEELEY. *Foreign Language Laboratories in Schools and Colleges.* Washington, D. C.: U.S. Government Printing Office, Bulletin 3, 1959.

KEATING, R. *A Study of the Effectiveness of Language Laboratories.* New York: The Institute of Administrative Research, Teachers College, Columbia University, 1963.

KREIDLER, C. J. and M. B. SUTHERLAND. *Flash Pictures: A Set of 252 Cards Used as an Aid to Teachers of English as a Foreign Language.* Ann Arbor, Mich.: Edwards Bros., Inc., 1963.

LEE, W. R. *Language-Teaching Games and Contests.* London: Oxford University Press, 1965.

———. and H. COPPEN. *Simple Audio-Visual Aids to Foreign Language Teaching.* London: Oxford University Press, 1964.

LUMSDAME, A. and R. GLASER. *Teaching Machines and Programmed Learning.* Washington, D. C.: N.E.A., 1960.

MARTY, F. L. *Language Laboratory Learning.* Wellesley, Mass.: Audio-Visual Publications, 1960.

———. *Programming a Basic Foreign Language Course.* Virginia: Hollins College, 1962.

ORNSTEIN, J., R. EWTON, and T. MUELLER. *Programmed Instruction and Educational Technology in Language Teaching.* Phila., Pa.: The Center for Curriculum Development, Inc., 1970.

QUILTER, D. *Dos and Don'ts in Audio-Visual Teaching.* Waltham, Mass.: Blaisdell Publishing Co., 1966.

RICHARDS, J. and M. POLIQUIN. *English through Songs.* Rowley, Mass.: Newbury House, 1973.

SMITH, W. I. and J. W. MOORE. *Programmed Learning: Theory and Research.* Princeton, N. J.: D. Van Nostrand Co., 1962.

STACK, E. M. *The Language Laboratory and Modern Language Teaching.* New York: Oxford University Press, 1966.

STREVENS, P. *Aural Aids in Language Teaching.* London: Longmans Green, 1958.

TAYLOR, A. *Equipping the Classroom.* London: Nelson, 1953.

357 Songs We Love to Sing. Minneapolis, Minn.: Schmitt, Hall, and McCreary.

VALDMAN, A. (ed.). "Programmed Instruction and Foreign Language Teaching" in *Trends in Language Teaching,* New York: McGraw Hill, 1966.

Visual Aids for English as a Second Language. Arlington, Va.: CAL, 1964.

Testing and Evaluation

DAVIES, A. *Language Testing Symposium: A Psycholinguistic Approach.* London: Oxford University Press, 1968.

HARRIS, D. *Testing English as a Second Language.* New York: McGraw Hill, 1969.

LADO, R. *Language Testing*. New York: McGraw Hill, 1964.
Modern Languages: Teaching and Testing. (filmstrip) Princeton, N. J.: Educational Testing Service, 1968.
Modern Language Association: *A Handbook on Foreign Language Classroom Testing: French, German, Italian, Russian, Spanish.* New York: Modern Language Association, 1968.
PIMSLEUR, P. "Testing Foreign Language Learning" in *Trends in Language Teaching,* (A. Valdman, ed.). New York: McGraw Hill, 1966.
UPSHUR, J. and J. FATA. *Problems in Foreign Language Testing.* Ann Arbor, Mich.: University of Michigan, 1969.
VALETTE, R. *Modern Language Testing.* New York: Harcourt Brace Jovanovich, 1967.

Appendix VII
Some Additional Resources

Agencies and Associations

American Council of Teachers of Foreign Languages (ACTFL). 60 Fifth Ave., New York, N. Y.
Association of Teachers of English to Speakers of Other Languages (TESOL). Georgetown U., Washington, D.C.
Binational Centers. Many countries; schools jointly sponsored by the United States and Ministries of Education in the host country
British Council. State House, London.
Center for Applied Linguistics (CAL). 1611 North Kent Street, Arlington, Va. 22209
Education Section of Ministries of Education, of Migration Offices, and of private educational and social agencies.
English Teaching Division. United States Information Service. Washington, D.C.
Modern Language Association (MLA). 60 Fifth Avenue, New York, N. Y.
National Association of Foreign Student Advisors. 809 United Nations Plaza, New York, N. Y.
National Council of Teachers of English. Champaign, Illinois.
Nuffield Foundation. Leeds, England.
UNESCO. United Nations Plaza, New York. (also Belgium)
U.S. Dept. of Health, Education and Welfare (HEW). Washington, D. C.
U.S. Office of Education (USOE). Washington, D. C.

Pen Pals

International Friendship League. Boston, Mass: 40 Mt. Vernon Street.
Letters Abroad. New York: 18 East 60 Street.
World Pen Pals. U. of Minnesota, Minneapolis, Minn.

Periodic Collections, Monographs, and Reports

Annual Bibliography on Teaching Foreign Languages. New York: MLA.
Britannica Review of Foreign Language Education. Chicago: Encyclopedia Britannica. (published yearly)
ERIC Clearinghouse on Linguistics. Arlington, Va.: CAL.
ERIC Focus Reports on Foreign Language Teaching. New York: ACTFL.
Georgetown Round Table Monographs. Washington: Georgetown U.
Language Research in Progress. Arlington, Va.: CAL.
Northeast Conference Reports. New York; MLA. (Reports available from 1954.)
Research in Education. U.S. Government Printing Office. Washington, D. C.

Periodicals and Journals

Anthropological Linguistics. Bloomington, Indiana: University of Indiana.
Archiv für das Studium der Neuren Sprachen und Literaturen. Braunschweig, Germany.
Audio-Visual Aids and Teaching of Languages. Antwerp, Belgium.
Audio-Visual Language Journal. Hertfordshire, England.
Babel. Journal of the Australian Federation of Modern Language Teachers Assoc., Melbourne, Australia.
Cahiers Ferdinand de Saussure: Revue de Linguistique Générale. Geneva, Switzerland.
Canadian Journal of Linguistics. Toronto, Canada.
Canadian Modern Language Review. (Ontario Modern Language Teachers Assoc.). Toronto, Canada.
Classical Journal. Columbus, Ohio: Ohio State U.
Contact. (Fédération Internationale des Professeurs de Langues Vivantes). Berne, Switzerland.
English—A New Language. Sydney, Australia: Commonwealth Office of Education.
The English Journal. Champaign, Ill.: National Council of Teachers of English.
English Language Teaching. Middlesex, England: IATEFL.

English Teaching Abstracts. London: British Council.

English Teaching Forum. USIA. Washington, D. C.

English Teaching Guidance. Tel Aviv, Israel.

English Teaching News. London: British Council.

Foreign Languages in School. Moscow, USSR.

Foundations of Language. Dordrecht, Holland: Reidel.

Français dans le Monde. Paris, France.

French Review. (Amer. Assoc. of Teachers of French). Baltimore, Maryland.

German Quarterly. (Amer. Assoc. of Teachers of German). Cincinnati, Ohio.

Glottodidactica. Poznan, Poland.

The Grade Teacher. Darien, Conn.

Hispania. (Amer. Assoc. of Teachers of Spanish and Portuguese). Washington, D. C.

The Instructor. Dansville Park, New York: Owen Publishing Co.

International Journal of American Linguistics. Bloomington, Indiana: U. of Indiana.

International Journal of Applied Linguistics in Language Teaching (IRAL). Heidelberg, Germany.

Italica. (American Assoc. of Teachers of Italian). Evanston, Ill.

Journal of English as a Second Language. New York: American Language Institute, New York University.

Language. Austin, Texas: U. of Texas, Linguistic Society of America.

Language and Language Behavior Abstracts (LLBA). Ann Arbor, Mich.: U. of Michigan.

Language Learning: A Journal of Applied Linguistics. 1522 Rackham Building, Ann Arbor, Mich.

Linguistic Reporter. Center for Applied Linguistics. 1611 North Kent St., Arlington, Va. 22209.

Modern Language Journal. Curtis Reed Plaza, Menasha, Wisconsin.

Modern Language: Journal of the Modern Language Association of the United Kingdom. London.

NAFSA Newsletter. NAFSA (National Association of Foreign Student Advisers), United Nations Plaza, New York City.

Programmed Learning and Educational Technology. London: Journal of the Association for Programmed Learning.

Publications of the Modern Language Association of America (PMLA). Modern Language Association, 60 Fifth Avenue, New York City.

Rassegna italiana di linguistica applicata. Mario Bulzoni (ed.). Rome, Italy.

Revista de Educación. Madrid, Spain.

Russian Review. The Hoover Institution, Stanford, California.

School and Society. 1860 Broadway, New York City.

Scuola e Lingue Moderne. (Official Bulletin of the National Association of Language Teachers). Rome, Italy.

TESOL Newsletter. TESOL, Georgetown University, Washington, D. C.

TESOL Quarterly, TESOL, Georgetown University, Washington, D. C.

Word: Linguistic Circle of New York, St. Peter's College. Jersey City, N. J.

Tests

Carroll-Sapon Modern Language Aptitude Test. New York: The Psychological Corp., 1959.

College Board Achievement Tests. Princeton, N. J.: Educational Testing Service (revised annually).

HARRIS, D. *Listening Test.* Washington, D. C.: American Language Institute, 1961.

______ and L. PALMER. *English Vocabulary Test* ...., 1963.

________________. *Listening Test, Form B* ...., 1962.

________________. *Vocabulary and Reading Test* ...., 1961.

LADO, R. *English Language Test for Foreign Students.* Ann Arbor, Mich.: U. of Michigan Press, 1962.

MLA Cooperative Foreign Language Tests. Princeton, N. J.: Educational Testing Service, 1964.

MLA Foreign Language Proficiency Tests for Teachers and Advanced Students. Princeton, N. J.: Educational Testing Service, 1962.

Pimsleur Language Aptitude Battery. New York: Harcourt Brace Jovanovich, 1966.

Pimsleur Modern Foreign Language Proficiency Tests. New York: Harcourt Brace Jovanovich, 1967.

TOEFL. Princeton, N. J.: Educational Testing Service (revised annually).

Index

8678-6
5-36

LIBRARY
FLORISSANT VALLEY COMMUNITY COLLEGE
ST. LOUIS, MO.

INVENTORY 1983